THE
HEROIC IMAGE
IN CHILE

THE
HEROIC IMAGE
IN CHILE

Arturo Prat, Secular Saint

by

William F. Sater

UNIVERSITY OF CALIFORNIA PRESS
Berkeley   Los Angeles   London

University of California Press
Berkeley and Los Angeles, California

University of California Press, Ltd.
London, England

Copyright © 1973 by The Regents of the University of California

ISBN:0–520–02235–1
Library of Congress Catalog Card Number: 70–189221
Designed by Bob Odell
Printed in the United States of America

TO MY MOTHER
AND
IN MEMORY OF MY FATHER

✝ ACKNOWLEDGMENTS

In my salad days I used to regard an acknowledgment page as almost superfluous. After my own experience, however, I have wilted considerably. My advisors were numerous, their assistance invaluable, and my gratitude boundless.

I am particularly indebted to the Ford Foundation and to the Universities of California and Chile for providing the financial support for my stay in Chile. My work in the Biblioteca del Congreso was enormously facilitated by the kind attention of Alicia Claro Marchant, Ximena Feliú Silva, and Jerado Welch Castillo. The staff of the Museo Pedagógico, in particular Luis Morales Gallegos and Carlos Omar Carvajal, were also very helpful.

My greatest debt of gratitude is to the staff of the Biblioteca Nacional in Santiago, especially its former director, Guillermo Feliú Cruz. Don Guillermo's assistance, his counsel, and enormous wisdom certainly made my task much easier. The constant good cheer and advice of my friend, Juan Uribe Echevarria, were also very much appreciated. There are many others to whom I am most grateful: Rodolfo Bustamante, Mario Medina, and especially Las Señoras del Seminario Matta Vial—doña Zulema, doña Isabel, and doña María—all of whom made the library not simply an institution but a home.

I thank as well Eugenio Peirera Salas, Cristián Guerrero Y., and Gonzalo Izquierdo, all of the University of Chile, for their friendship and valuable advice. Of all my Chilean friends, none were kinder than Dr. Arturo Prat Echaurren, his wife Elena, and Dr. Abraham Schweitzer, and his wife Clara. The hours spent in their beautiful home, their warm hospitality, and their unflagging interest in my work are enormously appreciated.

I owe a special debt of gratitude to Robert N. Burr, who not only supervised this work when I was a graduate student but also provided a willing ear and a ready mind when I encountered, as I often did, any difficulties. Earl Glauert of Central Washington College, as well as Stanley Wolpert, Albert Hoxie, and Phillip Borden, all of the University of California, Los Angeles, were extremely kind, offering their support and encouragement. E. Bradford Burns, also of UCLA, as well as my colleagues at California State University, Long Beach, Colin MacLachlan, James Starkweather, Keith Ian Polakoff, and Jaime Rodríguez also very kindly took time from their busy schedules to read and criticize this book. My brother, James C. Sater, and my friend of many years, Geoffrey Symcox, helped me revise this manuscript—neither an easy nor pleasant task—for which I cannot adequately express my thanks. Dr. Ralph R. Greenson, Clinical Professor of Psychiatry at the School of Medicine, University of California, Los Angeles, spent many hours discussing with me the various psychological materials used in this volume. His warmth, interest, and insights proved to be of enormous benefit. Finally, I should like to mention John J. Johnson who first introduced me to Latin-American history and who has since remained a constant source of encouragement.

For years my wife, Ana Lya Yaikin de Sater, has shared me with Arturo Prat. Despite the tempestuous times, the late hours, and the atmosphere of almost perpetual crisis, she has remained in good cheer. For this, as well as for her assistance in preparing this manuscript, I am eternally indebted.

William F. Sater

✝ CONTENTS

	Introduction	1
1.	The Heroic Moment	11
2.	Chile, 1876–1879: The Crisis Society	22
3.	The War of the Pacific: The Heroic Medium	34
4.	The Hero and His Time	48
5.	Arturo Prat and the Parliamentary Regime: 1880–1920	69
6.	Prat and the Established and Radical Press: The Hero 1920–1950	90
7.	Arturo Prat and Education	119
8.	Arturo Prat and the Military	134
	Conclusion	154
	Appendix I. Columns of Newsprint Devoted to Arturo Prat by Various Chilean Newspapers, 1880–1931	161
	Appendix II. Books and Materials about Arturo Prat Published between 1879 and 1950	163
	Notes	169
	Bibliography	211
	Index	239

INTRODUCTION

Valparaíso is Chile's San Francisco. It perches precariously on the bluffs overlooking the Pacific, a splotch of mottled red, yellow, and gray, which gradually sprawls down the hills to the water. It is a busy seaport town: foreign vessels crowd its wharfs, men of different nationalities climb its treacherously steep streets; the air smells of salt and is punctuated by the shrill cry of the perennial seagull. Plaza Sotomayor is one of the city's principal centers, a wide expanse of concrete, bordered by the ocean and flanked by massive buildings. At one end is the baroque nineteenth-century office of the provincial intendant; at the other, a three-tiered monument, surmounted by an imposing statue.

Each year, on the twenty-first of May, the plaza is deep with people watching the soldiers, the airmen, and the sailors of Chile march past this monument. Their standards dip, the officers arc their swords downward in salute, the men turn their heads smartly to the right, and the marching files goose-step as they come abreast of the marble structure. Despite the festive air, it is a bittersweet occasion commemorating an epic victory of Chile's navy and the tragic death of its principal hero, Arturo Prat, whose statue dominates the monument and who is buried beneath its marble pillars.

Although this ceremony occurs in Chile, it is reminiscent of countless celebrations held throughout Latin America—a continent whose cities, plazas, ships, schools, and even its cigarettes and beers, have borne the names of various heroes. Each nation has its pantheon of paladins and martyrs, men whose feats are perpetually frozen in bronze, whose acts are reproduced on postage stamps, whose faces stare out sternly from the face of the local currency. Indeed, there are so many heroes that they tend to merge into the background and, like the weather, be forgotten except on those special occasions when, in some deluge of historical nostalgia, it is impossible to ignore them.

When one visits the monuments of various heroes in Latin

America, a feeling of sadness, even depression, overcomes him. Perhaps this is not so unusual, for most Latin-American heroes have suffered enormously and died either in some titanic struggle between armies, or alone, hanging from a scaffold, standing before a firing squad, or wasting away in squalid exile. The independence leaders—Tiradentes of Brazil, Sucre of Bolivia, Manuel Rodríguez and the Carrera brothers of Chile, as well as Mexico's Hidalgo and Morelos—were all shot down or executed. Argentina's San Martín and Rivadavia perished in a European exile; Bolívar passed away while enroute to the Old World; Chile's O'Higgins also ended his days an outcast, as did Ecuador's Flores and Rocafuerte.

Later nineteenth-century figures, the men of various political persuasion who sought either to defend their countries or to introduce change, suffered similar fates. Rosas of Argentina died in exile, as did Pedro II of Brazil, Andrés Santa Cruz of Bolivia, and Chile's Francisco Bilbao. José Manual Balmaceda and the "Niños héroes" of Mexico took their own lives, while Ecuador's García Moreno and Eloy Alfaro perished violently as did Paraguay's Francisco Solano López, Cuba's Martí, Chile's Portales, and Peru's Grau and Bolognesi.

Twentieth-century leaders have fared no better. Perón, Guatemala's Arévalo, and Bolivia's Tórrez are now in exile. Brazil's Vargas and Chile's Recabarren committed suicide. Peru's leading intellectual figure, José Carlos Mariátegui, died at a tragically early age. The list of the murdered becomes longer each year: Madero, Zapata, Villa, and Obregón of Mexico; Colombia's Jorge Elicear Gaitán, and Bolivia's German Busch, all shot, as were the darlings of the Left—Camilo Torres and Che Guevara—and the protectors of the Right—Trujillo of the Dominican Republic and Sánchez Cerro of Peru. Gualberto Villarroel of Bolivia was an exception: he was lynched from a light standard in a city erroneously called La Paz. Obviously the Latin-American hero does not enjoy that most elementary of expectations: dying in one's bed—of natural causes and at a ripe old age—surrounded by weeping relatives, innumerable grandchildren, and mournful friends.

If, as the Visconde of Porto Alegre once wrote, "To know the biographies of all the outstanding men of a period is to know the history of those times,"[1] then the hero has been seriously neglected. Certainly there have been countless biographies—Guevara has been dead but a short time and already the list is impressive—but no one truly studies the hero. Instead, he is accepted as if he were another historical fact, a man who personifies some historical event just as an inventor is remembered for his feat of technology. This is a serious error. We must question why and then how a man reaches this status, instead of repeating the tiresome platitude that a hero is a hero because someone else said it first.

The literature dealing with the Great Man, unfortunately, rarely discusses the forces that generate the hero. Carlyle, for instance, skirted this fundamental issue while blithely affirming that "the history of what man has accomplished in this world, is at bottom the history of the Great Men who have worked here."[2] Such factors as environment, circumstances, and external forces are inconsequential, for the author had endowed the Great Man with the strength, and doubtless the ego, to subdue his surroundings.

Yet, environment, ambience, or society—however it is described —can restrict human activity. John Huss suffered martyrdom while Martin Luther, who espoused similar ideas, initiated the Reformation. Why did Luther succeed? Was Germany's intellectual climate more tolerant than that of Bohemia? Or, to paraphrase Richard Hofstadter, did its national psyche make it more receptive to new ideas?[3] The fact that Luther, unlike Huss, enjoyed the protection of the Elector of Saxony clearly demonstrates how vulnerable is the innovative man and how much he depends upon others for his success. Great Men do not operate in a void restrained only by their own whim and initiative.

Determinists would, of course, agree that Caylyle erred when he attributed so much influence to a single individual. Georg Hegel believed that "as a general rule, individuals come under the category of a means to an ulterior end,"[4] gray, faceless men who barely survived, whose actions were both limited and irrelevant. A few Great Men existed, souls who derived their *raison d' état* from "a concealed fount . . . from that Inner Spirit" whose message they transmitted to their less aware brethren. Such a philosophy accorded little significance to the individual who, at best, functioned as a conduit for a mystical force he could serve but not control.

Herbert Spencer seemed even more skeptical than Hegel about the ability of the individual to affect human development. The philosopher described man's growth from primitive and homo-geneous tribes to complex and heterogenous civilizations. This process, which he compared to biological evolution, developed a life force of its own, an inertia that inexorably pushed it forward. At one time the individual might have exercised some influence, but only when mankind existed at its most primitive level, the tribe. Once society had developed, however, it produced institu-tions, habits, customs, and ideas without the intervention of human action. Thus the Great Man could not exist in a mature society. Progress arose out of the interaction of social forces, not human endeavor. Only under the most favorable conditions might man accelerate these social forces, but create them, never.[5]

Marxists also strongly believed in determinism, "In the social production of their life, men enter into definite relations that are indispensable and independent of their will, relations of produc-tion which correspond to a definite state of development of their material productive forces."[6] The immutable force of mankind lies in the struggle between antagonistic economic systems. Human activity could do little to alter the outcome of this conflict for, as Trotsky implied, its conclusion was inevitable. Regardless of what Nicholas II did, "the development of events would have differed a little in form, but not in substance."[7] Men, therefore, could only temporarily deflect or accelerate the productive forces from their preordained ends.

George Plekhanov, another Marxist, unsuccessfully sought to expand this narrow interpretation of the individual's role. Yet, while arguing that a man could affect his world, Plekhanov contra-dicted himself by claiming that the structure of society limited all human activity. Regardless of how manfully one might strive, one's efforts were foredoomed, for although "influential individuals can change the *individual features of events and some of their particu-lar consequences*, . . . they cannot change their general *trend*, which is determined by other [economic] forces."[8]

Regardless of their ideological differences, determinists agreed that human endeavor could not prevent the inevitable: had Fred-erick III not died of cancer, Germany would still have evolved into a militaristic state and suffered the horrors of World War I; if Ludendorf and Hindenberg had not permitted Lenin to return to Russia, the Communists still would have triumphed; had a monkey not bitten King Alexander, Greece would somehow have lost its war with Turkey in 1920. These arguments utterly disregard the very real possibility that individuals can resist supposedly "overwhelming" social and economic pressures.

The soldiers of Charlie Company at My Lai constituted a group of men, all products of the same social and economic forces. They lived, furthermore, in an extremely rigid and stratified society. Unlike the theoretical world of the determinists, they obeyed not some elusive and unseen principles or life forces, but clearly defined laws which carried with them the sanction of force. Despite this, when ordered to "waste" unarmed men, women, and children, many of them balked, indicating that regardless of the circumstances, men can always refuse to obey an order.

Sidney Hook attempted to strike some balance between Carlyle's unrestrained individualism and the determinists' rigidity, arguing that alternatives do exist which can alter a society's development. The author divided Great Men into two categories: the eventful man and the event-making man.[9] The former, apparently a variation of the determinists' arguement, is a person placed in a vital situation and whose responses might alter society: the policeman entrusted with guarding Lincoln; the messenger who garbled the instructions to the Light Brigade; men whose casual reactions might, because of their accidental presence in a vital situation, have enormous consequences. The latter slightly resembles Carlyle's description of the Great Man: the individual who rises above class or social restrictions; the man who consciously and deliberately creates the preconditions that permit him to alter the course of humanity. A good analogy, perhaps, would be to compare a common hit-and-run driver with the assassin of Alexander II. The first, through the accidental confluence of events, may change the life of a small group of people; the second, after deliberate planning, sets into motion new forces which alter the physiognomy of the nation and perhaps the world.

Unfortunately, all the works earlier cited have little relevance to this study because they concentrate on analyzing Great Men—usually Great Political Men—and not the hero, which is, of course, an entirely different subject. The authors, furthermore, seem preoccupied with judging the efficiency of the Great Leaders: Did he govern well and democratically (Hook)? Did he accelerate or retard the impact of the economic forces (the Marxists)? Did he transmit the "Inner Spirit" (Hegel)? Did he contribute to the formation of the "social forces" (Spencer)? Pragmatic criteria, however, have little applicability to the study of heroes, especially those, like the Imperial Guard at Waterloo, the Spartans at Thermopylae, and, as we shall see, Arturo Prat, who died accomplishing nothing.

An analysis of the cult of the hero would reveal that his rise to prominence is dependent upon the needs of a society; that just as a fallen tree cannot be heard unless there is a human present, a man cannot be a hero unless some group or individual deems his actions worthy of praise.

An individual, X, for example, may be afraid to fly. At the completion of an air trip he has, by his own standards, performed heroically. It is doubtful, however, that people not afflicted with this phobia would consider his act so praiseworthy. Indeed, by their standards, X is simply acting normally. Yet, others who suffer from a fear of airplanes would acclaim him a hero. In essence, to understand the paradox of heroism, it is not the intention of the actor which matters, but the reaction of society to his act. Like beauty, heroism is literally in the eyes of the beholders who can sanctify any human action, elevating it from the mundane to the heights of glory. To understand the roots of heroism, then, we must study why societies require heroes.

It is a commonly held belief in psychological circles that the interaction of an individual with his family colors his later attitudes toward society. Thus, infantile ideals and values can become " ... the point around which all later social attitudes crystalize and thus it is the pattern of all later social behavior."[10] Some people may also project onto society the early important figures: frequently the mother becomes equated with the concept of the motherland—a symbol of fertility, warmth, and nourishment—to be both cherished and defended; a nation's leader may reappear as a father—powerful, harsh, but, one would hope, just and protective.[11] Freud, for example, noted this similarity when he analyzed the ties that bind the family to the father and the citizen to his leader.[12]

Often an individual, in repeating his childhood experiences in terms of society, will yearn to regress to that period of his early life when he felt blissfully secure, to return to a "social organization where he could not only find the same dependency but also the same protection that he experienced in his first years."[13] This drive is most likely to occur in people whose childhood was filled with dissatisfaction and frustration. Such hostility is compounded when the parent no longer appears to be the omnipotent figure he seemed in the early years of infancy.[14]

A child with such a background may not only search for a substitute for his lost idealized parents, but will also tend to be very unrealistic in his evaluation of later parental figures. This process of idealization will distort the real qualities of a leader and make him appear godlike and omnipotent. As a result, what emerges from this process is a benevolent leader, a surrogate father who replaces the individual's real father and who also has the power to treat the citizen like a child.[15]

> The relationship between the member and the leader is unequal. The status of the member is subordinate to that of the leader. There is inequality in ego structure, the leader superior the member inferior. The leader carries the authority and prestige symbolic of the parent. He is potentially a source of love, a protector or a source of hostility and a punishing figure. He may represent an ideal, a narcissistic extention of the member's self or the executive arm of the member's weak ego. He may assume the responsibility for the member's own guilt. He may in the last analysis attack and destroy the member. Like a child, the member seeks love and protection but fears betrayal and punitive injury. He may wish to depend on the leader as a magic helper. For this purpose he aggrandizes the leader and projects omnipotence to serve his own ends. The member accepts a dependent submissive position in the group but consoles himself, through magic control of the leader's aggrandized powers, the leader being obligated to use those powers on behalf of the member. The member identifies himself unconsciously with the idealized image of the leader. He shares the glory of the leader, derives pleasure from the leader's success and denies his own inferiority and helplessness.[16]

Despite this inequality in power, a leader's position can be quite tenuous, for it is conditional upon his playing a "loving and protective role."[17] If his followers believe the father-leader to be subject to authority or fear, the whole psychological structure that is erected around him will "tumble to the ground as surely as if he [the leader] has been removed by death."[18]

The destruction of such a father-leader can have severe consequences. If a society has too often totally delegated its decision-making powers to a leader, it may lose confidence in its own ability to function independently. Thus the transfer of power may not only corrupt the leader, but also weaken those who yield the power. Consequently, a member of the group may be "less able to control his fears and trust by reasoning power and responsible decision."[19]

A society, ruled by a leader whom its citizens no longer trust and confronted with an apparently insoluble problem, can become psychologically devastated. Anxiety gradually mounts to the point of panic. This is particularly difficult for the masses to master because all states of panic arouse a sense of helplessness. If this occurs when a society is confronted with an objective danger, it becomes imperative that it renew itself psychologically.[20]

This problem can become magnified if the idealized leader is gone. The loss of such a valued person, who had united the people in the past, may result in disorganized and irrational behavior. In desperation, people in such circumstances will search for a leader who will have the appearance of being omnipotent and omniscient.[21]

Very often people will attribute such characteristics to the hero, particularly when national circumstances are chaotic and confused. A distraught nation, its surrogate father humbled and disgraced, will seek another, a man who will actively undertake the protection of the motherland and consequently of its children. Such a man does not have to succeed: he must only act. Once he does, he is lionized and revered. His behavior resembles that of the former father, a standard of excellence worthy of being imitated. His virtues are extolled, enshrined in the nation's history for all to emulate.[22]

An alternative to the purely psychological approach is to consider the hero a manifestation of what social psychologists call a "value-oriented movement," that is, a collective attempt to restore order, stability, and progress in a society through the restoration, protection, or revitalization of a system of values. This movement often has the same etiology as its purely psychological counterpart: an insensitive or unresponsive government, coupled with a domestic or external crisis, produces in its citizens a sense of acute discomfort. A malaise permeates society; a feeling develops that the nation, once happy and progressive, needs to be purged. Many believe that the country has strayed from those bedrock virtues that had earlier brought the community happiness and contentment. The malaise ripens into a movement. It adopts a talisman—a slogan or a symbolic figure—or rallies around a leader to exorcise the evil forces and to return the society to its golden past by restoring the old and esteemed value system.[23]

The rise of Arturo Prat can be interpreted either as the search for a father figure or as the principal symbol of a value-oriented movement. The major difference between the psychological and the sociopsychological analysis is that the former seeks to explain mass behavior by applying the ideas of individual behavior to large groups, while the latter believes that group action can best be explained by empirical laws. Both these disciplines share a common point of agreement: that societies in stress often become victims of panic and that, under such pressure, they may seek some person or thing which they believe can, either objectively or symbolically, protect them.

This work will study the formation of Arturo Prat's heroic image. It will demonstrate that his growth was directly the result of the periods of crisis which overtook the nation in 1876–1879 and later in the years following 1891; that the loss of confidence in the nation's leaders produced a sense of anxiety which made Chileans yearn for a hero. It will be shown, furthermore, that Prat's popularity and usage were shaped by internal conditions and that, as these conditions changed, so the heroic image was altered to meet the nation's needs.

1 ⚔ THE HEROIC MOMENT

*In war one always
chooses the wrong hero.*

—GRAHAM GREENE

I

Iquique, a mining town located in the arid, dusty Peruvian province of Tarapacá, was built on a small sand strip sandwiched between the Pacific on the west and the Andes on the east.[1] Isolated from humanity, surrounded on three sides by the world's driest desert and on the fourth by the sea, the city lived a precarious existence, having to distill its water from the ocean and import its food. One substance attracted men to this parched, ugly land: nitrates, the magic chemical that, when sprinkled on the land, made crops grow and, when inserted into the breech of a gun, made men die; nitrates, a commodity more precious than gold in a world that seeks bumper harvests from both the farm and the battlefield.

Normally Iquique throbbed with activity. More than a thousand ships docked annually at its harbor, and usually there were from forty to fifty vessels lying at anchor at any given moment. The city was, comparatively speaking, large; it had six banks, a population estimated at between 20,000 and 25,000, and a disdain for morality which made one British missionary curse it as the Sodom and Gomorrah of the Pacific Coast.[2]

Since April 1879, the town had looked as if it had been visited by the plague. The nitrate fields were silent: no plumes of smoke, no explosions. The railroad was not running. The factories were mute. But for a few ships, all flying the tricolor of Chile, the harbor was empty. Iquique was a blockaded city. The Chilean ships were units of a squadron that had isolated Iquique from the rest of the world since Chile declared war on Peru on April 5, 1879.

Late on the afternoon of May 16, 1879, the waters of Iquique's bay were once again alive with motion. Like conspirators, alone and in pairs, the units of the blockading Chilean fleet slipped out of the harbor. The corvettes *Chacabuco* and *O'Higgins* sailed west. Within a short time the ironclad *Cochrane* and the collier *Matías Cousiño* followed, moving toward the south. The gunboat *Abtao* left after night fell, followed by the *Magallanes*, which had just returned from Valparaíso, and the other ironclad, the *Blanco Encalada*. As the squadron moved into the night, Iquique still was a captive city, policed by the old and decrepit corvette *Esmeralda* and the gunboat *Covadonga*.

The Chilean fleet, converging from all directions, rendezvoused forty miles off Pisagua. United, they steamed north to Callao to attack the Peruvian fleet while it lay at anchor. The Chilean navy was poised, soon to strike its first offensive blow of the war.

The Chilean commander, Rear Admiral Juan Williams Rebolledo, had devised a simple attack plan. The fleet should reach Callao at night. The *Abtao*, its magazines primed with black powder, manned by a skeleton volunteer crew, would then slip among the enemy fleet. Dropping anchor, the *Abtao*'s crew would first fire a broadside at the enemy, then after setting its ship afire, the Chileans would evacuate. As they rowed their lifeboats to their rescue vessel, they were instructed to shout that the *Abtao* was about to explode.

The Chilean ironclads were to commence firing once the burning *Abtao* silhouetted their enemies. Meanwhile, a makeshift squadron of torpedo boats, composed of the launches from the ironclads and the *Chacabuco*, was to capitalize on the confusion and fire its torpedoes primarily at the Peruvian ironclads. Then it was to retire.

The *Chacabuco* and *O'Higgins* constituted the fleet's rearguard. If possible—and only if it did not impede the actions of the ironclads—the corvettes were to fire at the enemy shore batteries or the city, preferably the latter. The *Magallanes* was to rescue the *Abtao*'s crew, as well as any other survivors of the explosion. The *Matías Cousiño* was to remain out at sea, so that its precious cargo of coal would not be jeopardized.

Williams's fleet left Iquique on the night of May 16. Almost immediately mechanical problems in the two corvettes and the *Abtao*'s boilers forced the convoy to reduce its speed. To make matters worse, the *Matías Cousiño*, which carried the fleet's fuel reserves, lost contact with the squadron. Still, the Chileans managed to reach Callao early on the morning of the twenty-first.[3]

The *Abtao*'s crew exchanged places with its replacements. As a result of some technical complications, it took longer than expected for the other ships to prepare the launches that were to serve as the torpedo boats, and it was not until 4:30 A.M. that all was ready. Although it was late, Williams ordered the *Abtao* into action. The crew could not respond immediately, however, and thus another half hour was wasted. Because sunrise was a short time away, and dawn would bring the loss of surprise and cover, Williams postponed the operation until the following night. He ordered the squadron to San Lorenzo Island, near Callao, to wait and make itself ready.

When the early morning mists cleared, the enemy's sanctuary was open. Foreign merchantmen had docked along the beach in orderly lines. The sloops *Pilcomayo* and *Unión* were anchored on the northern side of the bay. Nearby was one of the monitors. Otherwise the harbor was empty.

All of Williams's elaborate precautions, his baroque maneuvers, and his melodramatic predawn speech had been wasted. The *Independencia* and the *Huáscar*, the muscle of the Peruvian fleet— its two ironclads—had sailed. Both the Chilean fleet and its commander must have wondered what had occurred. Fate had intervened; as the Chileans had moved north, the Peruvian ships had been moving south. The fleets had passed one another unnoticed.

The Peruvian squadron left Callao the same day that Williams sortied from Iquique. The convoy was composed of three troop transports—the *Oroya*, *Chalaco*, and *Limeña*—escorted by the *Huáscar* and the *Independencia*. Enroute the convoy had anchored off the Chincha Islands because of mechanical difficulties. The remainder of the squadron resumed its southward course after detaching the *Independencia* to wait for the *Chalaco*, thrown off course by an erratic compass. They rendezvoused at a prearranged site on May 18, and once united, sailed southward.

The convoy coaled at Mollendo. On May 20, they docked at Arica and learned for the first time that the Chilean fleet had left Iquique. The *Independencia* and the *Huáscar* were ordered to attack, and after taking on additional supplies, sailed at eight that evening toward Iquique.[4]

Iquique's harbor was quiet that morning of May 21. Only two warships and the transport *Lamar* were at anchor. At 6:50 one of the *Covadonga's* lookouts sighted two plumes of smoke and sounded the alarm. Within minutes the smoke trails were recognized as ships, and then as the enemy. The *Covadonga* returned to report to the blockade commander, Capitan Arturo Prat, that the enemy had arrived.

II

Arturo Prat was the first son of an impoverished but cultured family. Born in 1848, on his maternal uncle's estate, Arturo was still quite young when the family moved to Santiago. Prat's grandfather had immigrated from Catalonia; his father owned a small business in the capital. The mother came from a relatively distinguished and well-educated family; her brother, Jacinto Chacón, was a noted poet and lawyer.[5] The family struggled financially because don Agustín, Prat's father, had suffered some business reverses and then was left partially paralyzed by a cerebral stroke.[6] Prat's mother ran a nursery school to supplement the family's income.[7]

These economic difficulties made it unlikely that young Arturo could have continued his secondary education. The family succeeded in overcoming this obstacle by enrolling their ten-year-old son in the Chilean Naval Academy which charged no tuition. Although initially he may not have been too enthusiastic, once involved Prat compiled an excellent record as a cadet. Later promoted to the rank of midshipman, he subsequently distinguished himself for heroism at the battles of Papudo and Abtao during Chile's 1865 war with Spain, for which he received a promotion and a decoration.

In many respects, Prat was not the typical naval officer. Early in his career, the young mariner decided to study to become an attorney. This was an extremely ambitious undertaking because he could not attend the University. He nonetheless persevered and received his degree in philosophy in 1871 and three years later, his bachelor of laws. Becoming a lawyer was just one of the acts that distinguished Prat from his brother officers. Prat was extremely independent and highly principled: he respected the unorthodox in an age of intolerance; he taught evenings in a free school for the workers of Valparaíso. Prat's professional career bore the scars of his individualism. Once he protested to the naval high command when two of his classmates were unfairly denied promotions. Twice he risked his reputation by successfully defending two other officers, Luis Uribe and Ricardo Owen, on charges of insubordination.[8] Devotion appears to have been a hallmark of Prat's character. Although he left home while still very young, Prat remained in close contact with his family.[9] He made a writing table for his father, and in his account book one reads that he purchased candy for a younger brother and gloves for his sister.[10] He supplemented his parent's small income with his meager naval pay, and when he received his share of some prize money, he sent most of it to his mother.[11] Prat was willing to sacrifice anything for his parent's comfort, often refusing to attend the theater, his one real pleasure, in order to economize on their behalf. He even postponed his marriage until a promotion made it possible both to support his parents and to establish his own family.[12]

This same sense of dedication wedded Prat to the Navy. Despite poor health, government economies that reduced his salary, and his wife's entreaties, he refused to leave the fleet although he could have become a practicing attorney: "I have no miserly ambition, neither honors nor glory attracts me, for I believe that I can serve my country in some way. . . ."[13] So Prat remained with the fleet—the first to board the "married man's" ferry from shore in the morning, and the last to leave it at night. In his professional relationships, Prat appeared somber and correct. Some officers claimed that he was a martinet; a superior once described him as a tyrant. Yet, his subordinates thought differently, even stating that if Prat were severe ". . . he acted like a father, worried about the welfare of his men."[14]

When the War of the Pacific erupted, Prat remained assigned to the Maritime Administration of Valparaíso, an inglorious position for a regular officer in time of war. Prat immediately requested sea duty, and when this transfer was denied, he felt so mortified that he refused to wear his naval uniform. In April 1879, Prat was trans-

ferred to the *Abtao* with orders to sail it to join the fleet at Iquique.
Upon his arrival, he was again reassigned, this time to the *Esmeralda*.

The new command made Prat despondent.[15] The *Esmeralda*
was easily the most wretched ship of the fleet, a fact the vessel's
earlier commander, Manuel Thompson, had noted in laborious
detail. Worse yet, Admiral Williams permitted other commanders
to cannibalize the *Esmeralda*, taking most of its crew in order to
strengthen their vessels. As a result, the ship was left in such poor
condition that many believed it incapable of defending itself.[16]

Beside stripping the ship of most of its experienced crewmen
and equipment, Williams apparently used both the *Esmeralda*
and the *Covadonga* as a dumping ground for officers whom he
either did not like or did not trust: many he considered malcon-
tents; others were recently recalled from retirement, while the
remainder were men who had held administrative positions before
the war.[17]

It is remarkable that Prat was so harshly treated. He had been
decorated for bravery under fire during the war and had further
demonstrated his heroism by saving his ship during a storm. He
had been rapidly promoted, and held the highest possible rank in
view of his age and years of service. Nonetheless, he was given
command of the worst ship in the fleet and was not permitted to
join the attack on Callao. Why then was Prat accorded such cavalier treatment?

It appears that Williams did this deliberately because he did
not like "literate sailors." Although Prat was clearly intellectually
oriented—for many years he had been a professor at the naval
academy and later was its interim director—this only partly ac-
counts for the antipathy between the two men. Prat was a quiet,
austere individual, and might well have appeared haughty—inju-
dicious behavior for a junior officer. Worse still, he had had the
temerity to defend two men against charges of insubordination
and had won acquittals in both cases. Finally, Prat had been a
member of a clique of naval officers who advocated a more aggressive war, a position that was the opposite of what Williams
desired.[18] The admiral, doubtless displeased, may well have retaliated by preventing Prat from joining the Callao expedition,
knowing full well that the hero wanted desperately to do so. It is

interesting to note that on the day the fleet sailed northward, Williams was heard to inquire in a "jovial" tone as to what Prat would do if the *Huáscar* attacked Iquique.[19] Prat replied that he would board the ship if such an occasion presented itself. They both knew, however, that such an opportunity was highly unlikely.

III

Unfortunately, Prat had become entrapped in his own bravado. Arrayed against him were the enemy's most powerful vessels while his own "squadron" consisted of two ships: the *Esmeralda*, a relic with twelve small guns and two patched boilers; and the equally weak *Covadonga*, under the command of the half-Peruvian Carlos Condell. Like the *Esmeralda*, this gunboat had also served in the war with Spain, but on the Spanish side, until the Chileans captured it at the battle of Papudo. The *Covadonga* might well have been a ship sailing under a curse. Its career had begun as a prize ship, then it became a lighter, and it was now faced with the almost certain prospect of destruction.

The enemy vessels were ironclads, protected by four and one-half inches of armor, and armed with twenty guns, only four of which were smaller than those of the Chileans. The Peruvians were swifter, almost twice as fast as their opponents, and had armored rams to slash what their guns could not explode. This would not be a battle but a slaughter.

The two Chilean warships shrank back into the harbor while the *Lamar*, flying the flag of the United States, fled. After learning that Condell's men had breakfasted, Prat commanded the *Covadonga* to follow in his wake. Condell was ordered to remain close to the shoreline, thus using the shallow draught of his vessel to best advantage, and to position the city of Iquique at his back. Prat had just repeated Nelson's famous demand, that each man do his duty, when the first shell from the *Huáscar* shrieked into the waters between the two Chilean ships.

Earlier, Captain Prat had assembled his crew and quietly informed them that never in history had a Chilean ship struck its colors, and stated that it would not happen at Iquique either. "While I remain commander, they [the colors] will fly, and if I die, my officers will know how to fulfill their duty."[20] The crew cheered its commander and nation, and then returned to its battle stations for the *Esmeralda's* last contest.

Unknown to Prat, a small launch met the *Huáscar* as it entered the harbor. The boat carried the captain of the port of Iquique who warned Miguel Grau, the *Huáscar's* captain, to be careful since a line of submerged mines protected the *Esmeralda*. Grau's informant was wrong; not knowing this, however, the *Huáscar* approached its enemy with a certain discretion.[21]

Prat, his ships without armor and his guns without either the range or the power of the enemy, maneuvered his ships close to the shore knowing that Grau would be reluctant to fire, for any overshot would hit the blockaded city. When the *Esmeralda* began to move, one of its overage boilers exploded, reducing its speed by half. The *Esmeralda* was still able to maneuver when suddenly it recoiled from a blast of rifle and artillery fire directed at it from the shoreline. Forced to move northward, the Esmeralda was caught in a crossfire which was slowly butchering its crew.

The *Esmeralda* was soon a floating charnel house. Although its decks were covered with corpses and slippery with blood, the Chileans returned their enemy's fire. After three hours of unequal struggle, Grau, perhaps tired, perhaps humiliated by the poor quality of his crew's gunnery, altered his tactics. Gathering momentum he rammed the *Huáscar* into the side of his enemy.

The *Huáscar* struck the *Esmeralda* near the bow and then fired its guns at point-blank range on the hapless Chilean ship before withdrawing. When the *Huáscar* struck again, Prat, accompanied by Sergeant Juan de Dios Aldea, screamed, "Al abordaje muchachos," and boarded the enemy ship.

The two men, virtually powerless, stood exposed on the *Huáscar's* decks while their enemies crouched behind armored turrets. For a few moments they remained motionless, perhaps searching for some weak spot to attack, in order to avenge their dead shipmates. Turning, they rushed headlong at the ship's armored bridge only to be cut down by rifle fire. Both men were mortally wounded and lay, like broken rag dolls, at their enemy's feet.

Their helpless comrades saw them die. Electrified by Prat's death and its sublime futility, the men of the *Esmeralda* readied themselves for the next attack. When the *Huáscar* again rammed the Chilean vessel, Lieutenant Ignacio Serrano and a dozen men boarded the Peruvian man of war. Like their commander, they too were butchered as they attempted to seize the *Huáscar*. Having been pierced twice, the *Esmeralda*'s powder magazines were flooded, its boilers extinguished, its gun batteries almost all dismounted. The ship was a hapless hulk when the *Huáscar* wheeled to deliver the *coup de grâce*. Still the crew fought back with rifles as the Peruvian ship once again rammed the *Esmeralda*. The Chilean ship was dying, submerging bow first, when Ernesto Riquelme, an eighteen-year-old midshipman, fired one last salvo. The *Esmeralda* sank at 12:30. Its colors were in tatters but still flying as the ship sank beneath the bloody waters. For the first time that morning, the bay was silent.

Carlos Condell, meanwhile, had fled southward, pursued by the *Independencia*. Unable to take to the open sea because the enemy could then easily destroy it, the *Covadonga* dodged amid the rocks and over the coastal reefs. Perhaps overzealous or impetuous, the *Independencia* became reckless. The ship's bow struck a reef, and it was torn open by the rocks off Punta Gruesa.

Condell returned leisurely to destroy his stranded enemy. The Peruvian ship had just struck its flag when the *Huáscar* sailed into the small inlet, forcing the *Covadonga* to flee. Condell wisely did not force his luck and continued southward. Doubtless he was content having just destroyed one of Peru's two ironclads thereby reducing its naval strength by almost half.

Chileans did not receive the news of Iquique until the *Lamar* docked at Antofagasta. The army area commander, General Arteaga, published an official communique on May 23, announcing that the *Independencia* had been sunk, but it provided no specific information on Chilean losses.[22] *El Mercurio*'s war correspondent substantiated this report but otherwise added nothing new.[23] On the morning of the twenty-fourth, Eulogio Altamirano, the civilian secretary assigned to the navy, telegraphed General Arteaga requesting a more detailed report because the president was almost as uninformed as the public.[24]

That same evening Arteaga replied that the commander of the Tocopilla garrison confirmed that a battle had taken place and that the *Independencia* had been lost. He also stated that the *Esmeralda*, overpowered by the *Huáscar*, had preferred to scuttle itself rather than capitulate. The *Covadonga*, he reported, had just docked at Tocopilla with more than one hundred wounded aboard. The *Huáscar* was said to have returned to Callao. It was not until the twenty-fifth, however, that the circumstances of Prat's death were known.[25]

The delay in learning about the battle confused the public and made them anxious. Aware that a tremendous struggle was taking place, but uninformed as to its results, the Chilean people waited, sure that both the *Esmeralda* and the *Covadonga* had been destroyed.

The streets and plazas of Valparaíso and Concepción were filled with people anxiously awaiting the news from the north.[26] In Santiago, Mauricio Cristi noted that the streets were traveled by "citizens carrying saddened hearts and souls grieving from an intense sorrow," for the bulletins from the north indicated that "two relics of Chile . . . were face to face with two colossuses of Peru," and no one doubted the outcome.[27]

When the news of the battle finally reached the capital, the city erupted. "Bells rang suddenly and numerous groups of citizens filled the streets, embracing amid sobs." People gathered joyously inside the Moneda, while outside crowds cheered before the presidential palace, where even Aníbal Pinto, Chile's usually taciturn president, was seen to be overjoyed.[28] Everywhere the nation acclaimed the brave men of Iquique.[29]

From the outset Arturo Prat was considered the preeminent hero. A subscription drive was begun to acquire another *Esmeralda* to lead the fleet, "as a regiment needs a standard in order to march into battle."[30] When the news of Prat's death became known, another subscription drive was initiated to pay for a monument to the *Esmeralda*'s last captain.[31] Petitions were presented in Congress to honor the fallen hero, to award his wife and mother pensions, and to make his children wards of the state.

The public's acclaim of Prat reached such a fever pitch that one Peruvian complained that Chile was in the throes of a madness called *Pratomanía*.[32] A regiment bore the name of his ship, while a fire company carried his. Streets, plazas, and even a beer were renamed in Prat's honor.[33] Even the young shared in the glory, for in Santiago alone an Arturo Marino and a Gloria Esmeralda were baptized.[34]

After reading a description of the battle, one is confronted with a bewildering and yet intriguing paradox: why is it that Condell, who triumphed at Iquique, is all but forgotten while Prat, who was defeated, became and still is Chile's favorite hero? The immediate response is that Prat became a hero because he sacrificed his life. But is this too simplistic an answer? Why, after all, should self-immolation be more important than victory? Before answering why Prat became a hero, it is first necessary to learn more about his time and the history of the nation that loved him so well.

2 ✟ CHILE, 1876-1879
The Crisis Society

Chile offers at the present moment a curious and apparently sad spectacle to those who had hitherto placed such confidence in her rulers and people, and it remains to be seen whether in this hour of trial, Chile has deserved the credit she has hitherto enjoyed, or whether such respect for this country arose solely for her honesty whilst in affluent circumstances, and the favor of temporary good fortune.

If properly administered this country is far from being insolvent but misgivings as to the administrative capability of the men who govern have arisen, and time alone can prove the result.
—British diplomat in 1878[1]

We are invaded by gangs of assassins and bandits of all kinds, and no one can call his property or his life secure. Stabbing and robbing are the order of the day . . .
—La Revista del Sur in 1879

Although for years considered the model of stability, by 1879 Chile was being destroyed by severe economic and political problems. While many predicted a rebellion, others actively encouraged it.[2] According to José Manuel Balmaceda, then a deputy in the Congress, it was only the outbreak of the War of the Pacific which prevented Chile from being plunged into a civil war.[3]

Many attributed Chile's crisis to its president, Aníbal Pinto, the son of a revolutionary war hero and former president, Francisco Antonio Pinto. The younger Pinto was a quiet, even laconic man, whose gentle face was dominated by a beard perhaps grown to compensate for a receding hairline. The president's earlier political career was not spectacular. He had served as a deputy and later as the minister of war in one of the cabinets of Federico Errázuriz, the man he succeeded as his country's first leader. Almost a political unknown, Pinto was distinguished solely by his personal rectitude and honesty: he was a model of domestic virtue whose private life was untainted by scandal. His professional life was equally exemplary. Indeed, Pinto was so honest that when he retired from public life he would have had no place to live had not a public subscription raised sufficient money to buy him a home. Still, because of this lack of notoriety, Pinto came to the presidency an enigma, a man whose "past is silent. His present is like a cloud. His future has all the mysteries of the shadows."[4]

For such an innocuous individual, the gentle Pinto aroused enormous antipathy, primarily, at least according to his enemies, because his candidacy had been assured through the direct intervention of Errázuriz in the electoral process. The critics claimed that the former president had distributed political patronage and had handpicked the delegates to the presidential convention in order to assure Pinto's victory. The less restrained called Pinto the least qualified and gifted of all the contemporary Chilean political figures, predicting that he would be the political tool of Errázuriz.[5]

The ultramontane Conservative party threw its support to Benjamin Vicuña Mackenna, a renegade Liberal who, after losing the Liberal nomination to Pinto, bolted the party to form his own political organization: the Liberal Democrats. Vicuña Mackenna was a well-known journalist, a prolific author, and a dynamic orator who waged a whistle-stop campaign, attracting large crowds throughout the nation.[6] Pinto, whose public speaking abilities were often lampooned, privately confessed that he doubted he could defeat such an opponent.[7]

In addition to his own skills, Vicuña Mackenna also enjoyed the support of the press which, unrestrained either by good taste or libel laws, described his opponent as a symbol of aristocratic decadence, an aphasic fool, and a effete fop.[8] The few pro-Pinto papers—one of which supported him because he was the lesser of two evils—[9] responded in kind, depicting the Liberal Democratic leader as without principles and a lackey of the wealthy and the Church.[10] For some, words were not enough: in Angol an obscure shoemaker shot and wounded Vicuña Mackenna. Although it could not be proved, the antigovernment forces claimed that the would-be assassin was one of Pinto's supporters.[11]

Despite his earlier promises, Errázuriz appears to have intervened in the election, although to what extent is hard to gauge.[12] Apparently the government was not the only one guilty of such behavior.[13] This, however, did not prevent the opposition press from comparing Errázuriz to various European and American tyrants and his protégé, Pinto, to an assassin of Liberty.[14] The American minister to Santiago, on the other hand, claimed that it was Chile's freest election and compared it favorably with political contests in the United States, a dubious compliment in view of the political corruption of the Grant administration.[15]

Sadly for Pinto, time did not mellow the opposition, which likened his administration to "a pool of stagnant water whose foul fumes were poisoning the life of the nation."[16] The man who had previously been called weak suddenly became endowed with almost demonic powers which permitted him to seduce the Congress from the path of virtue and to corrupt the nation's political parties.[17] All remained impassive while the motherland became the plaything of "bastard and unworthy ambitions."[18]

Pinto's unpopularity could have been predicted, for Errázuriz had saddled him not only with a bad political reputation but with economic problems as well. Under the Errázuriz administration Chile had enjoyed prosperity. The discovery of the Bolivian silver mines at Caracoles had stimulated the economy providing a market for Chilean labor and products. Within a short time, mining became the nation's most dynamic economic sector as the amount of capital invested in mineral extraction almost tripled in a five-year period.[19] The silver boom stimulated other areas of the economy as well, and the gross national product expanded yearly. Money begat more money, and capitalists increased their investments in the economy. An air of euphoria seized the nation as imports of liquor and perfume passed the million peso mark in 1875.[20]

From the onset, the boom of the early 1870s was flawed. The Errázuriz governments, in all the years but one, operated at a deficit, financing railroad construction and even acquiring two ironclads for the fleet. Imports, many of them useless luxuries, exceeded exports. The fever of Caracoles infected Chile with the virus of speculation as greedy credit institutions lent money for questionable projects hoping to make a quick profit.[21] According to one contemporary account, companies were founded more often to exploit the credulous investor than the resources of Bolivia.[22]

The bubble was bound to burst and it did in 1873 when first Germany, and then other European nations, switched to the gold standard. Silver, no longer the metal of monetary exchange, declined in value on the world market. Almost at the same time, the reserves of the Chilean mines began to dwindle and within two years silver production and profits were down.[23] Despite a few optimistic reports that the silver markets would recover, it was obvious that the boom was over: the Fever of Caracoles had broken. In Chañarcillo production declined by more than 70 percent. The same fate befell Chimbero and Lomas Bayas where more than half the mines were abandoned.[24] Copper production also suffered. In a three-year period, copper prices dropped by 50 percent.[25] Mine owners, facing declining profits and exploitation by rapacious exporters, began to shut down their works; the few who continued to operate did so on a reduced level.[26]

Chile fell victim not only to the whims of international trade but to nature as well. In 1876 the heavens opened up. Initially the farmers were pleased. In Concepción one newspaper rejoiced as the rains began to fall. Within two weeks its enthusiasm had dimmed, and after a month it lamented that the rains were destroying the fields.[27] If the south suffered from too much moisture, the north remained bone dry. The heat devastated once green valleys, turning years of labor into dust. One journal estimated that the nation's harvests would be down by 50 percent from the level of 1876 and, the paper noted, 1876 was a bad year.[28]

The winter of 1877 brought no relief. So much rain fell on Talca that the farmers could not sow their fields.[29] In the valley of Aconcagua more than 5,000 *cuadras* of land were submerged. "This year," warned *La Revista del Sur*, "after the 18th of September [Chile's independence day and the begining of Spring] comes the hunger."[30]

Famine did indeed come to Chile. There were shortages of wheat in Chillán. People in Cauquenes came to regard beans and potatoes as a luxury; in Valdivia, where the rains destroyed the crops, the inhabitants began to appear at the doors of a charity hospital afflicted with an illness known as starvation.[31] The bishops of Ancud and Concepción begged their parishoners to donate food for the starving and to offer their prayers for better weather.[32] Santiago's citizens also suffered. The price of beans, onions, potatoes, and bread increased so drastically that most people barely subsisted. "The terrible spectre of hunger," wrote one journal, "is now at our doors."[33]

The combination of poor economic conditions and the climate devastated Chile. The rains alone, it was estimated, idled over 300,000 people, paralyzing the economy.[34] In Concepción, commerce came to a halt and "for rent" signs appeared in the windows of once prosperous firms.[35] Mines in the north continued to stagnate.[36] In the south, when there was employment for the farm worker, it paid so little—between twenty and thirty centavos a day—that he could barely keep himself alive.[37] Beggars began to appear in substantial numbers on the streets of southern cities: Indians tried to procure jobs for their children as domestic servants.[38] The situation became so desperate, according to one paper, that the only alternative to starvation was for an honest man to become "a thief and a decent woman a prostitute."[39]

Many of the unemployed turned to crime. Hordes of bandits ravaged the countryside, stealing cattle and grain from the farms and even attacking railroad trains.[40] Life in the cities became equally unbearable. In Santiago men were not safe after nightfall.[41] The capital, however, was a haven of tranquility in comparison to Chillán and Tucapel where families feared to leave their homes in the light of day.[42] Lawlessness increased so enormously that *The Chilian Times* recommended the formation of vigilante committees; *La Revista del Sur* adopted a more extreme policy, advocating a return of flogging and, if necessary, the lynch rope, to restore order.[43]

Weakened by hunger, living in homes described as kennels and in cities where human ordure was left on the streets, Chileans sickened and died.[44] Smallpox decimated the countryside and the provincial cities; in Santiago so many fell ill that there was not enough room to house them in the municipal lazarette and there were too few carts to transport the corpses to the cemeteries.[45] When it was suggested that vaccination against smallpox be made compulsory, the Conservatives resisted, claiming that the state had no right to intervene in the private life of its citizens.[46] As a consequence, the epidemics continued unabated. Unfortunately, smallpox was not the only disease to plague the nation: diptheria, scarlet fever, measles, and dysentery also took their toll, especially among the poor and the young.[47]

In his first annual message to Congress, Pinto admitted that the nation was in the midst of a crisis. The economy, he noted, was being devastated by a depression which seemed to grow, not receed. The general economic decline, moreover, had reduced the government's revenues, thereby endangering the payment of Chile's foreign debt. Confronted with these problems, Pinto could propose no solution except the reduction of government expenditures, especially those of the military, in hopes of balancing the budget.[48]

The minister of finance, Rafael Sotomayor, was equally pessimistic, prophesying that 1877 would be another deficit year unless the government borrowed money, a measure he opposed. In addition, Sotomayor also objected to his nation's dependence on the *alcabala* and tobacco monopoly for revenue and hoped eventually to find a more stable source of income. But before implementing any radical changes in the nation's tax structure, he preferred to wait for the return of normal economic conditions. Until then, he preached economy to the government and patience to the people.[49]

Neither the remarks of Pinto nor those of Sotomayor pacified the nation. *El Pueblo* stated that the workers could not earn a living and demanded that the president remedy this situation.[50] Other critics, attacking the administration for being more concerned with political and religious issues than with solving the nation's economic problems, advised the government to reduce its expenditures, to cease involving the country in wasteful enterprises like international expeditions and the acquisition of warships. Economy in government and higher import duties, the pundits claimed, would solve Chile's economic dilemma.[51]

Some believed that there were more fundamental reasons for Chile's economic crisis: as long as the nation remained a producer of raw materials, depression would be inevitable.[52] Various politicians joined demonstrating workers to claim that a policy of protectionism and the development of national industries were as necessary to Chile's economic salvation as a balanced budget.[53]

Traditional economists rejected these arguments, claiming that the customs house was a source of revenue, not a regulatory device to protect domestic industry. The only result of such a system would be that the consumer would have to pay more for shoddy, domestically produced items than for imported ones. The worker, he claimed, should seek his salvation in hard work, not in government protection.[54]

This advice was little solace as the depression continued. Copper exports declined over 28 percent in 1877. The silver mines remained paralyzed. The agrarian sector was perhaps the hardest hit, as drought and rain alternately seared and drenched the wheat fields in the late 1870s. Even the little wheat that could be salvaged went unsold, because bumper crops from the United States glutted the world market. Eventually, production declined so drastically that wheat had to be imported from Argentina and Uruguay just to feed the population.[55]

Despite the advice of the finance minister, Chile continued to operate at a deficit. Pinto tried to remedy this situation by ordering economies and even authorizing his minister to France, Alberto Blest Gana, to sell Chile's two ironclads. Although these vessels were offered for less than a quarter of their original price, the European buyers declined the bargain. Unable to find new sources of revenue, Pinto tried to cover his internal debts by borrowing from foreign sources. Inflation and rumors that the government might default on its foreign debts, however, made British and American financiers reluctant to invest any additional money in Chile. The British bankers, furthermore, would not permit a conversion of the existing loans, piously claiming that this would only jeopardize Chile's economic reputation.[56]

Pinto was confronted with the problem of raising money in a paralyzed society. The essential industries, commerce, mining, and agriculture, not only could not pay their taxes, but demanded relief. The National Society of Agriculture urged a reduction in the levies on large landholders, claiming that any deficiency could be made up by assessing the previously exempted small farmer.[57] The copper industry wanted lower export duties on its products and the right to import necessary raw materials.[58] The coal interests also urged that export duties be reduced in order to permit them to compete with foreign rivals. Chile, land of free trade, was rapidly and radically changing its economic orientation.

With the traditional sources of revenue all but exhausted, in 1878 the government proposed direct taxation of income, real and fixed property, and invested capital.[59] Pinto also sought to float another bond issue to tide the government over the crisis. Some of the legislature objected to this method of obtaining government revenue. One congressional committee warned that continued borrowing would aggravate the financial situation and damage the nation's international credit. Restrict expenditures advised the committee members, adding, somewhat unnecessarily, that "a nation, like a private individual, should have its expenses conform to its resources."[60]

Despite such counsel, in June 1878, Pinto borrowed from his nation's banks more than 2,000,000 pesos, at 9 percent interest, for a two-year period. In return, the banks were permitted to issue their own notes, secured by a deposit equaling 25 percent of the total amount emitted, which the treasury had to accept. At least one congressman considered this proposal tantamount to the government's relinquishing its right to coin money, and denounced it as the begining of a paper economy that would depreciate the Chilean peso on the world market and cause internal inflation.[61]

The following month Pinto learned that one of the nation's credit institutions, the Banco Nacional, was almost bankrupt. In a series of secret sessions the Congress heard that only one bank in the entire nation was solvent, making the shift to paper money imperative if panic was to be avoided. Faced with the potential collapse of the economy, the Congress, therefore, decreed that the bank's notes were to be accepted as legal tender for the next two years. Chile had taken the first, and sadly not the last, step on the long road to inflation, a journey that still remains uncompleted. The gold drain was not the only cause of the banking crisis of 1878. Unsound fiscal policies on the part of the banks themselves contributed in no small measure to the poor financial situation. For years these institutions, hoping to profit from the silver boom, had extended credit without the proper metallic reserves, a practice that did not stop, even on the eve of the crisis. The Banco Nacional, for example, with cash reserves of 4,000,000 pesos, lent its own directors 7,000,000 pesos, nearly half of which had been granted only two months before the declaration of the inconvertibility of paper notes.[62]

This declaration did not solve the monetary dilemma. Mines remained below their 1876 levels of production. Commerce faltered and trade with Argentina, for instance, declined over 75 percent in just one year. One newspaper predicted that 1879 would be a year of mass business liquidations.[63] Despite hopes that production might rise, Chile was still importing wheat. The vineyards were plagued by a disease, *odium tuberi*, which one observer noted, "was all that was needed to ruin completely our agriculture."[64]

From all sides the critics assailed the administration with often contradictory attacks. *El Ferrocarril* declared that the government had initiated unnecessary tax reforms when it only needed to economize by reducing the number of public employees and curtailing military expenditures.[65] Provincial newspapers asserted that Pinto's delay in imposing the new forms of taxes proved him to be a lackey of the wealthy.[66] *Las Novedades* stated that the nation had survived a similar economic crisis in 1830, but, "then there was a Portales. And today, what do we have?"[67]

Economic problems were not the only divisive issues in Chile. Serious religious disputes exacerbated Pinto's already strained relations with his countrymen. Chile's ultramontane faction considered liberalism as the political arm of a Masonic conspiracy intent upon destroying the Church. As a representative of this movement, Pinto was suspect, primarily because his closest associates, Errázuriz and Domingo Santa María, were considered violent anticlericals.[68] For this reason the Conservatives had opposed Pinto's candidacy and viewed his election with something less than enthusiasm.

Almost immediately Pinto's cabinet antagonized the Church by advocating such radical changes as allowing work on Sundays and Feast days and the holding of masked balls. The state's attempt to control the schools, which at least one Catholic journal considered part of a Masonic plot, caused additional friction, especially when the government sought to educate women and to abolish the compulsory study of Latin.[69]

Nothing, however, disturbed the faithful as much as the attempt to secularize the cemeteries. The clericals claimed that the burial grounds legally belonged to the Church which had the obligation and right to preserve their sanctity by refusing to bury those whom it considered unworthy. Conservative deputies, the ultramontane press, and the hierarchy warned that the proposed cemetary laws were a prelude to open persecution of the Church and predicted a rebellion if they were passed.[70]

The anticlerical elements responded with equal zeal. Ultramontanism was denounced as the "black vomit of modern socieites"; priests were accused of hoarding food while others starved and of withholding the sacraments for political reasons. One journal even alleged that the Church wished to retain control of the cemetaries because it sold the plots to the poor.[71] By 1878 the level of invective reached such a point that a group of citizens issued a plea for moderation. A petition was published requesting that the outstanding issues between the Church and the state be resolved. The statement, *Espocisión a nuestros conciudadanos*, sought to protect the Church from anticlerical legislation on the grounds that the overwhelming majority of Chile was Roman Catholic. But the petitioners also defended the rights of dissenters, and sought to regularize the relations between the government and the clerical hierarchy.[72] Any attempt at reconciliation was stillborn, for the nation was plunged into another religious crisis over the nomination of a successor to the archbishop of Santiago, Ramón Valdivieso.

Valdivieso, a staunch defender of the prerogatives of the Church, died in June 1878. His passing did not displease some anticlericals, who believed that his demise would cripple the ultramontane cause.[73] The Conservatives, quite naturally, were upset: not only had they lost a powerful leader, they also feared that the government might use the archbishop's death as a chance to appoint someone who would not be as zealous about defending the Church against the state.[74] The nomination of Francisco de Paula Taforó, a priest notorious for his illegitimate birth and his liberal politics, seemed to confirm these fears. The clericals were scandalized, first by Pinto's refusal to consult with the Church hierarchy before making his decision, and then by his selecting an individual whom they regarded as totally unfit. Taforó might be acceptable to a "red pope," exclaimed the rabidly pro-clerical *Estandarte Católico*, but not to Jesus Christ.[75]

As soon as Congress approved Taforó's nomination and sent it to Rome for Papal confirmation, a delegation of the faithful left for the Vatican to fight against Taforó's appointment. When Blest Gana arrived in the Eternal City, he learned that his ultramontane countrymen had preceded him, armed with protests from both the clergy and the laity. Although Blest Gana was also equipped with recommendations praising Taforó, he lamented that not one was written by a priest. Just one clerical sponsor, he wrote, would be more valuable than anything said or written by secular authorities.[76] The Papacy subsequently rejected Taforó's nomination, and the issue remained unsettled for many years. In the meantime, however, the government became involved in an even more volatile religious problem.

Early in 1879, the police of La Ligua, a small town near Santiago, while looking for a criminal, searched the local rectory. The authorities later found the prisoners elsewhere, but the village priest, Francisco Lisboa, and his congregation became incensed at the violation of religious sanctuary. Lisboa led a religious procession to protest the actions of the police which he denounced as sacreligious. The authorities halted the parade, provoking a demonstration during which a provincial official was wounded. The police jailed Lisboa provoking the ultramontane press to claim that such actions violated the priest's clerical as well as civil rights.[77]

Beset by internal difficulties, Chile also became involved in a diplomatic dispute with Argentina over the control of the Strait of Magellan and Patagonia. Although this was a long-standing problem, it had never become a serious issue until Argentina, flushed with its victories in the Paraguayan War, began to press its claims to the disputed territory in the late 1870s. Adolfo Ibáñez had been Chile's foreign minister until 1875 when he was replaced with José Alfonso, a moderate who, unlike Ibáñez, was willing to cede Patagonia to Argentina in return for Chilean control of the strait.[78]

The government subsequently sent Diego Barros Arana to Buenos Aires to negotiate the boundary problem. To the nation's dismay, Barros Arana exceeded his authority by agreeing to a treaty in which Chile retained only partial control of the strait, thereby losing its outlet to the Atlantic. The negotiations became further complicated when Chilean authorities seized a foreign ship for violating its territorial waters. The vessel, the *Devonshire*, was operating within the contested area, but it had received permission to do so from the Argentine government. The latter, outraged at seeing its authority mocked, mobilized its fleet and sent warships to the Santa Cruz River to support Argentine claims.

Both nations hovered on the brink of war until they agreed to submit the issue to arbitration. Pending a final solution, however, Chile was to exercise its sovereignty only on the Pacific side of the strait. Pinto submitted this agreement, the Fierro-Sarratea Treaty, to the Chilean Congress for ratification where a large number of deputies attacked it, claiming that Patagonia was Chile's by virtue of an earlier Spanish land grant and by right of prior occupation. Adolfo Ibáñez stated at one point in the debate that the proposed treaty constituted a turning point in Chile's history, when a choice had to be made between its becoming either a rich empire or an American Switzerland. With the rich resources of Patagonia, he claimed, Chilean agriculture, pastoral activities, and industries would prosper, making the nation wealthy and powerful. Without these resources, Chile's major export would be soldiers who would serve foreign masters and farmers who would till alien soil.[79]

A substantial portion of the press joined the Congress in opposing the treaty. The most generous critics merely attacked Pinto for being misguided: the less restrained accused him of purposely betraying the nation's interests, staining Chile's honor, and cravenly capitulating to Argentina.[80]

Before the treaty was ratified, a handbill was circulated in Santiago urging the people to gather before the Congress to cheer "those valiant deputies who defended the honor of Chile, now so infamously besmirched with mud by a pact arranged by merchants."[81] Six congressmen voted against the proposed treaty, and twelve stalked out in protest, to be greeted by the cheering mobs below. Despite these melodramatic gestures, the bill received the support of the majority of the legislature which the press villified for having pushed Chile "on the via dolorosa of the nation's dignity."[82]

Within weeks of the Argentine crisis, indeed perhaps because of it, a border dispute with Bolivia plunged Chile into the War of the Pacific. Now, in addition to the burdens of internal dissent and economic paralysis, Pinto and his nation had to face the threat of extermination. For all too brief a moment there was unity: the politicians ceased carping, the citizens stilled their whining, and even the criminals stopped stealing[83] in order to rally around the leader they had previously excoriated. Lamentably these moments of accord were short-lived: the fragile bonds of sunshine patriotism could not withstand the dual burden of political animosity and a foreign war. Alienated in peace, Pinto's task was now more difficult as the leader of a Chile plunged into a fratricidal war.

3 ⚔ THE WAR OF THE PACIFIC
The Heroic Medium

*The so-called War of the Pacific, which erupted in
1879, was a conflict between Chile on the one side, and
Peru and Bolivia on the other. In simple terms Chile was an
energetic, economically expanding nation that coveted the
great mineral treasures, particularly in nitrates, found in
the coastal provinces of her neighbors, Bolivia and Peru.
Irresistibly tempted by these underdeveloped and sparsely
occupied areas, Chile took advantage of the customary
political anarchy in the Republics to take the provinces by
a war of conquest.*
—JOHN LLOYD MECHAM, A Survey of United States–
Latin American Relations

I

Bolivia precipitated the War of the Pacific when it imposed higher taxes on the Chilean-owned nitrate companies operating in the Atacama Desert. Since colonial times the Atacama had been considered worthless until the discovery first of guano, and then of nitrates, made this area extremely valuable. Suddenly Bolivia and Chile laid claim to this previously neglected strip of desert, and for years each nation engaged in fruitless negotiations hoping to have its jurisdiction recognized. In 1874, Chile signed an agreement relinquishing its rights to the disputed territory in return for which Bolivia agreed not to increase the taxes on the Chilean Compañía de Salitre y Ferrocarriles for twenty-five years. Although the Atacama officially became part of Bolivia, most Chileans still considered the area morally theirs, since the majority of its population and economic enterprises were owned by their countrymen, and resented the fact that their compatriots had to live under the uncertain rule of Bolivia.[1]

Following on the heels of the Argentine crisis, the increase in taxes antagonized the already touchy Chileans who considered the Bolivian action not only arbitrary but insulting to Chile's national honor. For this reason, when Pinto demonstrated a willingness to parley with the Bolivians, a substantial portion of the press objected. Bolivia, the journals complained, had never contributed to the development of the Atacama, and now it was using the issue of taxation as a pretext for the eventual expropriation of Chilean property.[2]

The Chilean press demanded that Pinto protect the nation's honor and enforce its treaty rights.[3] A public meeting even advocated the use of force to defend the nationally owned industries.[4] In February 1879, Pinto ordered his troops to occupy the littoral, basing his action on the concept of "revindication," a doctrine that claimed Chile was entitled to repossess its former territory on the grounds that, by raising the taxes, Bolivia had voided its 1874 treaty with Chile. Although this action led to a Bolivian declaration of war, the Chilean press almost unanimously supported its president's decision.[5]

Chile had other enemies besides Bolivia. Some feared that Argentina and Peru might possibly intervene.[6] This anxiety, at least that regarding Peru, was not illusory, for within a week after the seizure of Antofagasta, Chilean newspapers, noting that pro-Bolivian demonstrations were taking place in Lima, began to express doubts about their northern neighbor's neutrality.[7] Peru, in the meantime, sent a diplomatic mission to Chile to mediate between the two disputing nations. Although the Chilean government officially welcomed it, many newspapers doubted that it would be effective: Bolivia did not appear disposed to arbitration, and Peruvian demands for the withdrawal of Chilean troops from the littoral were unacceptable.[8] According to many Chileans, the return of the disputed territory would expose their compatriots in the north to the caprice of the Bolivian government's reprisals.[9]

While the Peruvian mission remained in Chile, the local newspapers continued to reprint the increasingly hostile statements being made by the Lima press.[10] The Chileans considered these editorials unjust. They denied that Chile had any imperialistic designs and sought to reassure the Peruvians that the occupation of the Atacama would ultimately benefit them, because industry in the disputed area would prosper more under Chilean than Bolivian administration.[11]

The Chilean press noted, however, that the Peruvians were arming their fleet and reinforcing their garrison at Iquique. Both the papers and the Congress asked the government to clarify the significance of these actions and their possible repercussions.[12] While some newspapers were willing to interpret the Peruvian moves as purely defensive acts against a possible Bolivian violation of its territorial integrity, they did not explain why Peru was readying its fleet when Bolivia had no navy, or why Peru was sending weapons to Bolivia.[13]

Within a few weeks, many believed that a Peruvian declaration of war against Chile was imminent and that Peru's diplomatic mission was merely a subterfuge to gain time.[14] Some claimed that Peru and Bolivia had signed a secret military alliance, an allegation both the press and the Congress wanted the Pinto government either to confirm or deny.[15] Before March ended, however, few, if any, doubted that such a treaty existed. On the contrary, most of the Chilean press argued that it was Peru that had encouraged the Bolivians to raise the taxes on the Chilean-owned nitrate company. The press theorized that the Peruvians had promised the Bolivians a favorable trade treaty in return for which the Bolivians would raise the taxes on the Chilean mines. The Bolivians, never expecting the Chilean company to pay the taxes, had planned to use the company's refusal as a pretext for expropriating its holdings, knowing that the Chilean government, already embroiled in a border dispute with Argentina, could not retaliate. The Fierro-Sarretea Treaty with Argentina, however, saved Chile, for it no longer had to worry about its eastern border. Bolivia, unfortunately, had committed itself and was past the point of no return.[16]

The final rupture in Chilean-Peruvian relations was almost anticlimactic and occurred when the Chilean government demanded to know whether there was a secret treaty between Peru and Bolivia, and, if so, whether Peru would remain neutral in case of war. When Peru replied that it could not declare its neutrality because of its 1873 alliance with Bolivia, Pinto, with congressional support, declared war on April 5, 1879.

II

Chile was seriously unprepared for war. The government, for reasons of economy, had drastically reduced its military expenditures and scaled down the size of the armed forces. The

Chilean military could muster only 2,400 troops, most of whom were protecting its southern border against the Indians. The National Guard, often considered at best a tool of political repression and at worst a useless extravagance, had also been gutted; by 1879, it numbered but 7,161 men, a 70 percent reduction over the previous year.[17]

The regular army's units were not only understrength, they were badly equipped with old Comblain rifles and American carbines, with little additional materiel should the army have to expand. The National Guard was in even worse condition, because its infantry units used the obsolete Minié rifle, which had a tendency to explode when fired, while the cavalry did not even have firearms, only lances and sabers. Only a few of the reserve artillery units possessed fieldpieces, but these were almost useless, because they were made of bronze. In essence the National Guard was militarily unimportant; it could not even clothe or arm its own members, let alone provide a trained reserve to supplement the regular troops.[18]

It is extremely difficult to evaluate the military potential of the Allies. As the years have elapsed the Bolivian and Peruvian historians have often exaggerated Chile's strength and underestimated their own nation's military prowess in order to excuse the Allied defeat.[19] Although there is some agreement on the size of Peru's National Guard—approximately 65,000 men—various historians have estimated the strength of that nation's army at anywhere from 2,000 to 7,000. Despite the discrepancy, it can be ascertained that the Peruvian army could muster at least 5,789 men at the beginning of the war. Like the Chileans, the Peruvians also had tried to reform their army by sending military missions to Europe to study new methods and to acquire weapons. These plans never came to fruition, however, because of financial problems. Again like Chile, Peru equipped its troops with a variety of weapons, relying mostly on the Casteñon rifle, a modified version of the Chassepot, and possessed a few artillery units, most of which were inadequately equipped.[20]

Bolivia's prewar military strength is also something of a mystery. Although the peacetime army numbered between 1,200 and 2,300 men, the nation also had a large National Guard of some 54,000, which was increased by mobilizing all unmarried men between the ages of sixteen and forty once war began.[21] The Bolivian army's equipment consisted of a bizarre assortment of different weapons of varying calibers and nationalities, although it received substantial numbers of new and modern weapons from Peru and Argentina.[22]

Whatever their material deficiencies, the Allied armies still outnumbered their enemy by more than two to one, a fact of which the Chileans were uncomfortably aware.[23] While some of the Chilean press might sarcastically describe the average Bolivian soldier as an illiterate Indian, they still feared him. The enemy, it was observed, was strong, well armed, and dedicated. Even before Peru's entry into the war, various Chilean news journals were already disturbed about fighting just Bolivia and cautioned the nation not to be too impetuous or optimistic;[24] Peru's involvement in the struggle increased these fears.[25]

Like the army, the Chilean navy had also suffered from economy measures. By 1879, one transport and a corvette had been sold, while two other warships, the *Covadonga* and the *Esmeralda*, were disarmed. The active fleet consisted of six vessels: the two ironclads, *Blanco Encalada* and the *Cochrane*; the corvettes, *Chacabuco*, *Magallanes*, and *O'Higgins*; and the transport, *Toltén*. Not all of the fleet, however, was battle ready. The *O'Higgins* and the *Chacabuco* required such extensive repairs on their boilers that one naval officer recommended that they be used only as sailing ships. The *Blanco Encalada* needed its armor repaired; and its bottom, like that of the majority of the fleet, was so fouled that its speed was reduced by almost one-half. Of the entire squadron, the director of arsenals considered only the ironclads, the *Magallanes* and the *Toltén* seaworthy.[26]

Additional problems plagued the navy as well. The fleet did not possess sufficient transports, making logistic support difficult. The navy also lacked both junior officers and ablebodied seamen because the government had closed the Naval Academy and the School for Mariners in 1876. For this reason, some of the ships were so understrength when the war began that Chile had to hire foreigners to man its fleet. Perhaps Luis Uribe, a survivor of Iquique and later an admiral, was correct when he subsequently declared that Chile triumphed in the War of the Pacific only because Peru was the more disorganized.[27]

The mainstay of Peru's navy was its two ironclads: the monitor *Huáscar* and the frigate *Independencia*. There were also two other ironclads, but these were so old that they had been relegated to coastal defense. Peruvian historians have claimed that Peru's navy was more decrepit than its army. Manuel Vegas and Geraldo Arosamena stated that the fleet had not participated in firing exercises for over five years. They also alleged that a substantial number of ships had been either disarmed or dismantled when the war began.[28] According to Paz Soldán, only the *Pilcomayo* was really seaworthy, while supposedly the rest of the squadron was in varying stages of decay.[29]

These later judgments do not agree with the reports of various contemporary observers. In 1878 the Peruvian government declared its fleet was the "best organized and disciplined of all the Pacific States."[30] While this might be dismissed as propaganda, in that same year the Ministerio de Marina pronounced the *Huáscar* in perfect condition.[31] In March 1879, two Peruvian newspapers were pleased to report that the *Manco Capac*, the *Huáscar*, the *Independencia*, and the *Unión* were ready for combat.[32] These remarks tend to indicate that Peru's fleet was a worthy adversary for the Chileans. Indeed, one might wonder if they had not taken on more than they could handle.

Both sides were aware of their respective deficiencies and tried to augment their naval strength by purchasing additional vessels. Peru sought to acquire an ironclad from Italy, hoping to sail it immediately to Callao. The Chilean government tried to block these transactions, and even considered ambushing any newly purchased Peruvian ship as it entered the Strait of Magellan.[33] Throughout the war, each nation waged a diplomatic struggle to deprive the other of munitions and supplies from abroad. Peru once hired an English torpedo expert, a former Royal Navy officer, to act as an instructor, but the Chileans successfully prevented him and his torpedoes from reaching the enemy. The Peruvians had similar luck when they stopped a shipment of torpedo boats, labeled farm machinery, from reaching Chile.[34]

In addition to these two avowed enemies, Chile faced the threat of Argentine intervention. Argentine naval vessels, operating out of Peruvian ports or launching an attack from the Atlantic, in conjunction with the Peruvians from the north, would have caught the Chilean navy in a vise.[35] The Chilean fleet, therefore, had to win some initial victory to demonstrate to its eastern neighbor that its intervention would be foolhardy.

III

Apparently, it was the lack of a clearly defined strategic objective, not material deficiencies, which prevented Chile from winning this necessary victory. Although there was general agreement that naval superiority was a prerequisite to the conquest of Peru, there was a crucial and costly difference of opinion on how to achieve this needed maritime supremacy. The president and his advisors had favored an immediate attack on Callao hoping to destroy or immobilize the Peruvian fleet after which the Chileans could then launch an attack against Lima, thus capturing Peru's political and military nerve center while bypassing its garrisons in the south.[36]

The commander of the Chilean squadron, Admiral Juan Williams Rebolledo, did not agree with his superiors. He claimed that the fleet was unable to launch an attack against Callao because it was too dangerous. He further argued that the navy did not possess the necessary logistic support to sustain a blockade so far from its base of operations. As an alternative Williams proposed to blockade Iquique, which he did on April 5, 1879. The admiral believed that this action, which would deprive Peru of its nitrate revenue, in conjunction with additional attacks on the Peruvian coast, would force the enemy to abandon his fortified port and come south to attack the Chileans.[37] This essentially passive strategy miscarried, however, for it permitted the Peruvian fleet to arm its capital ships and to fortify both Callao and Arica, an important port to the south.[38] In addition, the Peruvian naval commander, Miguel Grau, capitalized on the Chilean inertia by harrassing its lines of communication, knowing full well that as long as the Chilean fleet remained off-balance, Peru was safe from invasion.

Four contests marked Williams's tenure as fleet commander: Chipana, which was inconclusive; the assault on Callao, which was a farce; the blockade of Iquique, which was useless; and the capture of the *Rimac*, which was a disaster. Chipana occurred within the first weeks of the war, on April 15, 1879, when two Peruvian ships attacked the *Magallanes*. The battle was really only a brief skirmish because the Peruvians had to give up the pursuit when one of their ships blew a boiler. Despite the unheroic quality of the contest, both sides glorified the encounter—the Chileans for having escaped, and the Peruvians for having forced the enemy to retreat.[39] Except for the occasional bombardment of an undefended nitrate dock, it was not until mid-May that the Chilean fleet took any decisive action. Till then, it steamed off Iquique wasting precious coal, its crews riddled by scurvy and demoralized by inactivity.[40]

Suddenly, on May 16, without informing either his president, the minister of the navy, or his own officers about his destination, Williams embarked on his ill-fated attack on Callao. As noted earlier, his expedition was hardly a masterpiece of planning or execution. During the trip north, Williams managed to lose his fleet collier. He further handicapped the expedition by including in the attack force vessels whose slow speed substantially inhibited the entire convoy's rate of progress. Finally the admiral failed to deploy some of his ships to reconnoiter ahead. Had he done so on the evening of May 19, he might have intercepted the southward bound Peruvian fleet, thus averting the disaster of Iquique.[41] Having botched his earlier attack on Callao, thereby fullfilling his own prophecy that such a mission was impossible, Williams reverted to his old strategm of reinstating the sterile blockade of Iquique.

Although the loss of the *Independencia* drastically altered the naval balance of power in Chile's favor, both Williams and Grau ignored this fact, the first out of obstinacy, the second out of a sense of desperation. The Peruvian fleet continued to attack Chilean shipping and coastal cities, and even occupied Punta Arenas, a port more than 3,000 miles south of Lima. In the meantime Williams moped off of Iquique waiting for a glimpse of his enemy and perhaps secretly glad that he did not appear. Occasionally the admiral made some half-hearted attempt to capture the *Huáscar*, but each time he failed. This should have been expected: because he had refused to allow his ships' bottoms to be cleaned or their engines to be repaired, Williams's squadron was no match for the speed of the "Ghost of the Pacific."[42] In a fit of pique the admiral vented his frustrations by shelling more nitrate docks and once even bombarding the defenseless city of Iquique, claiming that the enemy had the effrontery to launch a torpedo attack against him.[43]

As might be expected, those who worked with Williams described him as a difficult individual. Independent to a fault, he rarely consulted with the president, let alone with his army counterpart or his subordinates.[44] He appeared to despise General Arteaga, the commander of the army expeditionary forces, and refused to coordinate his efforts with those of the military.[45] The admiral often behaved erratically, frequently countermanding his orders for no apparent reason.[46] Terrified of torpedoes (a reasonable fear but one inconsistent with his profession), Williams imagined them everywhere, and refused to anchor for the night unless assured he was safe.[47] This fearless mariner also suffered from ill health, supposedly syphilitic in origin, and used this as a threat to resign from command knowing that the government dared not replace him because the admiral was far too popular with the fleet.[48] Williams, moreover, enjoyed the protection of the Conservative party, which was considering running him as its candidate for the presidency in 1881.[49] Any move against him by Pinto, therefore, would have embroiled the president in political infighting, something he wished to avoid because he already had enough foreign enemies.

While Williams was vacillating, the army had been training and equipping its personnel. The weeks of inactivity became difficult to endure, and many soldiers deserted because of material shortages and poor pay. Condemned to wait upon the navy's pleasure, their officers complained about Williams's conduct of the operations.[50] Various high-ranking government officials shared the army's disdain of the admiral, accusing him of not actively pursuing the Peruvian fleet.[51] Plans were afoot to ease Williams from authority, political consequences be damned, when the capture of the *Rimac* finally forced him from command. The loss of the *Rimac*, a transport carrying men and equipment to the north, precipitated a government crisis and eventually led to the collapse of the ministry of Antonio Varas. His successor replaced Williams with the younger and more dynamic Galvarino Riveros. The new commander ordered his ships cleaned and repaired and, after dividing the fleet into two divisions, each built around one of the ironclads, began to search for the *Huáscar*.

On October 8, one task force sighted the *Huáscar* and the *Unión* sailing north. As the outnumbered enemy fled, the second Chilean squadron blocked its escape route. The *Unión*, capitalizing on its speed, outdistanced the Chileans. The *Huáscar*, however, turned to face its six pursuers off Punta Angamos. Within seventy minutes the Peruvian ship, an abattoir, struck its colors. Grau and the majority of his officers and men were dead, and with them perished Peru's chance of winning the war. Shortly after this battle the Chilean army invaded the Peruvian province of Tarapacá. By January 1881, Lima, the jewel of the old Viceroyalty, was in Chilean hands. The war was to linger on for a few years more before the diplomats finished what the generals had begun. In 1883, Peru ceded Tarapacá to Chile and gave it temporary control over the provinces of Tacna and Arica. Bolivia, which did not sign an armistice agreement until 1884, suffered the most, losing its coastal provinces and its outlet to the sea. Isolated in the *altiplano* it was to continue to harass Chile in hopes of regaining its lost territory. For Chile the happy conclusion of the war, however, tended to obscure the difficulties of the early days of the struggle, days that must be relived in order to understand the rise of Prat to popularity.

IV

When war was declared, the entire nation pledged its support to the Pinto government.[52] *El Ferrocarril* informed the public that the hour of sacrifice had arrived and that Chile demanded that each should fulfill his duty.[53] In a pastoral letter, the bishop of Concepción stressed the need for "abnegation, valor, and above all, obedience to duty, even unto death." Chile, he noted, had always abided by the motto of living with honor or dying with glory, and he expected this tradition to be honored.[54] La Serena's bishop reiterated these demands and ordered his clergy to preach that it was glorious to die when the motherland was in danger.[55]

It was not only the people who were to bear the burden. The press included the government in the need for sacrifice, enjoining it to be vigilant in equipping the soldiers and resourceful in directing the war effort and leading the nation. Pinto and his ministers were warned that they too must sacrifice to be examples of "unblemished patriotism, sacrificing everything, even their personal comfort," to conquer glory.[56] If the government fulfilled its duties, if it led Chile to victory, then it would be a "strong government . . . beloved . . . a government which the people of Chile and their representatives would forgive many failures."[57] The president was warned, however, that the nation would not tolerate any act that would besmirch the nation's honor; Chile demanded nothing less than victory from its leaders.[58]

The initial outburst of euphoric patriotic unity was short-lived, and the Chilean press soon found substantial reason for being discontented with Pinto. Initially the public complained about the government's failure to forestall an allied attack by establishing defensive positions in the north. Later it was the blockade of Iquique that excited the critics, who claimed this strategem was ineffective because it allowed the enemy to reinforce its southern garrisons at will and prevented the fleet's being used to best advantage.[59] Some of the press noted that while the fleet waited outside Iquique, the entire Chilean coastline was defenseless. The critics supported this allegation by citing the example of Chipana where, as a result of the government's mishandling, disaster had almost befallen the Chileans—a fate, it noted, that had been avoided only because of the intervention of Divine Providence and the skill of the *Magallanes*'s captain. The press, like the public, was unaware that it was Williams, not the president, who was the author of the blockade and instead blamed it on "the faint hearted and cowardly spirit . . . in the Moneda [Chile's presidential palace]."[60]

The sinking of the *Independencia* quite naturally encouraged the press to be more voluble in its complaints about continuing the blockade. After all, Chile had won naval supremacy and should assert it to best advantage. When it did not—when the blockade was reinstituted—the protests became more shrill. The government was accused of being both incompetent and deaf to the pleas for action, and of conducting the war without a "design, plan, or overall strategy."[61] While the government waited, the Peruvians continued to fortify their cities causing one source to wonder if the administration was waiting until the enemy was prepared before attacking.[62] When Peruvian arms shipments from Panama reached Callao unhindered, the government was congratulated for being so vigilant.[63] It was particularly galling that the Peruvian navy, supposedly inferior in ships and men, was still on the offensive. As it raided the Chilean littoral, some sarcastically recommended that the Chileans should copy Peruvian naval tactics.[64]

Throughout June and July the cries for an offensive filled the nation. The army, immobile since the seizure of Antofagasta, became demoralized. Recruits, who at the outbreak of the war rushed to enlist, now deserted with alacrity seeing that those entrusted with waging the war were failing in their duty.[65] The civilians became equally dissatisfied. The average citizen, it was reported, on encountering a friend in the street, no longer inquired after his companion's health, but on the progress of the war.[66] The public's attitude toward the government became increasingly hostile as newspapers fanned the fears of an anxious and frustrated people. The press blamed the government for not providing sufficient food, clothing, and amunition for the troops; for permitting incompetent officers to remain in command; for playing partisan politics.[67] These errors, along with the failure to seize the initiative, disenchanted the people who were described as being caught up in an "atmosphere of impatience, of disgust and restrained fury . . . owing to the inertia and confusion . . . of the directors of the war."[68]

The nation, it was asserted, had sacrificed for the war giving freely of its money, its blood, and its youth.[69] It was not with the people that the fault lay, but with the government, characterized as a "monopoly of blunders,"[70] and the ally of a criminally complacent and self-seeking Congress, which had plunged Chile into a pit of despair.[71] Nowhere, lamented one paper, was there a leader for if there were "a strong heart, a clear eye, and a vigorous arm in the Moneda, the war would have been over by May."[72]

The lack of confidence in the executive and legislative branches of the government made some yearn for the return of a Portales.[73] One anonymous citizen even suggested turning the nation over to a dictator who would rule for the duration of the war.[74] More significant were the threats that the people would act violently unless the government demonstrated its ability to lead. *Las Novedades* described the public's mood as being quite amenable to "popular action" and remarked that it would be very "easy to raise twenty or thirty thousand men to answer the cry of the motherland wounded by treachery."[75]

The *Rimac*'s capture seemed to be the final blow. Seized without firing a shot in its own defense, its flag still flying, the vessel was incorporated into the Peruvian navy and its crew and passengers, a crack cavalry unit, were interned. When the news reached Santiago, crowds gathered before the Congress building calling for the ministers to resign. That same evening, mobs chanted, "Death to the traitors," in front of the Moneda. Rioting ensued, and troops responded to the rocks of the crowd with bullets, wounding and killing many.[76] The public's protest had been in vain, for according to one newspaper, Pinto "in an excess of foresight and . . . cowardice . . . had fled to Viña del Mar.[77]

Although the press generally disapproved of the rioting, fearing that it might indirectly aid the enemy, it nonetheless sympathized with the people and considered the demonstrations a logical consequence of the government's incompetence, corruption, preoccupation with partisan politics, and outright treachery.[78] More rioting was predicted, even rebellion, unless the president and his government acceded to the public's demands for an aggressive war.[79] One paper was less optimistic over the prospect of Pinto's completing his term of office and pointedly reminded him that O'Higgins had abdicated rather than precipitate a civil war.[80]

The public, unaware that it was Williams and not Pinto who had stalemated the war, turned on the president, the Congress, indeed, the entire Chilean political establishment. The failures of the war were never attributed to the Chilean people, only to their leaders, who supposedly were incapable of comprehending the meaning of patriotism. The press stated that it was not in the Moneda or the Congress where patriotism existed, but in the north, with the army and navy. A populist movement began which attacked the moral bankruptcy of almost the entire Chilean ruling class. The public unfavorably compared the present war leaders with those who had lead Chile in its fight for independence and its later struggle against Peru in 1838.[81]

What the nation needed to do, it was claimed, was release this spirit, the spirit of the true Chile. The motherland cried out for patriotism, "not the patriotism of music, pomp, and song . . . but the patriotism of Montesquieu . . . a love of country greater than the love of self," a "pure patriotism abnegating, vehement, sincere, which knows how to sacrifice, and actually sacrifices all for the enrichment, the brilliance, the prosperity and the triumph of the motherland."[82]

As can be seen, the early months of the war frustrated the Chilean people, turning them against their leaders, who they suspected of being either unwilling or unable to lead the nation. This yearning for sacrifice and inspiration provided a climate of opinion that, when given the catalyst of Iquique, ensured the initial popularity of Arturo Prat and pushed him into national prominence.

4 ⚔ THE HERO AND HIS TIME

The Chileans have lost their minds. They have become idolaters of a new religion which is called Prat. *There, everything is* Prat. *The names, the ships, the battalions, the societies, the statutes: even the scapularies. This is real Pratomania.*
—Peruvian newspaper, 1879

I

It is often difficult for present-day scholars, especially foreigners, to comprehend the basis of Prat's fame. By pragmatic standards the dead sailor could be complimented only for having delayed the battle's inevitable conclusion. While this may have been laudable, still this is not the stuff of which heroes are made. The men who write history do so from the relative comfort of a library or archive, insulated from the ambience and spirit that permeated the societies they so closely study.

If Iquique were a theatrical production, it would have been produced as a tragedy with its three principal actors, Williams, Condell, and Prat, each representing specific human qualities: greed, timidity, and sacrifice. Of the three actors Williams was perhaps the most important because he initiated the chain of events which lead to Prat's death. As earlier noted, the admiral was incompetent, which the more charitable perhaps might attribute to senescence, not stupidity. But whatever the reason, Williams mishandled the attack on Callao, first by refusing to abandon the mission after losing his fleet collier and then, the most critical error of all, by returning to Iquique without having inflicted any damage on the enemy.

In view of this less than splendid performance, one may seriously question whether Williams wanted to attack the Peruvians. It is certainly curious that after weeks of refusing to move against Callao, on the grounds that it would be too dangerous, he had reversed himself. Strange behavior indeed, especially from a man who was notorious for not committing his forces unless sure, if not of victory, then at least that his life would be safe![1]

It would be pleasing to report that some distant trumpet had awakened the admiral from his paretic dotage, inspiring him to battle for his country again. Sadly the explanation is not so idealistic. Williams wanted to be president of the Republic, a fantasy both the Conservative party and the admiral's general staff encouraged.[2] Because of his earlier war record Williams doubtless believed that his chances for election were excellent, but his refusal to carry the war to the enemy began to cost him support. Furthermore the press became quite critical which, according to his associates, upset the naval commander and potential candidate.[3] If Williams did entertain political aspirations, a hostile press was capable of destroying them. Williams therefore had to seize the offensive in order to redeem himself and his budding political career. Thus it was not patriotism as much as the cloying odor of political spoils which sent the old war horse clumsily moving to the north.

Although political ambition might explain why the admiral suddenly became so spirited, it still does not clarify why he chose Callao as the target, an objective he had earlier refused to approach. Obviously Williams was under pressure and needed some dramatic gesture to redeem his career. Callao therefore was a logical target. Apparently another factor played an important part in his decision: he had learned that the Peruvian fleet was not in Callao or that it was planning to leave. Therefore he opted for Callao knowing that it was not only glamourous but, above all, a safe objective.

These are serious charges, but they are not made lightly. After the battle, a high government official wrote to the prime minister charging that the attack on Callao was a "farce" and claiming "almost to have evidence that he [Williams] knew from the commander of a ship, which he visited, that the Peruvian fleet had already left that port [Callao]. . . . "[4] José Alfonso, another civilian government official, substantiated this charge, writing that a Chilean naval officer, Juan Simpson, had been told by the capitan of an English mail ship recently arrived from Peru that the Peruvians soon would be sailing south. Simpson admitted that he had not relayed this information to Williams, but he nonetheless believed that either the mail boat captain or the admiral's chief of staff had informed the admiral. These charges seem to be founded in fact because Williams, in his memoirs, admitted having met an English merchant marine officer on the night in question, although he denied that he was told anything else.[5]

On the basis of this information one may reconstruct the events in the following manner: Williams, seeing his political future jeopardized, realized that he had to take the offensive. Fearful of failure, he resolved to attack where he knew there was little danger. When he learned of the forthcoming sortie of the Peruvian fleet, he decided to move north, confident that he was sailing to an almost empty harbor. This same theory might also explain why Williams did not attack those ships he found in Callao: he was acting out a charade, a show of force, demonstrating his dynamic leadership and assuring his political future at the same time.

The part of Carlos Condell is also quite interesting. Condell's naval career had been meteoric but unstable; twice he had left the navy, once involuntarily. Affable and somewhat volatile, Condell was notorious throughout the fleet for his good luck, a trait that had protected him although he had neither a naval specialty nor the desire to study for one. Nowhere, however, did he need this luck more than in the Battle of Iquique.[6]

At the beginning of the battle, Prat had instructed Condell to follow in his wake and to keep as close to shore as possible. Condell, however, violated these orders and left the harbor, causing Prat to exclaim: "What is the *Covadonga* doing?"[7] Had Condell been on the *Esmeralda*'s deck, he might have answered Prat as glibly as he replied to a survivor of the battle who had asked him the same question. "Because I saw clearly that one had only two alternatives: surrender or go to the bottom with her. This made me decide to try to find a better fate."[8]

The desire for a "better fate" and his good luck, combined with the incompetence or hasty judgment of the *Independencia*'s captain, catapulted Condell into the limelight. The new naval hero wrote eloquently to the naval ministry, savoring his victory, and explaining his hasty and uncalled-for exit from Iquique as a strategic maneuver.[9] An earlier report, written before he knew that he was a hero, was less facile and perhaps closer to the truth.

> Seeing the superiority of the enemy, who in addition to his
> ironclads employed thirty boats which were sent against us
> from the beach, and seeing that . . . it was not only difficult
> but impossible for us either to defeat or escape an enemy ten
> times more powerful than we, I resolved to sail southward,
> keeping as close to the shoreline as possible.[10]

Unlike his second report, this one contained no mention of saving the *Esmeralda*, only Condell's implicit admission that discretion was the better part of valor. Perhaps the captain was not
completely at fault for his later expansiveness. A telegram to the
president from a high-ranking civilian official wanted Condell to
rewrite the report because the first "belittles the battle, and . . .
this is due to the fault of the narrator and perhaps the stupid fear
of spending too much money on the telegraph. . . ."[11] It might
well have been the encouragement from the fleet secretary, or the
open account for telegraph expenses, which encouraged Condell
to alter materially his first appraisal of the battle. Yet, if Condell
became the darling of the people, among his brother officers he
seemed less than popular. Luis Uribe, a lieutenant who survived
Iquique, exclaimed, on hearing of Condell's "victory": "That is
typical of Condell's luck which has protected him all his life regardless of the difficulties confronting him."[12] It is also interesting
to report that Condell appeared to lose the esteem of many of his
colleagues who, while considering him brave, nonetheless believed
that he lacked certain moral qualities.[13]

Prat, of course, did not share in Condell's famous luck. After
four hours of unequal struggle, Prat, in his last desperate moments
of life, flung himself upon his enemy. Perhaps too brave, he died
well but futilely.

Had the Chilean people been aware of the lackluster performance of both Condell and Williams, there would be no mystery
about why Prat became so famous. With rare exception, however,
the majority of the nation, then as now, was almost totally ignorant
of the facts. All they knew was that Prat had died in a naval battle,
that Condell had sunk the *Independencia*, and that Williams was
still the nation's respected naval leader. We therefore are still
faced with the same question: Why was Prat chosen as a hero
when there appears no rational basis for doing so?

II

One must conclude that the Chilean people in 1879 did not choose Prat for his pragmatism, but for what he represented. Prat exemplified the spirit of sacrifice fulfilled. It mattered not what he accomplished but what he was. Prat died for Chile, and an analysis of various primary sources—the press, congressional debates, and public meetings—demonstrates that it was his self-immolation that made him a hero in the eyes of his countrymen.

One of the most persuasive examples of this attitude was an interchange during a congressional debate. A member of the Chamber of Deputies submitted a motion to award prizes to the officers and men of the *Magallanes* for their acts of heroism at Chipana and the second battle of Iquique. While many deputies were willing to strike a medal for the crew, they denied the request for pensions. The sponsor of the motion, Enrique Tocornal, compared the two engagements with the exploits of the *Esmeralda*, claiming that the *Magallanes* had also fought against overwhelming odds and that only the skill of its commander, Juan Latorre, had saved it from disaster. Tocornal noted that the Republic had previously rewarded the participants of battles which had brought glory to the nation and asserted that the men of Chipana were certainly as worthy of this reward as the sailors of Iquique.

Justo Arteaga Alemparte, another deputy, rejected Tocornal's claim, stating:

> . . . The battle of Chipana cannot be compared with that of Iquique, Captain Latorre has proved that he was ready to sacrifice himself, but still the occasion for him to do so has not yet arrived.
>
> Whoever carries a sword is a man who is ready to die; but in war, valor alone is not enough. In order to be a hero it is also necessary to have the opportunity to have the luck.
>
> Doubtless Captain Latorre would have jumped from his vessel and boarded the enemy ship. But the opportunity for doing so still has not presented itself.
>
> The battle of Chipana is a happy battle, but the battle of Chipana is not the battle of Iquique; it is not a battle of heroes.[14]

Apparently Arteaga had many who agreed with him, for *La Patria* noted sarcastically:

> . . . In Chile they [the officers and men of the Magallanes] are not worthy nor will they be promoted because their ship was not sunk with half its crew cut to pieces and horribly mutilated. Forward brave sailors: Chile will reward you after you are dead.[15]

Perhaps it was for this reason that Condell's actions, though praised, were not as highly extolled as those of Prat. Prat had faced his enemy, aware that he was doomed, but, afflicted "with the madness of valor [and] the delirium of heroism," had jumped aboard the enemy's ship and was killed.[16] Condell, on the other hand, not only survived the battle, but his triumph occurred under entirely different circumstances. Fleeing from the harbor of Iquique, he shrewdly lured his opponent onto a submerged reef perhaps giving the impression that he was lucky and nothing else. Certainly some of the press noted the distinction between his actions and those of the fallen hero. One newspaper called the *Covadonga*'s survival a "miracle"[17] while another, although admitting Condell's skill, partially attributed his victory to his enemy's "lack of prudence."[18] A third credited Condell's good fortune.[19] Some of the press even claimed that Condell owed his victory to Prat, asserting that the *Esmeralda* had saved the *Covadonga* by diverting the *Huáscar*'s attention or that the fallen hero had ordered Condell to flee the port, thereby saving him.[20] The priest Esteban Muñoz Donoso noted, while not wishing to depreciate Condell's acts, that the latter's victory was the result of Prat's sacrifice.[21] The *Chilian Times* was more candid, praising Prat for his heroism, but noting that Condell had triumphed only because "a splendid ironclad frigate, steaming 12 knots, stupidly went aground on a rock while chasing a sloop steaming four knots."[22]

Thus it was not only the quality of Prat's behavior but the aid he rendered which distinguished the two men's actions. Prat did not owe his victory either to guile, good fortune, or his adversary's error. Aware of the inevitable consequences of his acts, he did not hesitate. His was a triumph of the will, generated by his own raw courage.

It is still difficult to understand why self-sacrifice should be the prerequisite for being a hero. Quite possibly this might have been the result of the Church and its teachings. As indicated earlier, the bishop of La Serena had called it a glorious act to die for one's motherland,[23] while his colleague, the bishop of Concepción, drawing on biblical heroes to inspire his parishoners, stated that the Chilean soldier, as a warrior of Christ, "does not put aside his weapon . . . until his last breath."[24] Francisco Belmar's *Manual of the Soldier in Defense of Chile Against Bolivia* similarly stressed the need for the sacrifice of one's life, claiming that "to spill one's blood in her [the motherland's] defense is a divine precept" and whoever would deny this to her "makes himself a criminal before the God Who created him, Who preserves him and Who commands that he sacrifice himself for her when necessary."[25]

The giving up of one's life was not simply virtuous, but was the epitome of human feelings, for when one acted heroically, "the human miseries are forgotten, vile flesh is transformed into vestments of light and the image of likeness to God is evident." In a requiem mass celebrated in Prat's honor, a priest, Esteban Muñoz Donoso, called Jesus "the hero of heroes; He made the cross a symbol of divine heroism and Golgotha the peak of His infinite glory."[26]

In Prat's sacrifice and that of his men there was a purifying force which enabled them to attain immortality. One cleric, Joaquín Díaz, for example, described Prat as a saint;[27] Belmar, another priest, stated that God waited for Prat and for all who died for their motherland "at the door of heaven, to crown him with glory."[28]

Belmar even claimed that it was sacrilege to allow Chile's flag to fall into the enemy's hands. The tricolored banner, he stated, "brings to mind the most beautiful Trinity of the Sky; and its white star is a symbol of the Patron Saint of our arms, the Virgin Carmelo."[29] Religious motifs permeated the vocabulary of heroism. Providence, for example, "favored Chile's cause";[30] the nation's flag resembled the Virgin, and like her, was immaculate.[31] It was perhaps for this reason that Prat's insistence that Chile's banner should not fall into Peruvian hands was so well received in a predominately Catholic nation.

Prat himself was often referred to as a martyr.[32] This is curious, because Arturo Wilson, a survivor of the Battle of Iquique, objected to the choice of that word. He claimed that Prat was simply a soldier "who defended a noble cause which his government could not peacefully resolve, and which, as a result had to be settled by force of arms." The title of martyr, therefore, was inappropriate because "both belligerents were armed and well aware of what they were doing; they had no other motivating force than love of country, and were ready to sacrifice their all for her [Chile or Peru]." He dismissed as "the fortunes of war" that one of the contestants was more powerful than the other.[33]

Despite Wilson's complaints, the religious theme gained strength. Great emphasis was placed on the body and blood of Prat, which according to at least one account, was shed as a form of penance. Prat, it was said, was like a saint who had ascended to heaven,[34] and his name was invoked as if to intercede in Chile's behalf.[35]

The tendency to depict the war and Prat's death in religious terms may well have been the result of Chile's Catholic heritage. Because Jesus had voluntarily martyred himself for mankind, it would not have been unusual to describe others who also sacrificed their lives in the same manner. Chileans, confronted with an act such as Prat's, may have subconsciously reverted to a traditional form of expression when describing it, especially those who interpreted the war as God's punishment for Chile's moral decay and anticlericalism.[36] Thus the New Testament was reenacted in miniature: Prat was equated with Jesus; the *Esmeralda* became his Calvary; and Chile, represented by its flag, was humanity fallen from a state of grace.

Chile's cultural heritage may also have inspired the need for sacrifice. As Ramón Menéndez Pidal noted, Spaniards have historically lionized men who gave their lives for a cause.[37] Chile's indigenous peoples demonstrated a similar trait. Indian chiefs like Caupolicán and Lautaro showed that the Araucanian also preferred to sacrifice himself rather than surrender.[38] Thus the two cultures, the Spanish and the Araucanian, established a tradition that required death before dishonor, a tradition subsequently reinforced by O'Higgins who was reputed to have said that Chileans either live with honor or die with glory. This colonial-independence period imagery fused to produce a standard of conduct which had to be emulated if one were to be considered a good Chilean. Prat was the first to equal this standard and for this reason was compared not only with Pedro de Valdivia,[39] Chile's first conquistador, but with various leaders of the independence movement: the personification of the spirit which drove the Spanish from Chile, the sons of Carrera, Freire and O'Higgins, the heroes who had established the traditions of victory or death.[40] Another poet, Domingo Izquierdo, exercising the license of his profession, even depicted Prat rising to heaven where he was greeted by O'Higgins.[41] Prat apparently so exemplified Chile's martial past that one priest was to state: "No Chilean could remain indifferent to Iquique . . . without ceasing to be a true son of O'Higgins and San Martín, of Caupolicán and Lautaro."[42]

Thus Prat's popularity can, at least in part, be understood because he had emulated a traditional Chilean cultural value. By choosing death over surrender, he had become "a standard of what ought to be expected of the sublime abnegation of our men of war, the active dedication and vigilance which the public demands of its forces . . . the spirit of those who sacrifice their lives in the nation's defense."[43]

III

As will be demonstrated, the Chilean society employed Prat in four ways: to demonstrate that Chile's warrior traditions had not atrophied; to compensate for the loss of the *Esmeralda* and to bolster the homefront's sagging morale; as a rallying cry for revenge; and finally, for internal political purposes.

Although constant warfare was the hallmark of its colonial period, postindependence Chile generally enjoyed internal stability and harmonious relations with its neighbors. Only twice before had Chileans taken up arms: in the 1830s they waged a victorious war against the Peruvian-Bolivian Confederation; and later they joined other Pacific Coast nations fighting against Spain in 1868. Neither of these contests was particularly spectacular: the 1830 conflict was protracted and bitter; the war against Spain was a disaster culminating in the bombardment and destruction of Valparaíso by the enemy fleet.

The Chileans considered themselves a nation primarily interested in commerce and agriculture, more at home in the market-

place than in the barracks square.[44] After all, one did not earn the
title of the Englishmen of South America or convert Valparaíso
into the principal trading center of the Pacific by fighting, but by
hard work and judicious investments. Because of this historical
development, the 1879 war with Peru and Bolivia made many
Chileans question if they had not forgotten their martial skills in
their quest for profit. A youth organization, *Juventud Chilena*,
asserted that the nation would be victorious only "if its children,
inspired by the examples of their ancestors, show themselves
worthy of her name and her glory by giving proof of selflessness
and patriotism."[45]

On May 21, Prat furnished the proof that Chile was still a warrior nation. He was the first to imitate the older standards of conduct, thereby demonstrating that "the years of peace and progress
in the arts and a life of material well being and abundance, have
not sapped the strength of their character nor weakened . . . the
old fiber of the indomitable sons of Castille and of the Araucanian
Indian."[46] The fallen hero proved to the world that Chile's "old
military spirit, instead of becoming weaker in forty years of peace
has become stronger."[47]

After a period of self-doubt Prat had proved that these fears
were groundless. He had demonstrated that, regardless of the circumstances of battle or the nature of his equipment, there were
hundreds, perhaps thousands, "capable of dying for Chile, cover-
ing the beloved flag of the motherland with their bodies."[48] Chile
had thus proved itself still a nation of heroes, and as Eduardo de
la Barra said of the men of Iquique: "They are Chileans: they
know how to fulfill their duty; they know how to die at their
posts."[49] The press joined Prat's name to that of Chile's earliest
heroes and described him as the descendant of the men who had
liberated the nation, proving that the spirit that had freed Chile
from Spain still lived.[50] A priest, Muñoz Donoso, joyfully proclaimed in one of his sermons, "Rise, illustrious shadows of the
fathers of the motherland, and sigh, because your blood has not
been sterile."[51]

In their relief on discovering that they were still a potent force,
Chileans made hyperbole the standard for describing Prat. *El Ferrocarril*, for example, claimed that the dead hero had shown the
world that "heroism is a spontaneous product of its [Chile's] soil,

and that the same uplifting spirit fills our heart today, as it did yesterday."[52] The fallen mariner proved the Chileans were an "invincible people, with a vigorous soul . . ." destined to become the leader of Latin America.[53] Others claimed that Chile was the equal of other warrior states and compared the obscure naval officer with Leonidas at Thermopylae, Nelson at Trafalgar, and the French Guard at Waterloo.[54] Some Chileans believed that Prat had made Chile famous and proudly noted how the battle had attracted so much of the world's approval.[55]

The rather exaggerated nature of some of these remarks reveals, perhaps, how deeply the war had tested Chilean self-confidence. Beneath the patriotic overstatements ran a deep-seated and ill-concealed fear, the result of the static and unproductive war. As has been demonstrated, following the seizure of Antofagasta, the conflict had degenerated into a "phony war" occasionally punctuated by some near disaster like Chipana. That Iquique brought no relief to this situation can be seen in the words of various Chilean Journals which described the battle as a "disaster," a "calamity,"[56] a "tragic event,"[57] even stating that the Peruvians had been able to "impose on us an hour of mortification and shame."[58]

Some sought to divert attention from this aspect of the battle by concentrating on Prat's heroism, thus converting an otherwise disastrous event into the last resort of the loser: a moral victory.[59] The press took some solace in the fact that, despite its advantage, the *Huáscar* took four hours to sink the *Esmeralda* and claimed that, because of this overwhelming superiority, the Peruvian attack did not even merit the title of a battle, but should instead be called a "cowardly murder."[60] A rationalizing government proudly proclaimed that winning was almost trivial in comparison with Prat's example; anyone could win battles, "but sacrifice is known only by the great souls and can only be demonstrated by a strong race and by nations who have been fortunate in understanding the dignity and grandeur of patriotism."[61] The press joined in the attempt to gloss over the *Esmeralda*'s destruction and Prat's death, claiming that only the strong and courageous could sustain losses in war. A people that could not were "not born to be conquerors. Their victories will be fortuitous. Their defeat is inevitable. They will never conquer, and if they do they will never consolidate their victories."[62] In essence the nation tried to disguise the loss it sustained at Iquique: defeat became victory because in dying Prat showed the inner strength of the Chilean character converting the *Esmeralda* from a shattered hull into "an epic victory bejewelled with heroism and sacrifice."[63]

But Prat did more than establish that the Chileans were a heroic people and console them for the loss of the *Esmeralda*. He also became the leader of the crusade to defeat the Peruvians. The press, delighted that the nation could produce heroes, demanded that others imitate his feat of sacrifice.[64] As one newspaper observed, "The blood of the incomparable heroes demands vengeance and there throbs in the great heart of the Chilean people the burning hope that soon the efforts of our sailors will finish the work of the martyr."[65] A hero had emerged who compensated for the defeat at Iquique, a source of inspiration to encourage those still living to emulate his noble actions. Just as Portales's death had galvanized the Chileans in an earlier war against the Peruvian-Bolivian Confederation, Prat's death became a cry for retribution which, if obtained, would guarantee his nation's eventual triumph.

Unfortunately some Chileans were willing to make Iquique not only the battle cry in a war against Peru but also a slogan for a political vendetta against Pinto. The dislike of the president had not lessened and seemed to coalesce around the issue of Iquique and the ill-fated attack on Callao. The public had been appalled to learn that the *Covadonga* and *Esmeralda* had been left alone in the bay and demanded to know who was responsible for this grievous error which resulted in the loss of the famous ship and its brave captain.[66] The press appeared perplexed by the entire affair, unable to understand why the enemy had been able to attack so easily and was disquieted by the fact that, but for the "heroism of our sailors," the Peruvians would have been more successful. Some questioned if it was the president, his ministers, or the naval high command who had dreamed up the ill-fated scheme and demanded to know who, in fact, was its author.[67]

The press generally made the government the scapegoat for Iquique. "The sensation which the news has caused in Valparaíso has been immense. The indignation in the capital has not been less. And everyone blames the government for the loss of our ships because of its lack of foresight and for leaving them alone in

Iquique."[68] One reporter described a conversation he overheard in which one of the participants summed up the battle by stating: "Here are the results of the infallible plans of the Ministry. . . . The Ministry, yes the Ministry . . . that is the guilty one."[69]

Two theories developed both of which blamed the government for Iquique. The first claimed that the Peruvians had repaired the underwater telegraph connecting Iquique with Lima after the Chileans had severed it. Thus, when Williams sailed north, Peruvian spies had flashed the news to Lima which, in turn, dispatched the *Huáscar* and the *Independencia* to attack the weaker Chilean vessels. If this claim were true, as one newspaper charged, then the battle was the result of the skill of the Peruvian espionage system and "the lack of foresight of the government . . . whose responsibility for the battle cannot be more sad or more grave,"[70] because everyone knew that the Peruvians were cowards and would seize the opportunity to win an easy victory. The second claim was that the government, not Admiral Williams, ordered the attack on Callao. One newspaper even stated that Pinto had commanded the *Esmeralda* and the *Covadonga* to remain in Iquique because their reduced speed would slow down the convoy, lamenting, "What a tremendous responsibility for President Pinto, whose error caused such a tremendous misfortune to befall our nation."[71]

Regardless of the true circumstances, Iquique became synonymous with the government's incompetent conduct of the war. "The *Esmeralda* and the *Covadonga* . . . are two stanzas of a poem of glory to Chile which have been handed over to the fury of the enemy, either through torpor or criminal negligence."[72] *El Independiente* sarcastically commented, "Three hundred corpses are floating at this moment in the ocean. . . . [They] speak still higher of the Cabinet's foresight and practical wisdom."[73] In the Chamber of Deputies, Aníbal Las Casas noted "that the still warm bodies of Iquique were the result of . . . [the] lack of a foresight and [the] negligence of those entrusted with the duty of being wise and cautious."[74]

Henceforth Iquique became an instrument to taunt the government each time it erred. Unfortunately the enemies of Pinto had many opportunities to use this tool. In mid-July the *Huáscar* launched a surprise night attack on the Chilean fleet while it lay at anchor at Iquique. Although Grau did not succeed in inflicting any damage, his daring outraged the press. Once again, *El Centinela* noted, the enemy had made "sitting ducks" of the Chilean forces.[75] *El Independiente* recalled that the Peruvians had earlier surprised the fleet, on May 21, when, as a result of the government's inexcusable confidence, the fleet's two weakest ships had been left in Iquique.[76] *El Mercurio*, while describing the July engagement, sadly remembered the first battle of Iquique which occurred as a result of "negligence and lack of cunning." Chile had lost the *Esmeralda*.[77]

The capture of the *Rimac*, within two weeks of the second battle of Iquique, gave the press additional reasons for attacking the government. As one paper noted, were it not for the "puerile confidence . . . of our leaders the *Esmeralda* might not be at the bottom of the ocean, nor the *Rimac* in the hands of our enemies."[78] *El Centinela* professed amazement, not that the enemy had captured the Chilean ship, but that it had not happened earlier.[79] "Sad luck for a country . . . when its protection is entrusted to a stupid arm and a myopic eye," wrote another journal which quoted a member of the Council of State who said that the government's "stupidities" were destroying the fleet.[80]

In contrast to the bumbling government leaders, Prat emerged as a paragon of virtue, and was used to demonstrate that "the tremendous infamy of our leaders" has not equalled the "martyrdom of a man and the . . . justice of our cause."[81] Benjamín Vicuña Mackenna sadly noted that although the Chilean people had risen to the level of the warriors of Iquique, their president and his government had not, thereby committing a sin for which there was no absolution.[82] Prat was the example of "abnegation, valor, and sacrifice."[83] If Chile demanded perseverance, Prat had fought for four hours against incredible odds.[84] If the people required examples of obedience to duty, Prat had remained at his post until his last breath. Serenely he had faced and accepted death, and voluntarily had given his life. Benjamín Vicuña Mackenna wrote that Prat was Chile's "representative man," "a chosen and privileged human being who suddenly revealed himself to his nation, and who, identifying himself with one epoch, passed to the love and the veneration of other ages." Prat was the incarnation of Chile's true spirit, and 1879 was the "Year of Prat."[85]

The hero thus provided a means of exposing the government's deficiencies. While the administration was castigated for failing to provide adequate food, clothing, and ammunition,[68] Prat was extolled because he inquired if his men had breakfasted, thus demonstrating a concern for the people, a trait at least one journalist wished the government might emulate.[87] *El Mercurio* attacked the government for not seizing the initiative in waging war, while praising Prat for boarding the *Huáscar*. The same paper criticized the administration for sacrificing the nation to its personal interests, while depicting the fallen hero as a family man, who offered everything, even his life, for his nation. Prat was the man who preferred to die rather than betray his nation, while his government despoiled Chile by following a diplomatic policy based on "Americanism" and failing to lead the country as it deserved.[88]

Thus Prat was to the Chilean people what their government was not: abnegating, brave, and most important, sacrificing. His popularity was rooted in their need for these virtues. Exhausted by the prewar economic problems and political strife, frustrated by the war, the people needed some ideal to inspire them. Because their government could not provide this ideal, they turned to extragovernmental sources. It was in the waters of Iquique that they found an individual who personified not only the necessary virtues, but the dynamic and sacrificing leadership needed in war. Arturo Prat supplanted the legitimate government which, due to its wretched record, had forfeited the nation's admiration and respect.

It does appear that the use of Prat as an antigovernment symbol had political implications. Chile's prewar political cleavages ran deep; and, as one newspaper noted, "the honeymoon of patriotism" that occurred at the onset of the war lasted but a short time.[89] Perhaps it would have been naïve not to expect that Prat would become a tool in some politico's arsenal despite the protests of the well intentioned.[90] A conservative newspaper, doubtless to advance the faith, claimed that Prat was inspired by the Church's teachings to sacrifice his life.[91] Benjamín Vicuña Mackenna, an open enemy of the Pinto regime, alleged that Prat favored free elections in Chile, intimating that the government's supposed intervention in the last national election had displeased the fallen hero.[92]

This political manipulation of Prat becomes more apparent in some of the letters and proposals submitted to honor the Capitán of Iquique. The Chamber of Deputies sent a condolence letter to Prat's mother, for example, which bore sixty-eight signatures. Of these, forty-seven were of men who belonged to rival political parties such as the Conservative, Liberal Democratic, and Radical.[93]

Other events indicate that this was not an isolated event. Santiago's municipal government also sent a condolence letter to doña Carmela.[94] Of its twenty-three signatories, all but one were either anti-Pinto or had some affiliation with an antigovernment political coalition. Of the twenty-nine men involved in the project to build a statue to honor Prat, six had signed the 1878 petition against the government, seven were Conservatives, and two were Liberal Democrats, the latter a political party formed by Benjamín Vicuña Mackenna after Pinto had supposedly cheated him out of the presidency. Even men with no obvious political affiliation either had ties with opposition parties or were critics of many of the government's policies.[95]

The measures to award pensions and other honors to the *Esmeralda*'s officers and men followed the same pattern as the letters of condolence. Although Pinto had originally stated that he was planning to reward the families of those who participated in the battle, he claimed that the legislature should take the initiative in making proposals.[96] Congress took him at his word and submitted two measures for consideration before that of the president.

The first proposal suggested that the government purchase two naval vessels, one to be named after Prat and the second for the *Esmeralda*. It also requested that the *Independencia* be declared a prize, one-half of its value to be distributed among the families of the deceased and the remainder among the survivors. The bill also requested that a medal be struck in gold and diamonds for the commanding officers; in gold for the officers, and in silver for the enlisted men.[97]

The second bill was even more generous. It requested that the state adopt Prat's two children and pay 500 pesos per year toward their education. In addition, each child was to receive 25,000 pesos in bonds, while Prat's widow was to be awarded the pension of a vice admiral. The families of those killed were also to receive a pension equivalent to higher ranks than they held before the battle. The bill also granted Condell 50,000 pesos in bonds, and promoted the survivors two grades.[98]

On the same day that Pinto submitted his plan, a third measure was introduced in the Congress. It, too, was very generous. The state was to purchase a home for the Prat family, as well as to pay for the children's education. Prat's wife was to receive a pension of 4,340 pesos a year, and his mother, 1,500. The wife of Serrano, one of the officers killed on the *Huáscar's* deck, would also be given a pension of 2,462 pesos a year and a house. Finally, the mother of Ernesto Riquelme, a midshipman who had died so valiantly, was to receive an annual pension of 1,500 pesos.[99]

In comparison with these measures, Pinto's proposal was almost niggardly. He requested that the Prat family be awarded a settlement of 30,000 pesos to be divided among Prat's wife and children. The dead officer's son and daughter, furthermore, were to receive scholarships for their education. The government would also award pensions to the families of those killed, while those who survived were to be given a bonus.[100]

The Senate also submitted a proposal. Like those of the Chamber, it exceeded the provisions of Pinto's measure. Prat's mother was awarded a pension of 1,000 pesos a year; his wife, 3,000 pesos. His son was to receive 500 pesos a year for ten years, and the daughter, the same amount for fifteen years. Serrano's mother was to receive 600 pesos a year; his wife, 2,000. Riquelme's mother was likewise granted a pension of 600 pesos a year. Those who died were awarded pensions plus a bonus of 25 percent, and the survivors were also granted a special bonus.[101]

Most of the congressional proposals exceeded the amount the president originally requested, a fact duly noted by one antigovernment newspaper, *Los Tiempos*.[102] Enrique Tocornal, an opposition politician, accused Pinto of being reluctant to submit his proposals to reward the men of Iquique, and further claimed that the Council of State had rejected his original measure as being "too miserly."[103] Some congressmen attacked Pinto's ministers of treasury and justice for refusing to expedite the payment of some temporary relief to the bereaved families.[104]

It is probable that Pinto's proposals were made to appear stingy for political reasons. Certainly it does appear curious that all of the legislature's recommendations appropriated more money than did that of the president. The most striking fact, however, is that the majority of those who proposed the legislation, or who were its most avid supporters, were members of opposition parties. The first proposal, for example, had fifteen sponsors, fourteen of whom were members of the ultramontane Conservative party.[105] Manuel Novoa, a congressman from the National party and a signatory of the 1878 petition criticizing the government, sponsored the second bill.[106] The third motion was the work of Juan Mackenna, also a Conservative.[107] The Senate's proposal seems to be the only exception, but even here politics may have played a role. A three-man committee, only one of whom may have had an antigovernment bias, authored the Senate's first bill, which was the least generous of all save Pinto's motion. Later a second committee submitted an amended proposal which was far more open handed than the original. Of these seven men, at least four were known for their opposition to Pinto. Another interesting coincidence: the man who worked hardest to increase the provisions of the bill was Benjamín Vicuña Mackenna, a well-known enemy of Pinto.[108]

This analysis seems to indicate that there was a close relationship between the development of Prat as a hero and the maneuvers of opposition political parties. This is not to intimate that all those who supported Prat were enemies of the Pinto administration, nor should it be construed to mean that the popular reaction of the nation to Prat was politically inspired. It does demonstrate, however, an apparent correlation between opposition politics and the uses made of Prat.

These political parties utilized the fallen hero in two ways. The first was to accuse subtly the government of not being responsive and grateful to Prat and his men for their sacrifice. Pinto was depicted as a miser, his government as ungracious in recognizing the valiant dead hero. This might have been for the purpose of contrasting the massive public acceptance of Prat and the limited response of the hero's government.

Some politicians also used Prat's heroism to defend Admiral Williams. As earlier noted, many attempted to blame the death of Prat and the Battle of Iquique on the government. To a great extent the Pinto administration was considered responsible for the battle's taking place under such unfortunate circumstances. Some, however, questioned if it might not be the fault of Williams. *El Centinela*, for example, noted that prior to Iquique Williams had informed his officers that they were soon to undertake an important mission. In the meantime, the blockade would be maintained by the *Esmeralda* and the *Covadonga*. The paper ended its article by questioning if Williams "was the author of the abandonment? Or . . . did Williams receive an order to leave the weakest naval vessels of the Republic alone? Once again, deep mystery." [109]

The admiral had not been extremely popular with the public. *La Patria*, in April, compared Williams to Lord Nelson, associating the former with cowardice and the latter with heroism.

> Nelson lost an eye at Calais, an arm at Tenerife, the skin of his forehead at Aboukir, and his life at Trafalgar.
>
> (Williams) Rebolledo heard the broadsides of the battle of Abtao behind a rock; has blockaded the unarmed port of Iquique; has passed far from Arica . . . ; has bombarded undefended cities like Pabellon de Pica and Huanillo; has lost his honor in Mollendo, that is if he ever possessed it.
>
> Nelson and [Williams] Rebolledo: An impossible comparison. [110]

Iquique certainly did not enhance Williams's reputation. Some of the press complained that the admiral had taken too much time to return from Callao and therefore held him responsible for the battle's taking place. [111] In an open letter to President Pinto, an "Old Patriot" demanded Williams's removal from command, alleging that Williams had not satisfied Chile's needs, and that the country would be better served if it replaced him with someone more skilled and intelligent, "if not more brave." [112]

Williams, however, was not without defenders who claimed that his ships were decrepit, the result of imprudent economies, and that their bottoms were like oyster beds. [113] *El Nuevo Ferrocarril*, an antigovernment paper, noting that the *Huáscar*'s speed was almost double that of Chile's ironclads, wrote: "Now one must not only be willing to die like a lion, he must also be capable of overcoming this disadvantage as well. Such is the administration of the Moneda." [114]

Some of the press averred that the government ordered Williams north and that it demanded that the *Esmeralda* and *Cova-*

donga remain in Iquique.[115] Another paper even alleged that the government had learned that the Peruvian fleet was sailing south but had refused to inform the admiral.[116] Supposedly Williams had letters supporting some of these claims and was going to demand a public hearing to clear his name, but the confrontation never occurred. Some of the admiral's partisans were not so subdued, and accused the government of persecuting Williams and denying him, and the navy, its aid.[117]

These assertions sought to displace the responsibility for the loss of the *Esmeralda* and the death of Prat from Williams to someone else. If the admiral was not guilty, then logically it had to be the government. One of the most subtle methods of exculpating Williams was by cloaking him with Prat's mantle of glory. *El Independiente*, for example, called Williams the patriarch of the Chilean fleet, the man who had trained Prat.[118] Because Williams was responsible for Prat's heroic acts at Iquique, it was not very logically argued, the admiral could not therefore be guilty of any error. At a dinner honoring the men of the *Covadonga*, Salvador Reyes exclaimed: "Prat and Condell are two names which signify glory for our nation and we would be unjust if we did not join to them the name of their teacher [Williams]. . . ." On the same occasion, Benjamín Navarrete stated: "The sailors of the fleet acknowledge that their admiral is not only a model and example of glorious feats, but . . . a father who shows them . . . fondness as well as severity, the path of honor."[119]

The use of Prat to salvage Williams's reputation was in part politically inspired. Williams was supposedly going to be the Conservative party's candidate in the next presidential election, and apparently this group defended Williams in order to protect its political investment. There is certainly sufficient evidence to show that there was a close relationship between the admiral and the Conservatives. Williams's chief defender in Congress was Carlos Walker Martínez, a prominent Conservative leader and the man who met the admiral when he returned from his service with the fleet.[120] Conservatives also figured prominently among those who signed the various petitions being circulated to defend Williams's conduct of the war.[121] Finally, it was mainly Conservative journals like *Estandarte Católico* which vigorously defended the admiral. Other antigovernment forces also supported Williams: Benjamín

Vicuña Mackenna, for example, toasted the admiral, stating that he too shared in Prat's glory.[122] Certain newspapers, which had a decidedly anti-Pinto bias, were also noted for their pro-Williams stance.

Arturo Prat, therefore, became more than a mere symbol of Chilean heroism. He was also used to attack his nation's leaders by demonstrating that they were derelict in their duty. This does not mean that all who revered the dead hero were motivated by a desire to disgrace the government. Still, it does show that Prat was an ideal vehicle with which to malign Pinto, and it appears that the unscrupulous manipulated the dead hero to their own advantage.

5 ⚔ ARTURO PRAT AND THE PARLIAMENTARY REGIME 1880-1920

The north is a tumor on the healthy body of Chile, a tumor which always suppurates and attracts flies. Even politics has been poisoned by its contacts, morals decayed; earnings did no good to those who toiled and wealth flitted by to fatten a few purses, leaving a residue for the Public Treasury and irresponsibility to the souls.
—GUILLERMO SUBERCASEAUX, Chile o Una Loca Geografía

I am not frightened by the idea that, by increasing the powers of the President, a Bismarck might appear who would dominate the political situation and who would succeed in gaining in authority at the expense of the transitory interest of the political parties.

I am not frightened by the advent of a Bismarck; moreover, I want it . . . I am not frightened; the reinforcement of authority, as I visualize it, is the only salvation for the nation.
—JOSÉ MIGUEL ECHEÑIQUE, National Deputy in 1899

I   1880–1900: The Decline of the Hero

After 1879, despite the earlier promises of eternal love and devotion, the Chilean public's interest in Arturo Prat waned. The decline in his popularity began in 1880 and continued until the mid-1890s. As Appendix I indicates, the amount of newspaper coverage devoted to Prat and the Battle of Iquique followed a fluctuating but downward curve. Although the majority of the press still printed some editorials commemorating the twenty-first of May, these had the strained quality of a child's thank-you note, perfunctory, graceless, and usually a little tardy.

As Appendix II indicates other media reflected this decline. In 1879 four books praising Prat appeared; in 1880 there were three plus the symphony, *The Seizure of the Huáscar.* The following year Domingo Izquierdo's play was performed. In 1883 Ramón

Pacheco wrote a fictional account of the battle and, in that same year, a commemorative pamphlet was published. Two years later, Benjamín Vicuña Mackenna wrote his two-volume work, *El álbum de gloria*, a book commemorating the heroes of the War of the Pacific, which dealt with Prat only tangentially. In 1886, Alfredo Irarrázaval Zañartu read his poem on Prat at the dedication of the naval monument; Manuel Hidalgo Carrasco played his canto, "Arturo Prat"; and another book appeared. The following year, Rubén Darío's ode to Prat won first prize in a poetry contest held to commemorate Iquique. Finally, in 1888, Justo Abel Rosales wrote his biography on Prat. Apparently, however, no other books or pamphlets about Prat were published until the turn of the century.

From 1880 to 1895, the period of decline in Prat's fame, the popular press devoted a substantial amount of space to the hero only in 1886 and 1888. Although this appears to invalidate the downward trend in Prat's popularity, it can be easily explained. The first date marked the dedication of the naval monument in Valparaíso; on the second, two years later, the government ex-humed Prat's remains and those of his comrades at Iquique and buried them beneath the monument. Although officially the monu-ment was a tribute to the navy, in reality it honored Prat and those involved in the battle.[1] A statue of the fallen hero stood atop the marble-tiered tomb, his hand clasping the nation's flag. His last words were emblazoned below, in bronze, while statues of Ri-quelme, Serrano, Aldea, and the unknown Chilean sailor who died on the *Huáscar's* deck stood on the second level.

The Chileans appeared not to notice Prat after 1888 as if he had been relegated to some patriotic limbo. The press often failed to mark the anniversary, or if it did, it merely described the festivities commemorating the battle and not the hero. From the descriptions it appears that these celebrations did not do justice to the dead hero. *Estandarte Católico* compained that the 1889 festivities were not only "ungraceful and unattractive," but also ill attended and very badly organized.[2] A year later *El Mercurio* laconically commented that "today's ceremonies will be no better nor worse than those of other years . . ."[3] while *Estandarte Católico* noted that the newspapers were filled with the news of everything but Iquique. "Political passion," it lamented, "steals everything."[4] In

1892, *El Ferrocarril* claimed that the twenty-first of May "passed unnoticed, since no celebrations were organized; nothing was done to commemorate it. . . ."[5] Apparently Valparaíso's 1893 festivities were equally uninspiring, consisting of the singing of the national anthem, and the "Hymn to Prat" by school children, a *Te Deum*, and a military parade.[6] In Concepción, to the south, *El Sur* sadly noted: "The 21st of May passed among us like any other day of the week."[7] Two years later, *El Mercurio* reported: "The festivities which have commemorated . . . the greatest act in our history have been almost insignificant."[8]

Some of the press blamed the government and municipal authorities for the inadequate cerebrations. "Poor, very poor, are the official demonstrations which were held to commemorate such an important day," commented a Santiago paper in 1884;[9] while Valparaíso's most prestigious journal wrote, "On days like this one, the square [where Prat's monument was to be located and where the commemorative ceremonies were normally held] seems to us like one of those vulgar women who wear what is left over from better times, adorned with ribbons and ornaments, wrinkled and filthy. . . ."[10] In 1885, *Estandarte Católico* complained about the festivities, claiming that they were in bad taste and blaming it on the unpatriotic spirit of Santiago's municipal and provincial governments.[11]

Five years later, *El Mercurio* angrily noted that someone had varnished the bronze parts of the monument, including the statues, making the entire memorial look like "a chocolate cake . . . [while] each statue looks like a black Christy minstrel. . . ."[12] Again in 1894 there were caustic remarks about the size of the official government party and the "simple" festivities.[13] A señor Ramos demanded that the government encourage the people to honor the anniversary of Iquique and the heroes who made it famous.[14]

Despite these charges it is doubtful that the government was responsible for the poor celebrations. On the contrary, public apathy sems to have been the cause of the lack of enthusiasm. As early as 1885, Santiago papers described as "moderate" the number of people who attended the commemorative ceremonies and complained that the bands departed the celebrations with unseemly haste.[15] In the same year, *Estandarte Católico* stated: "Crowds have only gathered at the Plaza de Armas and the University. . . . The beautiful tricolor flag has been flown only over the Moneda, the University, and the military barracks."[16] Apparently the situation did not change during the next five years. *El Mercurio* claimed that the people who attended the festivities did so to see the fireworks, not to revere the dead hero,[17] while *El Estandarte Católico* noted that were it not for a few people, there would have been no celebration of Iquique's anniversary in the school system, let alone among the general public. "Without these, the 21st of May would have gone unnoticed by anyone."[18]

The downward trend in Prat's popularity began to reverse itself after 1895; the hero became more prominent in the press and in the nation.[19] In 1897 the ministry of education authorized the twenty-first of May as a school holiday. The naval journal, *Revista de Marina*, began commemorating the battle of Iquique in 1901. By 1910, a publisher reprinted Vincente Grez's book about Prat; other works followed, including a play by Miguel Urzúa, and numerous poems by Samuel Lillo and Antonio Orrego Barros. In 1915 the Congress declared the twenty-first of May a national holiday. Although it was called Navy Day, to honor the fleet and all its accomplishments, the wording of the legislation and the congressional hearings leave no doubt that the law was enacted to commemorate Prat's heroic acts.[20]

II   The Metamorphosis of Prat's Image

A study of Appendix I and of the other materials dedicated to Prat indicates that he was more popular in the twentieth century than in the nineteenth. In addition to this increase in prominence, Prat's image also changed. These alterations are important because they reveal some of the basic causes for the resurgence of the fallen hero.

Although his popularity diminished in the years following the war, Prat's image was not radically transformed. A substantial portion of the press continued to describe him in religious terms, asserting, for example, that he had made heroism into a Chilean religion, and that Iquique was its Jerusalem.[21] *El Mercurio* claimed that Prat's final speech was to the Chilean nation what the voice of Christ was to Lazarus, commanding them to "arise and go forth. . . ."[22] A Catholic newspaper even stated that it was the Church's teachings that had inspired the dead hero to make his unselfish sacrifice.[23] The press continued comparing Prat to Leonidas and Nelson reassuring the readers that Iquique was not simply a glorious page in Chile's history, but in the history of the Americas and the world.[24]

Still, some fundamental changes occurred after Prat's popular revival. One transformation was the use of Prat as a symbol of the *raza chilena,* a theory originally enunciated by Nicolás Palacios, who claimed that the Chileans were unique because they were an amalgam of two heroic peoples, the Araucanian Indians and the Spanish conquistador. Despite the questionable validity of this allegation, especially when applied to Prat, the press continued to call the fallen hero the symbol of the *raza chilena,* thus indicating how the hero reflected contemporary cultural trends.[25]

A more significant modification of Prat's image was the emphasis on his personal life. Although prior to 1900, this aspect of Prat's personality was rarely mentioned, after that date, the press increasingly described Prat as the perfect father, son, and husband, praising him for his austere private life, his devotion to duty, and his hard work.[26] The newspapers eventually transformed the professional naval officer into the epitome of civilian virtues,[27] employing him not only to encourage Chile's youth to study, but to avoid the temptations of alcohol, tobacco, and loose women.[28]

The emphasis on Prat's domestic qualities and personal life appear incongruous when describing a war hero. There was some justification for this shift, however. Prat's resurgence was based on a need in Chilean society for both leadership and moral example. His sacrifice in war and his spotless private life incarnated supposedly traditional Chilean virtues which had once made the nation prosperous and happy. The rise of the parliamentary regime was believed to have debased these virtues. The government, the leadership elites, and the commercial classes struggled among themselves either for political power or profit. It was felt that society had broken down and needed to be regenerated, and one of the figures chosen to lead this moral crusade was Arturo Prat. His life and death were catalysts which could be used to castigate public and private corruption. Prat's life had a redemptive quality as well, for underlying the remarks describing him was the assumption that Chile would regain its lost grandeur when it emulated Prat's virtues. It is necessary to understand what occurred in Chile during the period of the parliamentary government in order to see how this affected both the image of Arturo Prat and his return to popularity.

III The Parliamentary Regime

The 1891 revolution which overthrew President José Manuel Balmaceda radically altered Chile's national development. Since 1870, Congress had been steadily curtailing the powers of the president. While most of Balmaceda's predecessors accepted these parliamentary limitations, he would not, and on the contrary he tried to force his supposedly radical programs on an increasingly hostile legislature. Late in 1890 the Congress refused to approve Balmaceda's proposed budget for the coming year in order to punish him. Balmaceda, unwilling to compromise or accept legislative meddling, declared that the appropriations for 1890 would be carried over to 1891.

In January 1891, the Congress, with the support of some naval units, rebelled. The insurgent stronghold was Iquique, the center of Chile's nitrate industry, where, financed by the nitrate revenues and protected by the fleet, the rebels were able to mobilize an army and defeat the forces of the government. Balmaceda took refuge in the Argentine Embassy, where he remained until his term of office expired. His responsibilities ended, he wrote a final testament and then shot himself.[29]

Although the war did not permanently injure Chile's economy, it materially altered the nation's political structure. Having won the civil war, the Congress emerged as the preeminent political force in Chile. Thereafter, the president was merely a figurehead whose cabinet was viable only as long as it retained the confidence of the Parliament. More significantly, the national power base shifted from Santiago to the provinces. The Congress consolidated its position by passing laws dividing the nation into 267 autonomous communities which assumed many of the responsibilities previously exercised by the national government, the most important of which were the registration of voters and the supervision of all elections.

This division into autonomous communities had originally been proposed to protect the provinces from any interference by the central government. While perhaps theoretically sound, in practice it was doomed because of a lack of stability in the nation's political structure. Chile had too many political parties, none of which could command a majority in the Congress. As a consequence, Chile's destiny was in the hands of a series of coalition cabinets united by tenuous ties and subject to dissolution at any given moment. Thus there was little continuity in government policy; few cabinets enjoyed a sufficiently long political life to accomplish anything. Presidential interference in elections was replaced by the intervention of local authorities. Provincial political bosses converted the autonomous municipalities into virtual satrapies which continued the fragmentation of the nation's political parties and made the members of Congress beholden to purely local interests.

Besides political instability, fiscal mismanagement and inflation became themes of Chile's postwar development. Although numerous individuals had tried to return the nation to the gold standard, they failed for two reasons: lack of support during economic prosperity, and resistance by the landholding oligarchy and other vested interests after economic conditions worsened.

The first postwar president, Domingo Santa María, had chosen to launch various public works projects rather than convert the paper money issued during the war. Although Congress had appropriated funds for this purpose, by 1887 only a portion had been used. Subsequently, poor economic conditions prevented the complete implementation of this plan.

The value of the peso, which had been relatively stable following the war, began to weaken as a result of worldwide economic conditions; the price of gold was rising while that of nitrates, by then Chile's principal export, was declining. Internal fiscal policy only complicated the problem because it permitted banks to issue paper notes up to one and one-half times the amount of their deposits, which added to the inflationary spiral.

Following the civil war, the government made additional attempts to stop the inflation. By then, however, many members of Congress represented agrarian interests or those people who benefited from an inflationary policy. Thus, from 1892 onward, opposition to any monetary reform gained strength, especially from the farmers, who had mortgaged their estates for the purpose of re-paying their debts in depreciated paper currency.

Despite some prosperous years, the value of the peso continued to decline throughout the 1890s, in part as a result of the increase in imports, especially luxury items, which squandered Chile's gold reserves. This gold drain was aggravated by the already large amounts owed by the government to foreign creditors for debts incurred by both the rebels and the Balmaceda government during the civil war. Finally, many foreign capitalists, losing confidence in Chile's economic future, began to withdraw some of their in-vestments, thus worsening the already serious economic situation.

Sadly, conditions did not improve. The nitrate, copper, and sil-ver industries suffered periodic depressions while the wheat crops of 1894, 1895, and 1897 were among the worst in Chile's history. These factors tended to militate against any plans for monetary reform. In the late 1890s, tension with Argentina forced the Chil-ean government to spend huge sums abroad for military and naval equipment in case war erupted between the two nations. This un-productive expenditure increased the country's financial difficul-ties. The final blow to monetary reform was struck when the op-ponents of change engineered a run on the Banco de Chile, thus ending any hopes of returning the nation to the gold standard.

After 1900, even with the return of better economic conditions, there was little possibility of monetary reform. The landholding aristocracy, which controlled the government, would not support a policy detrimental to its own interest. Inflation gained momen-tum.[30] From 1890 to 1914 internal indebtedness rose more than 300 percent. The government either sold publicly held nitrate lands, or borrowed from abroad to finance its deficit spending. In twenty years, the parliamentary governments floated more foreign loans than their parsimonious ancestors did in the entire nation's history.[31]

Perhaps more debilitating than the economic aspects of the in-flation were the psychological ramifications. Mortgage indebted-ness of both urban and rural property increased at a startling rate.[32] Chile became obsessed by speculation. Business activities multi-plied. In the period 1904–1905, the amount of capital invested in various business enterprises increased tenfold as many formed corporations more often to exploit the investor than develop an industry.[33] Imports continued to rise with the emphasis on luxury items rather than on the machinery needed to modernize the mines or the nation's industries.[34]

If inflation was one theme of Chile's postwar development, nitrate production was the other. Annexation of the former Peruvian and Bolivian provinces gave Chile a virtual monopoly on the nitrate trade. By 1910, there were more than 154 nitrate companies in operation, employing more than 35,000 men.[35]

The nitrate trade was a very risky business. Because nitrates were the principal component of fertilizer and explosives, the demand for them fluctuated in direct response to the state of world agriculture and peace. The prices, moreover, were set by the purchasers, who attempted to depress them. Thus nitrates became "an object of gambling. The speculators' game is played in Europe, between a hundred dealers involved in the stock market. These traders become rich in a couple of years, if they are not ruined in a few months."[36]

The expansion of nitrate production tended to lower prices, seriously affecting marginal producers who worked the less lucrative deposits. Whenever the nitrate industry suffered from one of its periodic depressions, the producers formed cartels to stabilize prices by assigning quotas to member companies in proportion to their productive capacity. These measures brought only temporary relief; prices dropped catastrophically, for example, in the years between 1891 and 1893. The worst slump was in 1896, when a worldwide depression in the sugar industry, one of the principal consumers of nitrate fertilizers, plunged prices even lower than previous levels. Although the producers survived this crisis, depression continued to threaten the industry.[37]

One of the most important ramifications of the nitrate boom was its impact on Chile's tax structure, especially after the inceptions of the parliamentary regime. Before this time, the government taxed income, urban and rural property, and inheritances. Following the civil war the Congress, no doubt intent on saving its own money or that of special interest groups, systematically ignored these sources of revenue, placing the burden of taxation on imports and exports. By 1897, more than 75 percent of Chile's ordinary revenues came from taxes on foreign trade. The income tax, which in 1890 paid 45,331 pounds sterling into the treasury, paid the ridiculous sum of seven pounds in 1894. After that date it ceased to be implemented. Revenues from land taxes were worth £115,555 in 1890. These revenues dropped to £8,998 in 1894 and to £2 in 1902.[38] Thus the Chilean economy was precariously balanced on the customs house, which in turn was dependent on the whims of world demand.

Not only was the nitrate trade oriented toward overseas markets, but eventually foreigners came to dominate it. During the War of the Pacific, British mining interests had purchased the bonds of the Peruvian nitrate companies when these were depressed. External pressure forced the Chilean government to recognize these claims, as well as those of other foreign bondholders, thus permitting foreign capital, especially that of Great Britain, to gain a stronghold on the Chilean economy which expanded with each government-held auction of nitrate lands. In 1878, British and American capital controlled 13 percent of the nitrate industry. By 1884, Britain alone controlled 34 percent. By 1901, the combined British and European interests comprised 85 percent, making Chile "an industrial colony, for foreign exploitation and use."[39] This same process occurred in other sectors of the mining industry. Beginning in 1907, first British and later American companies expanded their holdings in the copper industry, while a French concessionnaire acquired control of Chile's iron deposits, which it later sold to an American steel company.[40]

With the emphasis on mining, the agricultural sectors of the economy suffered. Beginning in 1895, wheat production began to lose its importance in the Chilean economy for a variety of reasons. Natural disasters struck the wheat fields with such ferocity that exports fell to their lowest level in the nation's history. Chile's foreign markets also shrank in the face of competition from Argentina, Australia, Canada, and the United States. This decline was hastened by the opening of the Panama Canal in 1914, which brought these nations closer to their European markets. Chile, its merchant marine undercut by foreign competition, could only watch as its former customers took their trade elsewhere.[41]

Mining also adversely affected cereal production, displacing the traditional centers of wheat production from the north to the south, where communications were not as developed, nor the soil as fertile. The nitrate mines also attracted any excess capital that might otherwise have been devoted to mechanizing agriculture and increasing its productivity. Not only wheat farming but almost all sectors of agriculture stagnated. Production of barley, maize, potatoes, and beans increased only slightly between 1910 and 1930. Only tobacco and grape production expanded, the latter with disastrous social consequences.[42]

The landowners were primarily responsible for the decline in agriculture. Often absent, if not in Paris then in Santiago, the *hacendados* mortgaged their properties, investing the proceeds not in their farms but in expensive buildings and ostentatious parties.[43] Samuel Valdés Vicuña claimed that the farmer no longer lived from the produce of his land but from its mortgage value.[44] These loans, which were repaid in inflated currency, supported the tinseled age of the parliamentary government.

The masses did not share the wealth of the parliamentary regime. On the contrary, the cheap money policy of the government inflated prices and depreciated the purchasing power of the salaried classes.[45] The worker was crowded into mining and industrial centers to live in the filth and squalor of the *conventillos*.[46] Cheated by his landlord, his money inflated by the government, overworked by his employer, the Chilean worker took refuge in alcoholism.

The nitrate miners lived in zinc barracks in an area where the temperature was 100 degrees at noon and below freezing at night. Their employers paid them in company script and forced them to buy at the company store and to drink at the company saloon. Working conditions were hazardous, and the miner was without the protection of either accident or health insurance. Foreigners and government committees observed these conditions, but their reports did not lead to improvements in the miner's life. Paid two to three pesos a day, the miners of the Atacama and Coquimbo fared only slightly better because of the more temperate climate, and because they could purchase fresh vegetables.[47]

The tenant farmer, the *inquilino*, often lived under worse conditions than the livestock for which he had to care. His status was not unlike that of a serf, for he owed feudal duties to his landlord. In a fertile country which could produce ample food, one author attributed 90 percent of the agrarian worker's illnesses to malnutrition. In the city, 60 percent of the deaths of industrial workers' wives were the result of starvation. Uneducated, often fatherless or without a name, the *inquilino* wandered the countryside looking for work. If he was honest, he emigrated; if not, he became a thief.[48]

The life of the urban proletariat was equally bleak. A worker's salary was 3.80 pesos a day; his wife and children earned half that amount. After laboring five days a week, nine to twelve hours a day, he returned to a home which was filthy, ill-ventilated, and infested with vermin. His children died of disease before the age of reason, his wife expired from starvation, and he, often from alcoholism. Although he was spared being paid in company chit, his cost of living outstripped the purchasing power of his salary. In twenty years, for example, the price of his food almost tripled, as did the cost of his clothing and housing.[49]

Meanwhile, Chile's international power declined. Argentina, its population swelled by immigrants and its coffers by the proceeds of the beef and wheat trade, challenged Chile's continental hegemony. Strengthened by a revitalized army and navy, Argentina reopened the old boundary dispute between the two nations. It sought to eradicate any Chilean influence in the Atlantic, and even threatened Chile's control of the Pacific by encouraging Peru and Bolivia to resist Chilean attempts to end the still outstanding issues of the War of the Pacific.

Throughout the 1890s Argentina and Chile stood ready to do battle. Chile, seeing its eastern neighbor arming, attempted to compete by rebuilding its fleet. The economy, however, could not stand the strain, and the victor of the War of the Pacific was forced to capitulate. In 1902, Chile signed the *Pactos de Mayo* with Argentina which ended the naval arms race, but also restricted Chile's influence to the Pacific side of the continent.[50] The treaty aroused enormous public antipathy which contrasted the present government's diplomatic policy with that of Balmaceda, who knew, it claimed, how to deal with "Gaucho diplomacy."[51] Pax Chilena was fast expiring. Its pretensions to control the Pacific were jolted when it was forced to make concessions to Bolivia, which demanded and received a more lenient peace than would have been imagined earlier.

By the centenary of Chile's independence, the nation's mood was not one of jubilation. Many believed that the country had been declining since 1891, and neither the flags nor the martial music could dispel this pessimism. As early as 1896, Anjel Vicuña had described the state of the nation as:

> anarchy without brakes, sterile in its result, ruinous in its excesses, unpopular for only talking about the needs of the people but doing nothing to relieve them; disordered in administration; . . . an organized system of insult against everything which is good, holy, and respectable.[52]

The nation became tired of seeing itself the plaything of caudillos and hack politicians who preferred to pad their own pockets[53] rather than provide the country with an adequate school and transportation system. The workers called their leaders "dealers without conscience, ambitious and intriguing speculators," and *El Mercurio* noted that 90 percent of the Chilean people "are nauseated when they think of the way the nation is being ruled."[54]

Electoral fraud became common. The vote was merchandise to be sold for food, money, or liquor. The tenant farmer voted as his patron ordered, as did the dead, who supported those responsible for their temporary resurrection. Honest men who left public service because they had no energy left to combat corruption saw their places taken by those with friends in high places.[55]

A decline in patriotism accompanied the corruption. Ana Johnson, an educator, complained, "The sacred image of the motherland, the supreme deity which has inspired all our great political and military glories, has been erased from our heart, pencilled from our minds." Julio Savedra, also an educator, commented that "it is widely accepted that our sense of patriotism is declining. Today's Chilean is not the same one which was once reknown for his civic pride."[56]

Few doubted that Chile had declined morally; only the causes were in doubt. Some argued that foreign materialism had subverted traditional Chilean values and that all things Chilean, including national pride, were now despised. Tancredo Pinochet Le-Brun claimed that Chile was again being conquered, not by force of arms, as under the Spaniards, but by foreign capitalism and technology. "And Chile will be defeated in this modern battle of work and intelligence not because its troops were lazy or cowardly . . . but because of its treasonous generals who lacked patriotism," the oligarchy who preferred the culture and capital of the foreigner to the traditions and commonweal of Chile.[57]

To others the frenetic business activity was the cause of the nation's problems; they argued that speculation, "the quick profits, the miraculous business ventures, the improbable rise in property values" were demoralizing the nation. Work appeared superfluous. Thrift became an almost unknown virtue, for "wealth could be assured only by a lucky purchase." In this atmosphere, corruption flourished. Indeed, what had begun as a malady of the upper strata of society spread to the middle class as well.[58]

Yet others believed that the sudden wealth of the nitrate fields had engendered a reckless hedonism, a limitless selfishness, which undermined the nation's morality. Arguing from history, they claimed that materialism had always corrupted nations in the past and, unfortunately, Chile was no exception to this rule. "Its [materialism's] evil influence has manifested itself in the public powers, in the government, and in the life of the nation." The concept of duty was destroyed, and with it the complimentary virtues of patriotism, abnegation, objectivity, charity, and sacrifice.[59]

Julio Valdés Cange compared Chile to Rome in its decline. He described the lack of civic spirit and called Chile's moral decline a manifestation of this illness. A malaise had permeated society because a good man would not speak out for fear,

> . . . if he is a lawyer, of not being on good terms with the judges of the court and, as a consequence, seeing his clients disappear; if he is a farmer, fearing that the banks will close their doors to him; if he is a businessman, that credit will be restricted in the importing houses or the customs officials will bother him; if he is a politician, that he would lose the favor of the crowds or the party chiefs; if he is an artisan, fearing that the bosses or the contractors will not give him a job; if he is a worker, that he will be fired by his employer.[60]

Enrique Mac-Iver described the nation's mood as a malaise that permeated Chile regardless of class or place. Despite its wealth, its resources, its hardworking population, he claimed that Chile was being destroyed by the absence of morality, "which consists in the fulfillment of duty and the obligations of public leaders and magistrates, in the loyal and complete fulfillment of their jobs . . . [and] having as its purpose the general good and not the interests and objectives of another kind." The old morality that made Chile preeminent in Spanish America no longer existed. Government officials rejected the concepts of duty and public service "for personal ambition, hatred, vengeance, cupidity, and the interests of a small clique" which were ruining the nation.[61]

Numerous critics denounced the president, his ministers, the Congress, the judiciary, and the political parties of the parliamentary regime.[62] Anjel Vicuña called the chief executive a lackey of the parliament, a weakling when compared to a Balmaceda who had fought those who tried to subvert the 1833 Constitution.[63] Abraham König stated, "Today we have neither a president nor a Congress, and I can now state that they have not existed during the last period, and if they did they lasted but a short time and were an exception." The presidents were considered prisoners who "rule but do not govern,"[64] ornaments "who only lend their hands to sign the laws which are presented to them and who play the role of a host at public parties."[65]

The Congress received the lion's share of abuse because it had the power to remedy the nation's ills but refusd to do so. *El Ferrocarril* accused its members of being on pleasure trips abroad,[66] while someone else attacked those who stayed home for betraying the old principles in order to gain power "as an opportunity to distribute among themselves the positions, the honors, the jobs, the properties, the monies, and on many occasions, the most lucrative contracts of the State."[67] The legislature was depicted as composed of individuals representing parties without ideals,[68] whose self-interest took precedence over the interests of the nation, men who deposed ministry after ministry, thus becoming "a cancer which corrodes the respectability and prestige of authority."[69]

The political parties did not escape criticism. Without discipline or sincerity, they were excoriated for having substituted intrigue for ideals, for being without a sense of duty because they refused to correct the rampant corruption that was destroying Chile. One politician damned his colleagues as passive sheep, afraid to protest the orders of their corrupt party leaders for fear of being forced out of politics. "What are the ideals and programs of the political parties," he cried. "Pretenses and nothing more."[70]

The nation's problems had not changed toward the end of the parliamentary regime; only its critics were different. The two deputies who had protested that alcoholism was destroying the nation in 1899[71] would have been horrified to learn that alcoholism was still an outstanding social issue fourteen years later "because politics so occupies the Legislature that it prevents them from seeing the most serious illness of the national organism."[72] Eleven years after the *Diario Ilustrado* pleaded for the development of national protection for Chile's agriculture, *El Mercurio* was still begging.[73] In 1895, the two doctors who petitioned the government to take steps to lower the high child mortality rate[74] would later be able to read that "poor people continue, meanwhile, to live in underground dungeons and their children to lose their health and their life, due to the danger from filth, dampness and the lack of either air or sunlight."[75] Those who protested the wretched living conditions of the urban and rural proletariat[76] would later learn that the nation's leaders were willing to import everything from foreign countries except that which would improve the life of the worker.[77]

Frustrated by the present, the Chilean people throughout the parliamentary regime viewed their past with pride and yearning. They remembered presidents who labored for the common good and who were forces for morality in government and society; legislatures composed of the nation's intellectual elite, who disregarded partisan interests for those of the motherland.[78] One newspaper begged for a return to those years; for a president

> ... of work and administration, vigilant and austere, practical and tranquil, without passions and hatreds, a servant of his motherland, a regulator of all the parties and not a captain of one, a serene and impartial protector of the right of suffrage and not a director of electoral intervention in favor of his favorites.[79]

Aníbal Sanfuentes requested that the Congress return to the nation "the Golden Fleece of administrative and political morality which, like so many good things, disappeared in 1891.[80]

Some proposed new laws in an attempt to end the political corruption, to regulate elections and voter registration.[81] Others, however, did not believe that additional laws were the answer. The nation suffered, they claimed, from a lack of ideals for which the law was not a substitute. As Máximo del Campo noted, " ... if the forgetting of duty is the principal cause of our ills, the cultivation and the practice of the same will surely be the remedy which will restore us." The same author begged, "Would to God that the public powers of the nation, the magistrates, the citizens, each one in his own sphere of activity, would inspire us in the fulfillment of duty."[82]

Another social critic agreed, noting that nations, like families, needed a model to follow. "The bad example set by the head of state is as pernicious to the citizen as the bad example of a father within a family."[83] His judgment was seconded by a member of the League of Civic Action, an organization founded to combat the corruption in Chilean society. He too feared that there was no example, either in the present administration or the entire nation, worth imitating and instead advocated:

> Let us, for a brief instant, turn our attention toward the past. Let us open the pages of the book which contain the acts of those model administrations; let us read the sessions of the legislative bodies and the archives that preserve intact the generous and patriotic impulses of those statesmen, far seeing and modest, economical in spending the money of the nation and prodigal with the blood of their sons when they could see that a menace was growing on the continent against the solitary star [Chile];
>
> Let us turn, gentlemen, from the page where so many weaknesses and so many miseries are printed, and let us have confidence in the future. If it is true that the excesses of evil are starting to destroy the soul of our citizens, the soul which is still in good health and which preserves that patriotic love that our fathers cultivated and in which Chileans have pride, we must care for it as a delicate flower is pampered. Let us bear in mind that the desire for progress and civic virtues which generate prosperity in a country grow together with the love of country. These [virtues] make the inhabitants [of a country] happy and wealthy and their governors anxious for triumphs and glory.[84]

Thus, Chile corrupted and without a leader worthy of emulation, turned to its past to find inspiration, seeking a Golden Age when all men were patriots who sacrificed themselves for the motherland. It was at this time that the example of Arturo Prat was resurrected. He symbolized all that his government was not and seemed to prove that the individual, if properly motivated, could change the course of a nation's destiny. Chile turned to its past and, among other lost heroes, discovered Arturo Prat: the symbol of perfection, of civic virtues and, most of all, of fulfillment of duty, Prat hopefully would lead the nation to victory as he had done in the War of the Pacific.

IV The Hero Resurrected

As earlier noted, for a decade or so following his death, Prat had languished in comparative obscurity. Like an old love, he was remembered warmly but his image had blurred with time. After 1891 Prat slowly came alive. His image changed from some beloved folk hero to an antigovernment symbol. Since this change in image and increase in popularity followed the inception of the parliamentary regime, it would not be unreasonable to conclude that Prat's revival was intimately bound up with the failings of that government. As will be seen, it was the parliamentary government that created the moral climate needed for Prat's return to popularity. Like some paladin, the hero returned from his historical limbo to provide the Chilean people with a standard of leadership and a symbol of morality since the parliamentary officials could not.

One of the earliest examples of this trend was an 1892 editorial which compared the administration's partisan politics, avarice, and lack of idealism with Prat's life of virtue and his final unselfish sacrifice. The paper hoped that Chile's president, Jorge Montt, a former professional naval officer, could provide, like Prat, the necessary leadership to save the nation.[85] A year later *El Sur* also noted the general decline in Chile and pleaded that the government might find inspiration in the example of Arturo Prat.[86]

In addition, the newspapers used the fallen hero's example as a force for national unity and urged that the former supporters of the Balmaceda regime be welcomed back into the national fold. The anniversary of Iquique provided an ideal opportunity to accomplish this, for the twenty-first of May was a day of "concord and fraternity because it instructs us that we Chileans are all sons of the same glorious mother."[87]

After 1892–1893, the press discarded the theme of national unity for a while, later to revive it as the nation foundered amid additional economic, social, and political problems.[88] By the turn of the century, however, Prat was principally revered as an example of sacrifice. In 1903, *El Mercurio* begged the heroes of Iquique to

> . . . materialize before us, to encourage us in this hour in which the nation demands sacrifices from us, as a comfort

when spirits are low, and as a standard of future behavior.

Today when public spirit is depressed and sad, it needs as never before encouragement which can elevate it and a light to guide it. In order to fight the darkness which surrounds us we need the splendour of the glory of Prat and Condell and their immortal companions.

This lesson still lives and asks the Chileans to elevate their hearts, to put aside petty arguements and to disdain materialistic interests, when these endanger the nation's honor.[89]

This need for sacrifice became the leitmotif of Prat's revival. In 1904, *El Porvenir*, for example, contrasted Chile's present lack of patriotism with the deeds of Prat and his companions, suggesting that the government emulate the hero and sacrifice its interests rather than those of the people.[90] Eleven years later, however, another paper doubted if Prat's life could inspire the older generation, claiming that the nation's politicians were "narrow minded, involved in short-lived and niggardly interests, tenacious in what they believe to be their rights and what, in reality, are their passions."[91]

In 1912, on the anniversary of Prat's death, a reporter wrote that a public servant had asked him how could a simple citizen be heroic in time of peace. The reporter replied, "Any fulfillment of duty by a public servant in 1912 is both very unusual and heroic." The writer noted, however, that the public figure's stomach was distended from overeating; his personal attire, that of a *bon vivant*. "I can understand," the reporter cynically wrote, "a thin and pale hero, but not one who is fat and who has a very good appetite."[92]

In 1879, the press used Prat to expose the Pinto government's inability to lead the nation. During the parliamentary regime the newspapers utilized the fallen hero to denounce its corruption. An editorial in *La Unión* in 1913 contrasted the Chile of 1879 with that of the present. During the War of the Pacific, it claimed, Chile's governments were composed of austere men, dedicated to preserving the nation at the cost of their lives, unlike the present government which was unable to formulate or implement policy because

> ... the corruption which has invaded the administrative body demolishes many efforts and weakens many arms.
>
> ... Today at the end of 34 years, the anniversary of the battle of Iquique is surrounded by noxious clouds: Our moral

health has deteriorated; we find ourselves in a state of con-
stitutional poverty, of decadence. . . . The treasury is rich,
but the habits of waste fritter away its wealth. . . . Prat, not
being able to conquer, jumped aboard the deck of an enemy
ship, resolved to die, and died. Are there some, today, among
our men in government, who are capable of making decisions
which may hurt their political career simply to save the honor
of public administration?

Thirteen of Prat's men jumped aboard the *Huáscar*. They
also died on the enemy ship fighting for the glory of their
motherland. In our present political fights, if there is some
bold assault, it is made on the public treasury, not for the
purpose of defending it, but with the aim of living at the nation's expense.

The old frugality has disappeared. We are living in a
period of scandalous financial mismanagement. The spirit of
abnegation and of sacrifice has been replaced by a fierce
selfishness and a wanton audacity.

In the light of this anniversary, then, one sees a very sad
and discouraging picture.

Will we continue to decline? The appearance of our old
glories makes us recoil in horror at the present decadence.
Can this inspire repentance and an energetic resolution to
recover the moral health which we are losing?"[93]

In a sense, Prat's image had broadened to respond to the needs
of Chilean society. Throughout the War of the Pacific, Prat's heroism had been equated with dying for Chile. Although it served as
an antigovernment symbol at the same time, the hero's death was
used primarily to inspire other acts of military heroism. After 1891,
however, the concept of sacrifice changed. Formerly the model of
military honor, the fallen officer increasingly became celebrated
for his civilian virtues. The new image was used not simply to attack the government's corruption, but to combat the decline in
private morality as well.

According to many, the wealth of the nitrate fields had undermined Chile's moral fiber. As one newspaper noted, their grand-
fathers had taught their children to be poor but honorable; their
fathers had instructed the present generation to be patriotic and
hardworking; but the new generation has been taught only to
seek money. "And, of course, with the primary concern being
money and business, the virtues of the ancient and simple society

are dying, and with them that vibrant patriotism which today is only a memory."[94] Prat, obviously, represented an earlier, simpler and more honorable generation, one that knew how to sacrifice itself for the motherland. Many believed that his example was needed to inspire the nation to return to its old traditions of patriotism,[95] to lead them in a "moral war against its ills, [for] . . . the sublime idealism of Prat, the most practical, the most fertile of idealisms, is what will save the people."[96] *El Mercurio* recommended that the story of the battle be disseminated throughout the nation, in the factories and the fields, in the school and the home, "from generation to generation . . . as the best example of honesty and civic spirit . . ." to remind each Chilean to fulfill his civic responsibilities.[97]

Prat's heroism became a tool to teach the nation's youth that the motherland should take precedence over the quest for money. Each year, on the anniversary of Prat's death, the private citizen was asked to examine his conscience to determine if he had sacrificed for Chile since the dead hero's example "shows them, by comparison, their duties and . . . in this way, exhorts and invites them to return to the proper path and to cultivate again the old virtues."[98]

Roberto Mario wrote that Prat's death had more than military significance, for it was "the most eloquent lesson of civic spirit which could have been written in our history." Mario stressed that the nation must imitate Prat's life of duty if it was to survive, because only civic valor like his could save Chile.[99] A year later, Nicanor Molinare wrote that Chile should cease using foreign methods to solve its national problems. Instead, the nation should return to its traditional values, values that Prat epitomized.[100]

A moral crusade to reform Chile began, stressing the redemtion first of the individual and, through him, the salvation of society as a whole. The press called on the average citizen to remedy Chile's problems by beginning in his own home and in the school. As one paper noted, everyone should devote himself to his family and his work; then the nation would be saved, for the men who could sacrifice in their daily lives would save Chile.[101]

6 ✝ PRAT AND THE ESTABLISHED AND RADICAL PRESS
The Hero 1920-1950

Whoever saves us is a hero; and in the exigencies of political action men are always looking for someone to save them. A sharp crisis in social and political affairs—when something must be done and done quickly—naturally intensifies interest in the hero. No matter what one's political complexion, hope for the resolution of a crisis is always bound up with hope for the appearance of strong or intelligent leadership to cope with the difficulties and perils. The more urgent the crisis, the more intense is the longing, whether it be a silent prayer or public exhortation, for the proper man to master it. He may be called "savior," "man on horseback," "prophet," "social engineer," "beloved disciple," "scientific revolutionist," depending upon the vocabulary of the creed or party.
—SIDNEY HOOK

I Arturo Prat and the Established Press

Chileans became increasingly frustrated by the parliamentary regime. What Enrique Mac-Iver had once described as "unhappiness"[1] had reached the point that another likened the country to an overheated boiler and blamed this condition on a corrupt president, a venal Congress, and a jaded oligarchy.[2] As usual the press begged that its leaders demonstrate the heroic qualities and selflessness necessary to save the motherland—pleas that sadly went unanswered.[3]

There was, however, one glimmer of hope: Arturo Alessandri, a reform candidate, won the presidential election in 1920. By the time he took office, the postwar collapse of the nitrate industry had plunged Chile into an economic depression. The new executive attempted to alleviate some of the country's problems by introducing new social and economic legislation, but each time the Senate blocked his proposals by refusing to ratify them. After four years of stagnation, a military coup overturned the Alessandri government, putting to rest the already moribund parliamentary regime. A military junta seized power and pressured the Congress into approving the social legislation earlier proposed by the president. Weeks later the junta turned on Alessandri, forced him into exile, and disbanded the Congress. There was internal dissension within the military, however, and some radical army officers overthrew the junta and invited Alessandri to complete the remainder of his term of office.

In 1925 a new constitution was written which provided for a return to the presidential form of government and, what is more significant, empowered the government to regulate and control the nation's social and economic development. Alessandri, although equipped with broader powers, was not without opposition. Carlos Ibáñez, one of the army officers involved in the second coup, decided to run for the presidency in 1925. He refused to resign as minister of defense while campaigning, so Alessandri, in protest, resigned his office for the second time.

Alessandri's role in Chilean history is still quite controversial. Some believe that his regime was too radical; others, that it was a failure because it did not break the oligarchy's stranglehold on the economy. As one distinguished journalist wrote in 1923, "The country is disgusted . . . tyranny and fraud still prevail in order that the interests of a small privileged group may be better served."[4]

These failures seem to have maintained Prat's popularity. Since the nation's problems remained unsolved, Chileans still needed the example of an Arturo Prat. As *El Mercurio* noted:

> In times of uncertainty and anguishing anxiety, we need to strengthen our spirit and fortify our faith in Chile's destiny. . . .
> Countries, like families, no matter what is their ancestry, need the types of acts which make . . . [the country] aware of itself, which awaken its most noble virtues and put it on a course from which no obstacle . . . can deter it.
> Captain Prat is not only an immortal example, an inspiring symbol because of his glorious act, but also, because of his character. He is the most ideally perfect type which the nation could choose for a hero. His entire life, so brief yet so

noble . . . the figure of a great sailor, a spotless gentleman, a
public servant and private individual. . . . Arturo Prat epito-
mizes the entire race.[5]

The figure of Prat thus increased its hold on the popular imagi-
nation. Still an antigovernment symbol and an example of Chile's
lost morality, Prat's sacrifice also began to be equated with saving
the nation by ensuring that each citizen would enjoy a decent
standard of living. This broadening reflected the national concern
with social and economic problems. As contemporary events had
transformed Prat's original image as a military man into a symbol
for governmental reform and personal regeneration, so they had
changed it again. By the 1920s, the nation has become involved in
problems of a social and economic nature. Sacrifice included not
only the moral condition of the Chilean but his economic status as
well. Thus Prat's life was lauded to make the citizen aware of his
responsibilities to his less fortunate countrymen. One paper wrote
that, because the possibility of war was slight, the citizen must "try
to become a hero in peaceful endeavors, in sacrificing ourselves
for the comfort of our fellow man," and recommended that he
choose Prat as a model on which to pattern himself. Although this
might involve some risk, the paper noted, this was "a step forward
in the way of heroism."[6] Even the conservative *El Diario Ilustrado*
agreed that man had responsibilities to the collective state in which
he was born—responsibilities based on the concepts of social
justice.[7]

Besides becoming involved in the fight to assure social change,
Prat remained the standard-bearer in the battle to inspire patriotism. This became more important as Chile's economic problems
led many to Socialism or Communism, movements that had a dis-
ruptive influence because they sought to resolve the nation's problems by class war and revolution. Some employed Prat to combat
these ideas, preaching the need for national unity and thereby
demonstrating that the nation did not need a foreign philosophy.[8]
In 1924, *El Mercurio* of Valparaíso wanted the story of Prat's
death to be circulated throughout the nation to explode the myth
that the War of the Pacific had been fought to preserve the interests of the wealthy. The journalist praised those who labored, likening their efforts to the struggles of the 1879 war, and hoped that,
instead of allowing themselves to be seduced into a class conflict,

the workers would learn from the lesson of Iquique that "union and fidelity between those who command and those who obey is the basis of triumph and progress."[9] The following year, another article appeared on the twenty-first of May entitled, "The Solidarity of the Race." Like the others it praised the nation for remaining true to its traditions and proving, by celebrating the day of Prat's martyrdom, that anarchy had not seduced it.[10]

There was a need for such soothing remarks because Alessandri's resignation plunged the nation into political turmoil. Although earlier quite anxious to become president, Ibáñez agreed not to run for that office if the nation's political parties could choose a compromise candidate. A coalition was formed which supported the candidacy of Emiliano Figueroa Larraín. Figueroa easily defeated his only opponent, a candidate of left-wing labor groups, and assumed control of the nation. The new president could not govern because of continued congressional opposition. Perhaps feeling himself inadequate to the task, Figueroa became increasingly dependent upon the support of Ibáñez who remained in the government as minister of war. Ibáñez slowly expanded his control over the government, first becoming minister of the interior and later vice-president. Aware that his power was diminishing, Figueroa resigned in May 1927. Elections were held, and this time Ibáñez was not so coy, winning by a landslide his race for the presidency.

As his country's first leader, Ibáñez implemented numerous reforms: he modernized the bureaucracy, initiated projects for industrial development and agrarian reform, and instituted changes in the nation's educational system. Despite these achievements, the Ibáñez regime was not economically sound. The nation's economic boom rested on raw material production and huge foreign loans, both unstable sources of revenue. Even worse, Chile was no longer a democratic nation. Unused to and unwilling to tolerate dissent, Ibáñez replied to domestic criticism by jailing obstreperous politicians, curtailing the activities of the nation's parties, and muzzling outspoken newspapers.[11]

The live general capitalized on the dead captain by using him to clothe his government with the mantle of respectability. For the first time since the parliamentary regime, Prat ceased to be used as an antigovernment figure and was, in fact, utilized to support the administration. The twenty-first of May became an occasion on which the nation praised not only Prat but the president as well. Numerous attempts were made to identify the dead hero with the living dictator. *La Unión* printed the picture of Ibáñez beside that of Prat in 1929.[12] Like Prat, Ibáñez was described as a man with no personal ambition, only "an eagerness to serve the motherland which is the sainted and noble cause of the citizen."[13] The public learned that the president was similar to Prat because he had saved Chile from corruption and had returned it to its traditional ways, thus demonstrating that he was anxious to uplift Chile's moral tone.[14]

Not unnaturally the Ibáñez government also used Prat to still any internal dissent by appealing to the nation's conscience to work and to obey.[15] The Patriotic League of Chile, for example, called Iquique's anniversary an important date because it marked the day when the president received greater power.[16] Before, as another journal noted, patriotism meant battles, sacrifice, and hardship; "today, it is synonymous with the love of order, peace, work, our institutions, our history, even though there are many who would curse them."[17] *La Unión* wrote that Prat had saved Chile in 1879 by obeying his orders and urged the nation to emulate the hero, claiming that respect for authority would again salvage the country.[18] Even Admiral Wilson, the living symbol of Iquique, was mobilized to encourage popular support for and obedience to Ibáñez:

> Whatever people say, the truth is that the civilians did not have the guts to impose the social order which we now enjoy thanks to the well organized government which we now have. I wish that all who are sincerely patriotic and who love the nation, as I do, could get together and cooperate with the actions of the supreme government.[19]

Perhaps Prat's influence had a salutary effect for, unlike other South American leaders, Ibáñez managed to survive the first year of the Great Depression. By 1931, however, the economic pestilence that had already devastated most of Europe and the Americas struck Chile and caused very severe economic dislocation. Agricultural products went unsold, and mining production all but ceased.[20] By July 1931, the minister of finance announced that the government verged on bankruptcy.

The economic situation ignited the fires of political rebellion. Students seized the buildings of the University of Chile and went on strike. Ibáñez retaliated with his usual brutality by ordering the police to fire on the demonstrators. On July 24 the police murdered Jaime Pinto Riesco, the editor of an anti-Ibáñez paper. Pinto's funeral became the occasion for a political demonstration. Later the nation's doctors, lawyers, and other professionals joined the student strike. Unable to withstand the mounting pressure, Ibáñez resigned on July 26, fleeing to Buenos Aires where the political climate was perhaps more to his liking.[21]

An interim president assumed control of the nation until elections could be held. Two principal candidates emerged from the ensuing upheaval: Arturo Alessandri and Juan Esteban Montero, a candidate of a coalition of the Liberal, Conservative, and Radical parties. Montero easily defeated his opposition, but despite this overwhelming victory, his regime was short-lived. Five months after his election, three Socialists—Marmaduque Grove, Eugenio Matte, and Carlos Dávila—overthrew Montero, dismissed the Congress, and ruled the nation by decree. The triumvirate apparently suffered from internal dissent, for within days Dávila forced his former colleagues from office.

Dávila proclaimed Chile a Socialist Republic and proposed to nationalize the nation's copper, coal, and nitrate industries. Quite predictably neither the conservative nor moderate elements were too enthusiastic about Dávila, his government, and most especially, his decrees. Isolated from left-wing support because he had banished Grove to an island in the Pacific, Dávila was easy prey. On September 12, 1932, General Bartolomé Blanche forced Dávila from office and assumed control of the nation until a caretaker government could be established and elections scheduled for the following October.[22]

The elections of 1932 were an exercise in individuality. Chileans were anxious to express themselves after the vacuum of Ibáñez, and there was a party for every subtle nuance of political opinion. Like quicksilver struck by a hammer, the parties divided and redivided. Seventeen different groups won representation in the Congress, not including 4 percent of the electorate whose parties had been unable to win a seat. The presidential election reflected the same diversity of opinion as the congressional elections. Five candidates ran: a Communist, a Socialist, a Liberal, a Conservative, and the eventual victor, Arturo Alessandri, the candidate of a coalition of center and moderate groups.

Alessandri announced that he would form a cabinet composed not only of his supporters—the Radical and Democratic parties—but of the right wing as well. This angered his allies who resented having to share political power with their former rivals. Alessandri's motives were quite understandable: the right wing controlled the Congress, and if the president wished to govern, it was necessary to cooprate with these elements.

Alessandri's second term was neither as dynamic nor as radical as his first, mainly because he feared that the Left might overthrow his government. At his behest, the Congress passed new legislation which suppressed leftist activities. Many radical newspapers were raided, and various opposition leaders were exiled. The president even gave his blessing to the formulation of the *Milicia Republicana*, a paramilitary organization designed to preserve public order. In view of the chaotic events of the early 1930s, perhaps Alessandri's fears were justified. To many, however, it seemed that the nightmare of Ibáñez had returned.

The president became increasingly dependent upon the right wing for support. The Radical party, in 1934, tired of Alessandri's restriction of political freedom and his inability to solve Chile's social problems, demanded that he dismiss certain members of his cabinet and replace them with individuals chosen by the Radical party. Alessandri refused, for he claimed quite correctly, that only the president could choose members of his cabinet. The Radicals retaliated by withdrawing their support from the president. Alessandri's other political mainstay, the Democratic party, also withdrew from the cabinet, leaving him with only the support of the rightist Liberal and Conservative parties.[23]

Another Alessandri blunder that alienated the Left was his choice of Gustavo Ross as minister of finance. Supposedly a genius, Ross had the unhappy faculty of alienating almost everyone, especially Alessandri's Radical supporters. Ross was not without some redeeming characteristics: he reorganized the economy, liquidated a portion of Chile's foreign debt, and even revived the nitrate industry by abolishing COSACH, a government monopoly established by Ibáñez, replacing it with the *Corporación de Ventas de Salitre y Yodo.*

Despite these successes, Ross's performance failed in other, perhaps more vital areas: inflation continued unabated. The cost of living increased almost 100 percent during his term of office. Foreign economic interests not only retained their disproportionate control over the nation's economy, but even acquired additional holdings in Chile. The agricultural situation fared no better. While the amount of land under the oligarchy's control increased, the *inquilino's* real wages and the amount of agricultural production declined.[24]

Alessandri's methods, his restriction of political liberty, and his anachronistic economic policies displeased a substantial portion of the nation. The nation's railroad unions declared a strike in 1936. Alessandri, believing that the movement might spread and fearing a coup, declared a state of siege and dissolved the Congress. Although legally empowered to act in this manner, the president exceeded his authority by persecuting various left-wing parties. Once again the government closed certain newspapers and exiled various political leaders.

Alessandri's repressive actions forced the Left to unite. The Communists and Radicals, as well as various elements of the Socialist movement, formed the nucleus of what eventually was to be Chile's first, and only, Popular Front government. The new movement was immediately successful. In the congressional elections of 1937, the Front won ten of twenty-two seats in the Senate and sixty-six of 146 in the Congress. The Front redoubled its efforts in preparation for the forthcoming presidential elections, actively seeking support not only among the laboring classes but among discontented members of the middle sectors. The Radical, Socialist, Communist, and Democratic parties, as well as the Chilean Confederation of Workers, held a convention in April 1938. After some debate, the assembly nominated Pedro Aguirre Cerda, a Radical, as its candidate.

The right's champion was Gustavo Ross. His choice was perhaps an unfortunate one for the Conservatives, for in a period characterized by social turmoil and economic discontent, Ross appeared as a defender of the privileges of the oligarchy and the Church, thus alienating moderate voters. Ross's personality did not improve his chances. A haughty, almost icy individual, Ross did not actively campaign, perhaps believing that it was beneath him. In a cynical parody of the democratic process, he expected to win the presidency by purchasing the requisite number of votes.

Despite his lack of personal charm there was still a substantial possibility that Ross would win the election because the left wing was not solidly united behind the Popular Front candidate. Carlos Ibáñez, who had returned to Chile in 1937, had also declared his intention to run for the presidency, representing a splinter of the Union Socialist party. His new party gained additional support when it allied with the small but vocal Nazi party, forming the Popular Liberating Alliance. Although Ibáñez was still an authoritarian personality, his platform included some rather radical economic reforms, and for this reason, many believed that he might lure from 20,000 to 30,000 votes away from Aguirre Cerda. At the last moment, however, the political situation drastically changed.

On September 4, 1938, the Popular Liberating Alliance paraded through Santiago. The following day a group of Nazi students seized part of the University of Chile, as well as the Social Security building. If the Nazis expected to receive support from the army, they were soon disappointed. The military rousted the students from the university and surrounded the remaining center of resistance. After a short battle, the Nazis surrendered. The *carabineros* disarmed them but, instead of taking them into custody, murdered them. The senseless death of the rebels infuriated Ibáñez and the Nazi leader, González von Marées, both of whom had been jailed when the rebellion began. After a discussion with Aguirre Cerda, both men ordered their supporters to vote for the Front candidate. When the election was over, Aguirre Cerda had beaten Ross by a mere 4,000 votes.[25]

Throughout the 1930s the various editorials published on May 21 reflected a concern about the nation's unstable political situation. One newspaper, *La Unión*, even described Chile's internal situation as one of "anarchy and doubt" and compared the entire nation to a new *Esmeralda*.[26] *El Mercurio* was similarly distressed by the domestic turmoil and wistfully hoped that the people would respond to the domestic crisis by conquering "the difficulties which are momentarily weighing on our progress and our development."[27] By 1934, however, both *El Mercurio* and *La Unión* were pleased to note that a semblance of political stability had returned and predicted that this period of calm would permit the nation to rebuild.[28]

The emergence of the Popular Front, however, aroused new fears. To many the new government meant that Communism was soon to engulf the nation. *El Diario Ilustrado* fearfully wrote that a "malignant virus" had been introduced into the nation and predicted dire consequences.[29] The fact that Chile did not become a Russian satellite did not reassure certain sections of the press. *La Unión* attacked the dissident new doctrines which had split the nation,[30] while *El Mercurio* sadly remembered when the nation was not divided by class distinctions, when a spirit of fraternity had united it.[31]

Many of the various newspapers attempted to persuade Chileans to repudiate the new ideas. *El Mercurio* wanted the nation to return to its traditions, "the substratum on which nationalities are erected . . . the inexhaustible source from which nations gather energy and their direction for the future."[32] *El Diario Ilustrado* begged the government to cultivate a return to patriotism, that "index which shows us our duties and our obligations."[33] *La Unión* described "the ideal of the motherland and the cultivation of the collective society in which one was born."[34] A year later another newspaper noted the need for "union, racial solidarity" and hoped that a patriotic involvement "would persist and become even greater in the hours of civic struggle."[35]

The traditional press—*El Mercurio* of Santiago and Valparaíso, *La Unión*, and *El Diario Ilustrado*—in an effort to preserve the nation, used the figure of Prat in two ways: to inspire sacrifice for the motherland and to instill a sense of national unity. The use of Prat to inspire selflessness, the fulfillment of responsibility, was already a traditional theme. Prat's name had become a talisman, which if invoked, it was hoped, would inspire others to sacrifice, a force that could "disperse the clouds which in this time of tribulations, obscure the future, which prevents thee [Chile] from achieving thy great destinies."[36]

The press followed the traditional theme by emphasizing that

Chile would be richer, stronger, and more powerful if only its citizens would emulate the hero of Iquique. Each individual, regardless of his station in life, was encouraged to place the interests of his nation above his own wants. The press admonished the worker, the businessman, the teacher, and the student to preserve Prat's heritage by working for Chile. The government was not excluded from these demands. Numerous articles noted that May 21 was an auspicious date on which to open the Congress, and prayed that the legislators and the government, imitating Prat, would devote themselves to laboring for Chile's benefit.[37]

The use of Prat for political unity was a relatively new theme and appears to have developed in response to the growth of radical political movements which favored revolution. The press regarded Prat as an antidote to these new and unhealthy ideas and used Navy Day to rally the nation. *El Mercurio*, for example, called the twenty-first a time for national reconciliation, an event that bound the Chilean people together: "Now more than ever, we need the love of the motherland. . . . Its light and warmth can help us so that we may look with objectivity at that which divides us and so we can take refuge in that which unites us."[38] The same newspaper, a a year later, stated that Prat's sacrifice "constitutes the best bulwark in the fight against the tendencies of the present hour."[39] *El Diario Ilustrado* observed that Prat's glory not only elevated the spirit but "fortifies the feelings of patriotic unity which served as our nationality and which will be the most solid base of stability and national greatness." Each observance of Iquique "is a shield against those who wish to undermine the ties which sustain the fundamental institutions of the Republic."[40] This same journal later noted: "Today the battle is also unequal—the battle which is being fought in order to defend the patriotic ideas threatened by strange ideologies which are without either a juridical or philosophical basis . . . ideas which capitalize on the open and irresponsible support from within our frontiers." The only solution was to look "toward this luminous past which we evoke on today's date and whose lessons surmount all the divisions and fissures in our patriotic faith."[41] *La Unión* also hoped that Prat's example might dissipate, or at least soften, the political acrimony. On the twenty-first of May, the paper noted, "Rancor is forgotten; partisan struggles come to a halt; the fire of burning passions is quenched and only one feeling dominates the heart and stirs the soul: patriotism."[42]

Chile's conservative elements seemed the most prone to use Prat to attack the Left. Members of the *Milicia Republicana,* for example, took their oath of allegiance to Prat, promising like the fallen hero to sacrifice all, even their lives, to protect Chile.[43] The Anti Communist Student Federation used the anniversary of Iquique to beg the nation to repudiate radical ideas and return Chile to the concepts of the motherland, "home, honorable work, civic consciousness, and the law of duty."[44] The ultraconservative *El Diario Ilustrado* also attempted to lure the country away from the sirens of the Left and return it to its traditional ways, claiming that the twenty-first was a day for all Chileans, regardless of political ideology, a day on which they should resolve their political differences and work for the motherland.[45]

Other newspapers used Prat to efface social and economic distinctions. One editorial noted that all citizens, whatever their social origin, were attracted to the martyr of Iquique.[46] *La Unión* wanted everyone, regardless of his economic or social status, to be devoted to Prat. It warned against the insidious alien doctrines that preached class hatred, claiming that they led only to the destruction of society, and sought instead a common ideal to unify divergent groups.[47] Obviously its pleas went unheeded for the same journal later warned that the "example of Prat, who gave his life for an ideal which was the Republic, is lost in a foul mist of hatred and opposing interests which struggle with one another thus losing sight of the collective interest."[48]

Although the 1940s marked a new decade, there was no significant change in Prat's imagery perhaps because political instability still plagued Chile. Soon after its election, the Popular Front's unity began to fray. Radicals and Socialists fought for political patronage. The leftists, battling over the control of the union movement, split farther apart when the Chilean Communist party supported Russia's nonaggression pact with Germany. By the time Aguirre Cerda died, three years after his election, the Front was neither popular nor unified. Although it did not last, the former government had sought to modify certain aspects of Chilean society by passing numerous laws providing for increased participation of the state in the nation's economic development. Despite these attempts, the economy appeared to stagnate while the inflation increased. To make matters worse, one of Chile's principal cities, Chillán, was devastated by an earthquake in 1939.

A coalition of Radical, center, and leftist parties elected Juan Antonio Ríos as Aguirre Cerda's successor. The new president was neither as radical nor as imaginative as his predecessor. Chile enjoyed a small degree of prosperity during the Ríos administration, not as the result of any brilliance on the part of the president, but because the war had increased the demand for Chilean raw materials. Despite the superficial appearances of growth, the nation's economic situation remained basically unchanged: inflation increased at a higher annual rate than did the nation's productive capacity.[49]

The political situation did not improve either. The thirteen political parties that participated in the congressional elections of 1941 became fourteen in 1945. Four years later there were eighteen. The death of Ríos, in 1946, further complicated the situation. Four men sought the presidency: Gabriel González Videla, a candidate of a Radical-leftist coalition; Eduardo Cruz Coke, nominated by the right wing; Fernando Alessandri, the former president's son and the choice of the Liberal and Conservative parties; and Bernardo Ibáñez, a Socialist. González Videla triumphed but his victory was hardly resounding: he won only slightly more than 40 percent of the total votes cast. Lack of a firm mandate combined with a weak power base within the Congress made González Videla's position difficult. He did not improve it when he expelled three Communist ministers from his cabinet and ordered all Communists struck from the voting rolls.

It is perhaps still too early to judge González Videla's administration. The few conclusions that can be drawn are hardly laudatory: The plight of the poor remained the same; agriculture continued to be dominated by a small minority of landowners; industry did not materially advance. Only in one area did González Videla excell: keeping the inflationary spiral moving upward.[50]

The lack of political stability and slow progress in areas of social reform and industrialization dismayed many Chileans. As in the previous decades, the newspapers continued to use Prat to instill in their readers a sense of abnegation and sacrifice. Primarily Prat became a moral force, not to attack the government, but to elevate the people, to arouse them from their lethargy "to the peaks where the winds of glory blow."[51] The twenty-first of May ceased to be merely a patriotic festival, a perfunctory courtesy to the past, and became instead a day of contemplation when the citizen was exhorted to compare his behavior with Prat's example and to promise to work for the improvement of Chile. The words usually associated with the fallen hero, sacrifice, fulfillment of duty, responsibility, were employed to call upon the people to dedicate themselves to the motherland.[52]

The press persisted in using Prat as a symbol of national unity. Distressed by the political bickering, fearful of Communism, numerous editorials tried to unify the nation by encouraging its readers to return to Chile's honorable and patriotic traditions. The people were chided to rise above banal political differences by focusing on Prat's sacrifice and the motherland for which he died.[53] One newspaper even referred to Iquique as the "communion and ciborium of the motherland,"[54] perhaps hoping that May 21 would become a day when the nation would literally assimilate Prat's spirit and body and thus would become united in some spiritual bond.

From 1892 to 1920, the hero of Iquique was utilized to attack the government and to stimulate public and private morality. This usage subsequently changed during the first Alessandri administration. The press began to tone down the antigovernment aspects of Prat's image and instead to employ him as a force for national unity. This transition was completed during the Ibáñez regime; and henceforth the hero, with a few exceptions, was used to inspire Chileans to respect and support their government. Prat's image divided into two contradictory parts: Prat the pacifier, the symbol of sacrifice and national unity; Prat the militant, the symbol of antigovernment sentiment.

This division appears to have been the result of the severe economic and political upheavals precipitated by the Great Depression. Though Chile was historically a stable nation, revolutions, counterrevolutions, and coups engulfed it in the third decade of the twentieth century. The nation had seen its military rebel, its unions declare general strikes, its parties splinter. Radical political movements became more powerful, and the possibility of a leftist or radical right coup appeared imminent. The established press, that is, the nonradical papers, reacted to this threat by using Prat to unify the nation, seeking to preserve traditional society by emphasizing the heritage common to all Chileans. The traditional press dared not use Prat to attack the government because the political situation was too unstable. Bad as a government might be, it was far superior to any radical alternative.

The press did not use Prat only to solidify public opinion. It also sought to change Chile and for this reason emphasized Prat's sacrifice in hopes of encouraging the people to work for the nation. The change the press desired, however, was to be within the context of traditional Chilean society and was to be accomplished by "acceptable," that is, nonrevolutionary means. In almost a parody of economic liberalism, which seeks prosperity through individual initiative, the established newspapers wanted each Chilean to emulate Prat, thereby improving the nation's general condition.

The image of Prat the militant was entirely different. For the radical elements of society, Prat was an avenging angel, a symbol of civic virtue to attack a system that had been unable or unwilling to heal the ills of Chilean society. Unlike the traditional press, which offered no solution other than individual initiative, the militants had new alternatives: Socialism, Communism, and Nazism. It was these groups that continued the tradition of Prat as an antigovernment figure in order to demonstrate the faults of the old order and the need for change.

II Arturo Prat and National Socialism

The *Movimiento Nacional Socialista,* Chile's Nazi party, was the youngest and most short-lived of the nation's radical parties. Founded by a lawyer, Jorge González von Marées, in 1932, the party continued to operate until 1941.[55] The Nazi party was antiestablishment, rejecting *laissez-faire* economics and parliamentary democracy of liberalism in favor of a fascist style corporate state. Unlike the Marxists, the MNS did not believe that Chile's problems were solely economic in nature; the country also suffered from a moral dry rot which had to be rooted out if the nation were to survive.[56]

It is difficult to describe the MNS perhaps because it did not use the words nationalism and socialism in the traditional sense:

the party's socialism was not that of Marx, but of Spengler; its nationalism was not the egalitarianism of the French Revolution but the elitism of Diego Portales. According to von Marées, Portales was nineteenth-century Chile's guiding light. Conservative and fearful of popular unrest, he had devised a centralized, authoritarian government which excluded all but a few. An oligarchy administered Chile, but an elite, according to the Nazi leader, which was composed of dedicated, sacrificing citizens who were willing to work for their nation's welfare. Under their aegis, Chile enjoyed stable government while its neighbors wallowed in chaos, a Golden Age von Marées hoped to recreate.

Von Marées believed that this system began disintegrating following the War of the Pacific. The easy money of the nitrate fields and the rise of liberalism corrupted the oligarchy. Greed replaced austerity and sacrifice. The debased oligarchs, driven by a desire to dominate the government and devoid of any ideology except that of personal gain, rebelled against Balmaceda in 1891. The civil war represented a watershed in Chile's development. Gone was the virtuous upper class of the past. In its place was a new form of government, the parliamentary regime, run by a small clique for its own personal enrichment.

Chile, according to the Nazi leader, suffered enormously under the new government. The rich dominated society; the people, without a strong leader to protect them, were defenseless. The restoration of the presidential form of government in 1925 failed to solve Chile's problems. Alessandri was a man without vision, at best only a third-rate caudillo; and although von Marées praised Ibáñez for rebuilding Chile, he too was considered a failure for not having established in "the national consciousness the principle of authority, incarnated in a strong but impersonal government which will nourish a strong collective spirit."[57]

The Nazi leader now claimed that Chile had reached a crucial moment in its history. The country was afflicted with the same ailment that had afflicted Europe following World War I. The old remedies were inadequate. If Chile wished to survive, it had to imitate Germany and Italy by accepting an authoritarian leader and a new philosophy: the collective will, "a mystique of sacrifice and solidarity for the cause of national resurrection which would replace the . . . venal and selfish appetites."[58] Once established, a

new corporate society would emerge, a nation in which one labored for the benefit of his fellow citizens and not for his own
advancement.[59]

The Nazi party had some difficulty convincing the nation that
it was a truly nationalistic movement. Although its leaders in-
sisted that the party was not a copy of either Italian Fascism or
National Socialism, the movement clearly resembled its European
counterparts. Instead of a Fuehrer or Duce, the party had its
Jefe. Instead of the Brownshirts or Blackshirts, it had the *Tropas
de Asalto*, the TNA. Its members used the Roman salute and, like
their European brethren, were anti-Semitic.[60] Ironically this had
to be toned down when the MNS joined the Popular Front. Suddenly the "'Jew' Communist Marcos Chamúdez" became an ally
and, for a while at least, the Nazis and Communists were friendly.[61]

The MNS was quick to exploit Arturo Prat, perhaps hoping to
demonstrate that the Nazis were truly nationalists. *Trabajo*, the
official organ of the MNS, demonstrated the party's reverence
for Prat by publishing numerous editorials praising the hero of
Iquique. The party always celebrated Navy Day with elaborate
oath-taking ceremonies, often supplementing these with paramilitary exercises. Special trains carried the party faithful to Valparaíso where the *Jefe* laid a wreath on Prat's tomb and his uni-
formed followers passed in review. Provincial units also conducted
commemorative ceremonies, once on the decks of the *Huáscar* as
it lay at anchor in the port of Talcahuano. The party also held
torchlight parades, à la Nuremberg, and by 1936, *Trabajo* reported
that 2,000 Nazis participated in the ceremonies honoring Prat.[62]

As well as being a symbol of patriotism, Prat served the party
as a standard of conduct for its members. *Trabajo* claimed that
Prat was a means of inspiring the Nazis to give their all for the
motherland in order to save her from the "negative forces"[63] operating inside the country. In 1935, Sady Zañartu claimed that
Prat had "identified himself with the sense of the collective being"
and hoped that he would ignite the same spirit in the Nazi youth.[64]
An article entitled, significantly, "El guía máximo" stated that
Prat incarnated all the Chilean virtues. The author noted that
Prat had expected his officers to fulfill their duty and claimed that
his command was being faithfully followed by the Nazi youth
"who know how to follow in his indelible footsteps . . . in order

to restore to Chile its former grandeur."[65] The following year another author reminded his readers that Prat's sacrifice was a lesson for all generations: ". . . only the sacrifice of the Chileans, only the most absolute abjuration of the dearest affections and selfish habits, will provide our people with the necessary vigor in order to triumph over destruction and ruin. This is the lesson which will be perpetually extracted from Prat's gesture."[66] On May 21, 1937, *El Jefe* himself used the ceremonies commemorating Prat's death to call upon his followers to remember the hero's sacrifice and to swear on his tomb to consecrate themselves "totally and forever to the grandeur of Chile."[67]

In addition to being a source of inspiration to the Nazi party, Prat also served as a vehicle to attack the government. Verbal barrages were leveled not only at the ideological basis of liberal democracy, a system that supposedly had cast Chile into the "abyss of the lowest moral abjection and physical misery,"[68] but also against Alessandri, whom they appear to have detested. The dislike of the president was fairly deep-rooted. Early in his administration Alessandri attempted to pass legislation forbidding the wearing of the Nazi uniform and generally restricting the party's activities. To add insult to injury, the provincial intendant of Valparaíso, Fernando Lira, refused to permit the Nazis to parade before Prat's tomb.[69] Although the intendant subsequently rescinded his order, the MNS never forgave the government and used every opportunity to attack it.

Trabajo, for instance, called the opening of the Congress in 1936 a profanation of the memory of Iquique, claiming that the present government had delivered the nation into the sweaty palms of International Jewry.[70] A year later when the government again attempted to deny the MNS a parade permit, the party newspaper stated that the Liberal administration was in such a "state of putrefaction [that] it is even obstructing the citizens who wish to render homage to the motherland's heroes." The editorial noted that this demonstrated the difference between the venal Alessandri government and the idealistic Nazis who were "ready to realize whatever sacrifice for the purpose of social justice in Chile." The paper admitted, however, that it could not expect a man who had betrayed Chile to foreign economic interests to revere the sacred dead of the War of the Pacific.[71] Jorge González von Marées claimed that the government believed itself threatened by these patriotic demonstrations.

> The regime, rotten to its core, falters before an act of patriotic homage. Its agents tremble because there is a possibility that a group of Chileans exist who are capable of responding to the memory of the motherland's heroes.
> Dedicated for decades to dragging down to misery and hunger the entire nation, calmly subjugating the nation's sovereignty to the yoke of foreign imperialistic capitalism, and systematically prostituting what was so noble and worthy . . . they cannot tolerate a youth which raises up in a gesture of protest against so much infamy.[72]

Trabajo stated that the selfish, individualistic Liberal politicians could not comprehend Prat's sacrifice. For these wretches, Iquique was only a device to distract the people from the misery of their daily existence.

> Blinded by selfishness and eagerness for profit, they have never been able to learn from the lesson provided by Prat. For the morally materialistic and venal men of the Right all ideals, all heroism, only serve their own personal advantage, in the same way that they have played upon the patriotic feelings of the people in order to guarantee socially inequitable regimes.[73]

In contrast the members of the party had cultivated Prat's virtues and thus were "ready to give their life for the collectivity, and to renounce all individuality for the common good." The Nazis vowed to return Chile to its honored position and to punish those who had forgotten the lessons of Prat. Though the hero of Iquique may have been shunted aside in the mundane race for wealth, the MNS promised to struggle to "revive the forgotten virtues which gave to the nation incomparable heroes, eminent statesmen and upright and abnegating citizens."[74]

The following year *Trabajo* again accused the government of failing to show proper respect on the twenty-first of May. The paper called upon all to examine their consciences to determine if they had fulfilled their duty toward the motherland. Chile, the paper claimed, needed Prat's spirit of abnegation to combat not only its foreign but its domestic enemies, "these traitors to their own blood, those vendors of their own land, those who threaten the life and the future of the Chilean people."[75] It was against these men who had undermined the nation's traditions of austerity and virtue that the Nazi party directed its efforts.

Once the Popular Front achieved power, antigovernment sentiment declined. *Trabajo* was pleased to note the difference between Aguirre Cerda, a man of the people, and Alessandri, a prisoner of the plutocracy. In 1939 the paper used May 21 to commemorate not only the death of Prat but also those of the young Nazis killed the year before. It considered both actions sacrifices, "the exhaltation of the purest and deepest patriotism." The men of the *Esmeralda* had died for the flag; the men of the MNS, "for the triumph of the ideal which signified the grandeur and welfare of Chile."[76]

Despite this patriotic rhetoric, the movement did not gain many adherents and finally collapsed a few years before the regime on which it patterned itself died a fiery death in Berlin. The German Reich lasted 12 of a prophesized 1,000 years; its, Chilean namesake even less. In retrospect one can see certain similarities between the MNS and other radical movements, Communism and Socialism. All were basically foreign imports although the MNS seemed the most preoccupied with proving itself a truly nationalist party. All rebelled against liberalism, seeking to replace it with a different system of government. Like the Communists, the Nazis were not democratic, but sought to impose on Chile a stratified elitist society.

Perhaps the kindest judgment that can be made on the National Socialist movement would be to call it a combination of contradictory ideas. More nationalistic than socialist, more xenophobic than nationalist, the MNS represented a radical right movement for ill-defined change. When one sets aside the blustering remarks about foreign and especially Jewish capitalism, the party's program remains without much substance. Its affection for Prat may have been genuine. Still, one might cynically conclude that at best its praise of the hero of Iquique was merely an attempt to cloak an unpleasant political movement under the guise of supernationalism. Devoid of a theoretical foundation except that borrowed from abroad, the MNS attempted to compensate for its lack of ideology with jingoism. Indeed it is quite probable that the liberal, intellectual, and democratic Prat would have been repelled by the movement and its implications.

III Communism and Arturo Prat

Unlike the MNS the Communist party was an older and more established political organization. The nucleus of the party was the *Partido Obrero Socialista*, founded by Luis Emilio Recabarren in 1912. Disenchanted with the Democratic party, Recabarren had established his own political organization convinced that Marxism was the only solution to his nation's problems. Although the *Partido Obrero Socialista* joined the Third International in 1920, it did not formally adopt the name of the Communist party of Chile until two years later.

At first the party was quite successful. It participated in the congressional elections of 1921, winning two seats in the Chamber of Deputies. The movement was strong enough by 1925 to present its own candidate for the presidential elections held that year. Although it lost, the party did win additional representation in the Congress, as well as a seat in the Senate. During the Ibáñez regime, the Communists went underground.[77]

Because of its revolutionary nature, the Communist party traditionally had remained aloof from political alliances with established parties. This self-imposed exile ended in 1935 when the International ordered its members to ally themselves with any progressive group in order to combat the rising influence of National Socialism and Fascism.

The following year the Comintern sent one of its agents, Eudocio Ravines, to Chile to implement its orders. Operating under the cover name of Jorge Montero, Ravines began establishing closer ties with the Radical and Socialist parties, even supporting their candidates for the congressional elections of 1937. Ravines also attempted to nationalize the party's image in Chile, and to tone down its pro-Russian bias. The party, for example, was ordered to display the Chilean flag at all its functions. Ravines also founded a newspaper and, consistent with its new conciliatory policy, called it *Frente Popular*, instead of the usual Red Banner.[78]

Because of the need to nationalize the party, one might have expected that Arturo Prat would have become the darling of the *Frente Popular*. The dead officer, however, was rarely if at all mentioned. In 1937, for example, the paper made but one fleeting reference to the hero of Iquique.[79] The next year the paper did print a longer editorial praising Prat's sense of duty, calling him "the national hero par excellence."[80] Despite these remarks, it appears that the newspapers interest in Prat was slight. The journal's editorials were more concerned with denouncing the war in which Prat died than in praising the dead hero. In both 1937 and 1938 the paper accused the oligarchy of fomenting the 1879 conflict to further its own economic interests. The paper not only attacked the upper class for failing to provide adequate pensions for the veterans of the war, claiming that once the struggle had been won its victors had been forgotten, but also used the issue of foreign domination of the nitrate fields as a means of attacking the Alessandri government specifically. When COSACH was dissolved and replaced by a new organization which permitted foreign companies to preserve their investments, the paper described this action as "the unconditional surrender of the heritage of the Chileans killed at Iquique, Angamos, Concepción, Morro de Arica, Chorillos and Miraflores, to the greed of foreign capitalism."[81]

Frente Popular's real hero appears to have been José Manuel Balmaceda. It was his picture and not that of Prat which appeared on Navy Day in 1937. The paper praised Balmaceda's attempt to nationalize the nitrate fields and lamented his death at the hands of foreign capitalism.[82] Arturo Prat, it seems, was almost superfluous.

This lack of interest in Prat was quite consistent with Marxist theology. The Communist party, both psychologically and ideologically, was unable to praise the hero of an imperialistic war. Noble though Prat may have been, his heroic act had been in the defense of capitalism and therefore beyond the pale of Marxist orthodoxy. For the Communists the twenty-first of May was an opportunity to praise the real hero of the movement, Balmaceda, and to flay the oligarchy that had destroyed him. It is true that the *Frente Popular* did write at great length about Prat in 1938. This was, however, the year that Aguirre Cerda assumed the presidency. For this reason the party may have devoted more attention to the dead hero as some concession to the spirit of the Popular Front. As will be noted, once this political alliance ended, the party dropped its nationalist trappings and again ignored Arturo Prat and his role in Chilean history.

Frente Popular ceased publication in 1938, and until 1940, when *El Siglo* was founded, the Communist party was without a paper. In the interim the tenuous alliance between the Left and the Communist party began disintegrating. This process was accelerated when Russia signed its nonagression pact with Germany in 1939.[83] From a certain point of view this isolation had some benefits. The Communist party could return to its ideological purity and cease playing the charade of being simply another Chilean political party.

This return to a hard line was amply demonstrated in *El Siglo*'s editorials of May 21, 1941. Once again it damned the 1879 conflict, calling it the War of Nitrates and attributing its origins to the greed of the Chilean upper class and its foreign allies. The paper deviated from its earlier position only slightly: instead of blaming the War of the Pacific on British and French capitalists, it now claimed that it resulted from conflicting British and American economic interests. Needless to say there was no mention of Arturo Prat. The day of his death served the party merely as a vehicle to attack capitalism in general and the Chilean oligarchy in particular.[84]

The newspaper radically altered its editorial policy the following year. Navy Day became an important event; the fleet was praised for its democratic spirit and its role in liberating Chile and South America from Spanish domination. Suddenly "Nazi barbarism" was discovered lurking about, and *El Siglo* demanded that the fleet be modernized and join the war against Fascism. The paper hoped that eventually all the American squadrons would be incorporated under one command and that Chile would join the Anti-Fascist League.[85] This was an interesting reversal of editorial policy. Only the year before the war against Germany had been described as a conflict precipitated by the greed of international capitalists and the merchants of death.[86] The reason for this change is not too difficult to determine. In June 1941, Germany invaded Russia. Once the Soviet Union became involved, the conflict became a holy crusade and the Chilean Communist party did all it could to aid its spiritual mother.

Throughout the remainder of the war, *El Siglo* faithfully commemorated the twenty-first of May. The newspaper ceased describing the war as imperialistic, and instead complimented the

navy for its democratic organization, thanking it for winning independence for Chile and encouraging the fleet to protect this freedom against the onslaught of the Nazis and their Japanese hench-
men.[87]

Some of this newly found enthusiasm even included Arturo
Prat. In 1942 the paper briefly noted the heroic exploits of the
Esmeralda and the *Covadonga*, but refused to describe the battle
in detail, claiming that it might antagonize Chile's neighbors and
thereby benefit the Nazi cause.[88] One year later the paper hoped
that the tradition of sacrifice established by Prat would be "present more firmly than ever in the Chilean sailors, since today they
have a great and difficult task to realize."[89] In 1944 *El Siglo* printed
a picture of Prat, and acknowledged his spirit of sacrifice, discipline, and valor.[90] In the last year of the war Prat was mentioned
again, and the Battle of Iquique was cited by name.[91] In comparison to earlier editorials, the attention *El Siglo* gave Prat during
the war years amounted to almost hysterical praise; but when it
is compared to the space given to O'Higgins, the founder of the
fleet, and to Lord Cochrane, its first commander, Prat comes out a
poor third.[92]

Essentially the paper was more concerned with praising the
navy as an institution rather than its principal hero, pursuing an
editorial policy consistent with its political views. Although the
periodical was willing to follow the Soviet line—even going so
far as to compliment the navy—it could never really accept Prat
because of his participation in a "dirty" war. The paper seemed to
concentrate more on the fleet's role during the war for independence, perhaps because the issues were more clearcut: the struggle
between Chilean nationalism and Spanish imperialism. Anything
after that time seems to have been overlooked. It is interesting to
note, for instance, that never once did *El Siglo* write about the
role of the fleet in its wars against the Peruvian-Bolivian Confederation or against Spain. Only the independence heroes appeared
important. Prat, it seems, was cited only because the paper would
have had difficulty not mentioning the man whose death Navy
Day commemorated.

Once the war ended, *El Siglo* returned to its traditional editorial policy. Arturo Prat was conspicuous by his absence. The
paper even turned on the fleet, condemning it for being undemo-

cratic and criticizing its military code as being incompatible with modern concepts of liberty and democracy.[93] Although the Battle of Iquique was specifically mentioned in 1947, the anniversary seemed to serve only as a launching platform for a diatribe against foreign imperialism and the domestic oligarchy. It was the latter, for example, who had deposed O'Higgins, Freire, and Balmaceda. The editorial stated that once again the nation was involved in a battle led by the Communist party in defense of its freedom and sovereignty.[94]

Subsequent editorials did not demonstrate any spectacular changes. Although the navy regained its former position of prominence, still there was no mention of Prat. As before, the articles heaped praise on Balmaceda; the man who made the day famous went unnoticed.[95]

It is impossible to complete the study of Prat's image in the Communist press beyond 1948 when *El Siglo* was closed by order of the government.[96] One might conclude, however, that in comparison with other newspapers, *El Siglo* was not the most enthusiastic booster of Prat. The paper's treatment of the dead hero falls into essentially three periods. During the first and third, from 1937 to 1941 and 1946 to 1948, Prat was almost totally absent from the editorial columns of the Communist papers. Only when Russia became involved in World War II did the paper deign to notice Prat. One must conclude, therefore, that the second period constitutes the exception and not the rule in the paper's editorial policy. Because of the war and the need for Allied unity, *El Siglo* condescended to mention the hero of Iquique.

As earlier noted, the neglect of Prat appears to have resulted from his participation in a war the Communist party found repugnant. It might also have been that the party considered Prat too bourgeois. A symbol of Chilean, not revolutionary virtue, the dead hero was perhaps too parochial and archaic for the party to accept. The men whom the Communists seemed to admire, O'Higgins, Balmaceda, and Recabarren, were all rebels against the traditional society. Prat's virtues, if imitated by his countrymen, could possibly reconcile the nation and cure its social and economic ills. This, of course, would undermine the Communist belief in the necessity of class war. Perhaps for this reason Prat was ignored and neglected: a rebirth of his virtues would delay the day of social justice and the revolution that promised to bring a happy life on earth.

IV Socialism and Arturo Prat

The Chilean Socialist party, unlike the Nazi and Communist counterparts, was not a monolithic movement. The party drew upon various ideological sources for its inspiration and early in its history began splitting into various factions.[97] Because of these internal divisions, perhaps it would be more correct to speak of Chilean Socialism as a movement rather than a party.

The discussions of Prat in the Socialist journal, *La Opinión*,[98] like those of the Communist papers, fall into three distinct periods: 1933 to 1942, 1942 to 1945, and 1945 to 1950. This similarity is only superficial, however, for if the Communist paper rarely mentioned the hero of Iquique, the Socialist journal never failed to devote a substantial amount of attention to Prat and his exploits.

In many respects *La Opinión*'s descriptions of Prat resembled those of the traditional press. Both agreed that Prat's sacrifice had enormous moral value, and believed that his death represented the apogee of Chilean heroism and virtue. Both stated that his life was one of sacrifice and dedication to the nation's welfare. *La Opinión* compared Prat to Leonidas and, like its traditional counterparts, praised Prat's virtuous private life.[99] Unlike the Communists, the Socialists refused to brand the 1879 war as imperialistic, claiming instead that it had been fought to preserve Chile's honor. The paper objected neither to the war nor to its outcome. Indeed, if *La Opinión* had any reservations about the struggle, it was because it believed that the nation's upper class had squandered the nitrate revenues acquired after the war and had failed to lead the country properly.[100] Not unlike the press during the parliamentary period, *La Opinión* used Prat to expose the nation's leaders as greedy and incompetant men. For the Socialists, Prat was the symbol of virtue; the oligarchy, greed incarnate.

In this respect, *La Opinión* appears to have believed that patriotism could have a salutary effect on the country. Love of the nation was more than a moribund remnant of nineteenth-century romanticism. Patriotism was a passionate devotion to one's nation, implying not only a reverence for the past but also signifying a readiness, indeed an eagerness, to work for its present needs. It was a force that stimulated Chileans "to love our soil, to be each time more useful, to try to obtain, by all the means possible, the defense of the individual's liberties and our economic independence and to work for the greatness and the general prosperity of our nation."[101]

Much as *La Opinión* loved Chile, it could attack its leaders for undermining the very spirit of patriotism so necessary for the nation's survival. The newspaper accused the government of having become weak, even effeminate, of permitting the country to stagnate, and of having refused to rescue it from the morass in which it wallowed. *La Opinión* complained that the upper class had failed to emulate Prat's nationalistic example[102] by permitting foreign capitalists to dominate the nation's natural resources thus "sucking all the vital sap of the nation and precipitating us into misery."[103] The Chilean people, the paper declared, had been defrauded. They had fought the War of the Pacific to save Chile, but because of government venality and corruption, only the bankers of Wall Street and London seemed to be enjoying the fruits of their victory.[104] The government was urged, in the name of Prat, to better the people's situation by improving their standard of living and to rid the nation of its foreign economic masters.[105] The people were exhorted to emulate Prat by fighting for a Chile "great, generous, prosperous and free."[106]

Subsequent editorials did not vary from this pattern. Prat's sacrifice at Iquique was used to expose the oligarchy's failures and to shame them into making reforms.[107] The paper became somewhat more optimistic in 1936, the year of the Popular Front, hoping that the new government, inspired by Prat, would free the nation from economic bondage and, like the fallen hero, dedicate itself to Chile's salvation.[108] Two years later the paper noted that on the morning of the Battle of Iquique Prat had asked Condell if the men had eaten breakfast. "Yes," *La Opinión* wrote, "the people who gave us glories and riches have breakfasted. But after half a century could the people now answer affirmatively this unexpected question of the Captain of Captains?"[109]

Throughout its editorials, *La Opinión* tried to compare Prat's actions during the war with those of the oligarchy. The hero, according to the journal, was a man of the people who had died at Iquique while the wealthy had remained at home, protecting their economic interests and assuring their future by war profiteering.[110] A few years later *La Opinión* stated that only two groups of Chileans had participated in the famous battle: the middle class and the proletariat. The paper also emphasized the importance of Juan de Dios Aldea, noting how this man of working-class background had fought beside his officer to save Chile.[111] The implication of these remarks is obvious: Chile had been saved by its humble sons; its upper class, however, had not participated.

The paper altered its editorial policy slightly when the World War II erupted. Although *La Opinión* continued to commemorate Iquique's anniversary, it explained that by rendering homage to Prat it hoped that it was not offending either Peru or Bolivia. This new sensitivity was doubtless the result of the war, for the paper explained that all American nations needed virtues like those of Prat "at this moment in the work of unity and continental solidarity." The hero, the paper observed, was needed not only to rebuild his own nation but for the "joint and fraternal concept of great continental unity."[112]

The war also appears to have subtly modified the newspaper's reactions to its own government. Perhaps for the first time *La Opinión* used Prat as a unifying force. The newspaper claimed, for instance, that all classes of society had participated in the Battle of Iquique and urged Chileans to "put aside for some moments our political hatreds and unite in order to give thanks to the Almighty for having given us the 21st of May, for having given us a man, a symbol which might make victory possible for us." Despite these concessions, the paper continued to recommend that the government model itself on Prat and strive to imitate his sacrifice.[113]

Even after the war had ended, the paper continued to strive for continental unity. The Socialist journal emphasized that Prat had been fighting for his motherland and expressed its admiration for the Peruvians and Bolivians who had also fulfilled their duty during the War of the Pacific. For a while the paper did not renew its attacks on the government. *La Opinión* remained critical of the oligarchy's way of running the nation, but preached a policy of toleration, perhaps fearful that the political situation might worsen.[114]

La Opinión eventually returned to its prewar policy of using Prat to unmask the government's inability to subordinate its needs to the people's benefit. In 1947, for example, the paper stated that the nation could best render its homage to Prat by casting out those who had forgotten their sense of responsibility and patriotic duty.[115] Two years later, *La Opinión* again praised Prat's acts as the purest manifestation of civic virtue and hoped that it might inspire the nation to emulate the fallen hero. The paper observed that May 21 was also the day for the opening of the Congress and hoped that Prat's sacrifice would be remembered.[116]

As can be seen then, the Socialist party was a vocal protestor against the *status quo*. Unlike their radical Right or Left competitors, however, the Socialists appear less the captive of a foreign ideology and more a domestic reform movement, apparently taking up the standard in the struggle against the faults of the government which the more traditional press had long since discarded.

7 ⚔ ARTURO PRAT AND EDUCATION

*'Tis education forms the common
mind:
Just as the twig is bent the
tree's inclined.*
—ALEXANDER POPE

I Arturo Prat 1880–1890

Educators, unlike other sectors of Chilean society, emphasized Prat's moral qualities, filial devotion, and scholastic achievements more than his wartime actions. Even before the war had ended, Enrique Montt told an audience of school children that the battlefield was not the only test of man. A citizen, he asserted, could best prepare himself for war by learning to fulfill his civilian responsibilities. Montt claimed that Prat's acts at Iquique were the logical consequence of the earlier sacrifices he had made as a dutiful son, responsible husband, and loving father.[1]

Miguel Luis Amunátegui, a prominent politician and educator, seemed to agree with Montt, claiming that it was because of his education that Prat triumphed at Iquique. Cannons, the educator said, were but the slaves of intelligence; problems in gunnery, merely questions of mathematics. Without the skills acquired at school, Prat would never have boarded the *Huáscar* and thus become Chile's preeminent hero.[2]

Three years later, at another commemorative ceremony, Pedro Acuña told a group of young students that it was at school that Prat first learned to love his motherland and to sacrifice. Acuña informed his audience that if they wanted to emulate the fallen hero, they too must begin in the classroom. The speaker concluded his address, stating:

> Children: the school shows you the path you must follow in
> order to imitate Prat. Your books and your teachers will teach
> you how to love your country; loving your country makes

heroes: love your school books, and the future generations
will do for some of you what today you are doing for the
"Martyr of Iquique."[3]

At the same celebration, a precocious seven-year-old, Luis Gorigoitía, urged his classmates: "Like Prat let us try to achieve victory
over a formidable enemy who pursues us; error and ignorance, so
that we might, in one day not too distant, offer the support of our
arm and our blood to our beloved motherland."[4]

Chilean textbooks, unlike the various public speakers, were not
overly enthusiastic about Prat. Orestes Tornero, for example,
barely mentioned the Battle of Iquique, let alone its principal
hero, in his brief description of the war. Although a subsequent
edition of Tornero's book discussed the war in greater detail, it
still did not stress Arturo Prat.[5] Tornero's works seem to be typical
of the various texts published immediately after the war. Miguel
Luis Amunátegui's *Compendio de la historia política i eclesiástica
de Chile*, for instance, also failed to mention Prat. A later edition
did acknowledge the battle and Prat's role but not in any significant manner.[6] The works of other contemporaneous authors, Esteban Muñoz Donoso and Gaspar Toro, followed this same pattern.[7]

The reason for this omission is quite simple. The textbooks published during and immediately after the war did not stress Prat
because school books generally are slow to incorporate recent
events. Authors merely added a few additional facts to bring their
earlier works up to date. School books published for the first time
following the war, however, were substantially different. Gaspar
Toro's *Compendio de historia de Chile* (1492–1884), for instance,
not only gave a comprehensive description of the Battle of Iquique, but also included pictures both of the battle and of Prat.
Toro did not attribute Chile's ultimate victory in the war to the
spirit of Prat, as did subsequent books, but rather to Chile's organization, its racial homogeneity, its habits of work, and its
solidly established institutions.[8]

*Lecciones de historia de Chile para el uso en las escuelas públ-
icas*, published in 1887, was the first book to emphasize Prat's
role. It minutely described the battle, quoting from the fallen
hero's last words. The book's unknown author stressed Prat's academic skills as much as his military prowess, stating that his final

sacrifice was the result of his having led a life subordinated to duty.[9]

Chile's educators, at least between 1881 and 1890, accentuated Prat's scholarly qualities perhaps to encourage the nation's youth to study. Certainly there was nothing unusual in these actions; the battlefield is always more spectacular than the classroom. Indeed, fighting for one's country makes the school appear superfluous if not effeminate. Prat dispelled the image of clumsy intellectuals. If the teachers were correct, it was the school that forged the hero. This rather limited role subsequently changed. Prat's popularity not only increased, his image changed as well, and these modifications resulted in part from the growth of new ideas among Chilean educators.

II Changes in the Philosophy of Chilean Education

Beginning in the 1890s, educators joined other segments of Chilean society in manifesting their disdain for the corruption and materialism of the parliamentary regime. Educational journals joined the popular press in complaining about Chile's decline. As early as 1893, one author denounced Chile's leaders for failing to set the proper example, stating that patriotism had become a word used by politicians to rationalize their squabbling for power.[10]

These complaints became more strident as the year progressed. By the mid 1900s, educational journals ceased being simply professional magazines and began criticizing the social system as well. Ana Johnson and Julio Saavedra[11] lamented the collapse of Chilean patriotism. The Association of National Education published an open letter to the president demanding that he put an end to the nation's political immorality.[12] Apparently this request went unheard since this same article was repeatedly reprinted.[13] Tancredo Pinochet Le-Brun wrote *La conquista de Chile en el siglo XX* in 1909. A year later an obscure teacher, using the pseudonym Julio Valdés Cange, wrote *Sinceridad: Chile íntimo en 1910*, a scathing attack on Chilean society.[14] These works also protested against the parliamentary regime and, like other protests, must have been ignored, for by 1912 Luis Galdames concluded:

> . . . as a State, as a nation, we lack social, economic, political, and international ideals. We lack, in essence, an ideal which affects the people's vitality and their future. And since these ideals do not exist, we are proceeding in a hesitant manner, always vacillating, seeking progress and a grandeur which we do not know how to achieve. Because of this, the national character is diminished and each day an even deeper apathy pervades us.[15]

In part Chile's crisis was ideological. Many educators believed that foreign ideas were culturally undermining the nation. These feelings were somewhat justified. The government had sent a mission abroad in 1885 to study foreign teaching methods for the purpose of revising Chile's educational system. Chile invited foreign professors to revamp the nation's schools and their curriculum.[16] Initially these reforms were well received. A quarter of a century later, however, many believed that these imported ideas were ruining Chile, depreciating its traditional values and endangering its very existence as a separate cultural entity.[17]

Amanda Labarca warned that Chile was in danger of becoming a foreign enclave, "more European than Chilean, more French than European."[18] Julio Saavedra attacked a phenomenon he called, "exotismo," the cultivation of foreign habits and customs in preference to those of Chile.[19] A book reviewer called the same idea "snobismo,"[20] and Luis Galdames warned: "The truth is, gentlemen, that in organizing our educational system we have forgotten that we are Chileans."[21]

If foreigners caused Chile's decline, the solution was obvious: purge the nation of all alien influence, return Chile to its traditional folkways, and instill respect for its customs. The response was almost xenophobic. Even the Spanish language was suspect. Julio Saavedra was but one of a few who demanded that the Spanish used in Chile should conform only to the needs of the nation and not to the rules of the crusty Royal Spanish Academy.[22] Others agreed with Saavedra, claiming that a national language was imperative to the nation's cultural survival.[23]

The movement for cultural nationalism gained momentum. Foreigners were to be forbidden to teach certain subjects.[24] All things Chilean were considered good. Even the Araucanian Indian, for years a dreaded enemy, became a romantic figure.[25] The government was encouraged to stop foreign immigration because there were still landless Chileans.[26] Educational journals pleaded for a government program to improve the nation's health and a campaign against the use of alcohol.[27]

As nationalistic feeling grew, it eventually began to focus on foreign economic domination. Many educators concluded that the nation must fight back. Luis Galdames urged changes in the educational system to permit the nation to defend itself against foreign economic interests. He demanded that Chile cease emulating the outmoded ideals of Ancient Greece. Chile, he claimed, needed new heroes, not the soldier or politician, but someone who would work for the country's economic welfare.[28]

Francisco Antonio Encina argued that Chile's Spanish and Catholic heritage had stunted the nation's economic growth stifling the instinct for business and economic competition. Chile's youth, he lamented, preferred the humanities and liberal professions to the marketplace. The only way to regain control of the nation's resources was to develop an educational system that would train men for commerce.[29]

The educational journals and societies encouraged economic nationalism. It was at a meeting of the Association of National Education that Encina presented the lectures that were subsequently published as his famous work *La Educación económica y el Liceo.* This same organization published his *Nuestra inferioridad económica,* as well as Galdames's *Educación económica i intelectual.*[30] Some educational articles urged the introduction of courses to prepare Chilean youth for business.[31] Others chastised Chilean consumers for purchasing foreign-made items and criticized domestic manufacturers for being too ashamed to print "Made in Chile" on their products.[32] Guillermo Subercaseaux urged that the nitrate industry be taken from foreign control and advocated laws for the protection of Chilean industries.[33]

Despite the gratuitous advice, Chile's economic situation did not improve. The outbreak of the World War I only brought additional hardships. Educators redoubled their efforts to change the nation's social, political, and economic structure. With enormous numbers of people unemployed and many suffering, they beseeched the president and his Congress to work for the nation's welfare.[34] The parliamentary regime remained unmoved. When it collapsed, there were few mourners among Chilean educators.

While the teachers were demanding cultural and economic nationalism, they also were attempting to revolutionize the nation's
educational system by introducing courses on civic education. Although the movement for civic education began around the 1880s,
it is questionable whether it developed in response to the parliamentary regime. Quite possibly issues other than political initiated
this movement. But even if civic education did begin as a separate
entity, it appears to have merged with the other movements critical
of the parliamentary regime and to have sought as its goal the
abolition of corruption and decay in Chilean society.[35]

Formerly education was simply the transmission of knowledge
from one generation to the next. Civic education changed this
outmoded concept. Henceforth education had to be based on concepts of morality and civic responsibility.[36] The new courses sought
not only to enlighten men but to make of them virtuous and patriotic citizens. Civic education was to instill a variety of attitudes:
respect for the Constitution and national institutions, obedience
to the law and authority, a sense of national unity, and understanding of the individual's sense of civic responsibility. Perhaps the
most important goal of civic education was to inculcate in the individual a sense of morality, honesty, and duty so he might better
serve his nation.[37]

Numerous educators believed that the best way of teaching
civic education, of inspiring a love of the motherland, was through
the study of Chilean history. That subject provided examples of
virtuous and self-sacrificing men, proving that civic education was
not an illusory platonic ideal but a realistic goal that could be
achieved through discipline and hard work. Thus just as a child
learned to function within his family by imitating its members, so
he would learn to assume the responsibilities of belonging to an
even greater family, that of Chile, by imitating its greatest sons.[38]
An one teacher noted:

> At each step we find in our national history men whose char-
> acter, virtues, honesty and patriotism can be a precious guide
> for the child's future conduct.[39]

The study of history encompassed more than the memorization
of fact. Indeed, according to one educator, rote memorization destroyed history's intrinsic value. History was thus more than a func-

tion of the memory; it was a morality play, teaching what was good and bad, laudable and despicable.[40]

> History should educate the child morally as well as seek the development of the intellectual faculties. It should cultivate in the student higher feelings, awakening a love of virtue, friendship, justice, generosity, the desire to imitate the great actions and the resolution to be useful to his fellow man; the hatred of vice in all its manifestations, of tyranny, fraud, selfishness, envy, ambition, of all base motives and ignoble actions. To awaken these feelings history makes use of examples: it presents us with virtuous men and wicked men, praiseworthy actions and detestable actions; it shows us, by means of the consequences of acts, the moral sanction which all human actions have and shows us the path of duty and the virtue of practicing good and avoiding evil.[41]

Chile's teachers needed examples, living symbols, to inspire and indoctrinate its youth, men who died for the motherland, men of character who labored for their families and for their nation.[42] It was with these examples that the teaching profession hoped to reform society. Unlike some nations, Chile did not have to manufacture some paradigm of virtue; it already had Arturo Prat.

III Arturo Prat and Cultural Nationalism, 1890–1950

Prat's popularity increased as the forces of cultural nationalism and civic education gained new adherents. A good example of this change is found in the works of Francisco Valdés Vergara. In 1888, Valdés Vergara wrote *Lecturas infantiles preparadas para niños de ocho a doce años de edad*, a primer designed to encourage Chilean youth to emulate the lives of various worthy men. Among those mentioned were George Washington, Abraham Lincoln, and Benjamin Franklin. Arturo Prat, alas, was absent.[43]

Within ten years Valdés Vergara wrote *Historia de Chile para la enseñanza primaria*. This volume devoted six pages to the Battle of Iquique and included not only a picture of that contest, but of its principal participants: Arturo Prat, Carlos Condell, Ignacio Serrano, Manuel Orella, and even Miguel Grau. Valdés Vergara also wrote an extensive biography of Prat which later was incorporated by the authors of various compilations of reading material.[44]

There were other indications that Prat's popularity was increasing. Domingo Villalobos wrote *Lecciones de historia de Chile*, which included not only portions of Prat's final speech, but some biographical materials as well.[45] Chilean educational journals began reporting on the commemorative ceremonies at various public schools, especially those of the Escuela Normal de Preceptores de Santiago, which were held regularly after 1887.[46] The ministry of education declared the twenty-first of May a school holiday in 1897.[47] Educators began recommending that students visit Prat's tomb.[48] Teachers not only incorporated Prat into history lessons, but into other disciplines as well.[49] In an article on the significance of Chile's flag, one author noted that Prat had won fame defending that sacred banner.[50] When José Bernardo Suárez died, he was remembered not only for his contributions to education but also for having been one of Prat's professors.[51]

The concept of duty perhaps best explains Prat's resurgence in popularity, as well as the changes that occurred in his image. As in the rest of Chilean society, many teachers became disenchanted with the parliamentary regime. The educators offered constructive criticism, which was ignored or rejected. Unable to cajole the nation's leaders into change, the schoolteachers sought to rebuild the nation by educating their children. In a society supposedly bereft of symbols of morality, the school turned to the nation's past. Like the popular press, it found in Prat not simply a symbol of nationalism but a life of dedication and sacrifice. Thus just as Prat became a fixture within civilian society, he became one within education as well. Prat was an ideal choice, a superb vehicle for the spiritual reeducation of the nation's youth and national regeneration.

This attitude was best demonstrated in an article entitled: "El 21 de mayo i la educación cívica de los niños de las escuelas públicas." The article's unknown author not only praised Prat as an example of "discipline, of stability, and of abnegation in the fulfillment of a citizen's duties," he also explained how the school could use the fallen hero to stimulate patriotism:

> The Chilean school has always known how to cultivate in our school children the civic notions of the severe fulfillment of duty. Day by day, hour by hour, it has emphasized the need to form some day, through the virtue of its citizens and the

hard work of its children, a greater and more powerful motherland . . . the school, in addition to enriching the child's intellect with knowledge, also nourishes his generous impulses and feelings. It also cultivates and develops a feeling of love for the motherland which is personified in the civic virtues of good citizens and in the actions of our heroes.

In summation, civic education in the public school will try, in the future, to dispell the shadows which have deformed our culture. It will seek to intensify in the soul of the future generations, the model figures of the social organism, who have written on the pages of their life, the most honest code of patriotism. It is in this way that our nation can rest tranquil. The characteristics of our people are preserved and will be transmitted with great intensity in the formation of the future generations; the schools uniting the past and the present, and building on such a foundation that will ensure the future greatness of the Republic.[52]

The emphasis on Arturo Prat shifted. The schools no longer portrayed him simply as a scholar but as a dedicated servant of the motherland. One of the first manifestations of the shift in emphasis in Prat's image was a speech given at the Escuela Normal de Preceptores in Santiago. The speaker, a student named Víctor Hernández, noted:

We always have to remember that one of the greatest fathers of the motherland, the immortal Carrera . . . understood that the motherland's destiny did not rest solely in the mouth of a rifle or in the breast of brave soldiers. Also necessary were the wise lessons of the school . . . the luminous torch which should lead its children to the greatest acts of which a virile people are capable.

Hernández claimed that a new generation of patriots—men not only ready to defend the motherland in war, but perhaps more important, to lead it toward a life of education and progress—could be produced if only Chile's students would imitate Prat. It was Chile's teachers who were to bear the enormous responsibility "to inspire our youth in Prat's example, which is an inexhaustible fountain from which flows the greatest act of Chilean patriotism."[53]

Another commemorative celebration was held two years later. The speaker again praised Prat, describing him not simply as an illustrious and self-sacrificing patriot, but also as a man "studious and inquiring in peace . . . the perfect type of citizen." Like Hernández, the lecturer emphasized the role of the teacher in molding the youth in Prat's image. "We, the men of the present generation, have the imperative duty of giving a sense of awareness to those who follow us, stimulating them to imitate this life full of abnegation and civic virtues, of heroism and undying glories." If their efforts were successful, then Chile's youth would be capable not only of triumphing in war, but of gathering "the fruits of study and of honorable work in peace."[54]

Romildo Colombo also stressed the importance of indoctrinating the nation's youth in the virtues of Arturo Prat. He alleged that, by celebrating the twenty-first of May, the nation's students learned what "is good, beautiful, and great . . . how to love the motherland, how to cultivate science and how to render homage to the arts." Ideally this education had to begin while the student was still young, for "a child who will admire the motherland's heroes will also be a hero." Colombo admonished the younger generation to respect the country's heroes, "Chile's true aristocracy," and hoped that "the example of Prat may awaken your enthusiasm and that you will become good citizens and learn to fulfill your duty."[55]

As has been seen, Chilean educators reflected the popular discontent with the nation's social and economic conditions. Like the press, teachers began to stress the need for a society in which the individual worked not simply for himself but for his nation.[56] A prominent educator, Darío Salas, believed that the aim of education was not simply to enlighten the individual but to "benefit the community, and that its object is to make each man a factor of collective betterment, to enable each one to give to society the best service which his natural aptitudes permit him to offer."[57]

This tendency became more pronounced in the second decade of the twentieth century as educators began using Prat as the example of the citizen who gave his all for his motherland's improvement. A señorita Muñoz told her classmates at the Liceo Superior de Niñas that by imitating Prat's virtues Chilean youth would learn how to love work and duty.[58] Félix Gonzáles, in 1917, used the occasion of the Battle of Iquique to exhort the nation's youth to "promise to work for its [Chile's] aggrandizement, to fulfill faithfully our student duties, to protect and develop the national industries, and to run to its defense when some enemy might offend it or try to attack it."[59] Four years later, Bórquez Solar told Chile's youth that there was little probability of their dying on the battle-

field. War, he claimed, was a thing of the past, and if Chile's young
desired to become heroes like Prat they must do it by working.

> . . . in truth I say that you can achieve heroism, as worthy of
> remembrance and of praise as that of Prat, in a simple life,
> in whatever position which Destiny might have reserved for
> you: working the fruitful land, digging in the bottoms of the
> mountains, at the anvil, in the factory, in the workshop.
>
> Look at the modesty of Prat. . . . He could find greatness
> under the most disadvantageous conditions. Put all your
> heart, all your soul, into whatever work you may choose to
> undertake. And, you can be sure that when you fulfill that
> duty towards your motherland and your brothers, by working
> without regard for yourself, you are already on the road to
> heroism.
>
> . . . we should exert ourselves for the welfare of our fellow
> man. You can make yourself great in the redemption of the
> proletariat, a hero of justice and truth, by consoling the sad,
> helping the needy, not out of a sense of charity, but human
> solidarity. Cure the spirits sick with hate who swarm in the
> *conventillos* because of ignorance, a criminal lack of atten-
> tion, and an abominable inequity.
>
> You must understand that in future history will exalt new
> heroes: men who surely will not carry swords but perhaps an
> armful of wheat or tools, or the pen of a writer.
>
> These are but brief reflections on Prat which I wanted to
> tell you today. You see now, of course, the path which you
> will have to follow in order to imitate or surpass him.[60]

Prat's use as a symbol of sacrifice and reverence for the motherland became more obvious as Chile became tainted with radical
ideas—Socialism and Anarchism—and saw its workers in the north
and south participate in bitter industrial strikes. These movements
began to sow doubts as to the validity of Chilean society, its traditions, and its very foundations. The educators were perhaps
quicker to respond to this threat than the press. As early as 1902,
Ruperto Oroz warned:

> What is important . . . is to put our children on guard against
> the sophisms of those *without a motherland*. Beneath the
> beautiful names of cosmopolitanism and internationalism,
> these apostles of a new ideology are definitely attempting to
> blind us to our duties and to consecrate cowardice.[61]

In 1909 José María Muñoz feared that "universalist ideas which
believed in a universal motherland" were gaining a foothold in

Chile. He saw labor unrest as the cause of the nation's internal problems and believed "it was the duty of all good citizens to oppose seditious movements, the strikes, and the infamous conspiracies of unworthy opponents."[62] These complaints did not cease as the nation suffered additional social and economic upheavals. Chile's educators tried to counter these "subversive" movements by emphasizing nationalism in education. They sought to create the idea of a Chilean family to preserve the nation from divisive forces.[63] It was only natural that the twenty-first of May and Prat would be used to inspire unity.

Prat's name was again linked to that of the "fathers of the nation." The hero of Iquique was mentioned in conjunction with Caupolicán, O'Higgins, and many of the leaders of the independence movement.[64] On May 21, 1913, before the First School District of Santiago, one man spoke out against "the forces of social dissolution and individualism which threaten the nation's destiny." In an address to the children of workers, the lecturer hoped that the twenty-first of May would provide an occasion for his audience to manifest their appreciation for a moment which was to unite all citizens in the love of the motherland.[65] Luis Berrios, in 1919, attempted to combat any foreign influences when he stated:

> . . . we are content with the poem of Ercilla and the tradition and lessons contained therein. We believe in the motherland of O'Higgins, Carrera, Portales, Bulnes, Pinto, Prat and Balmaceda. Teach then, that we do not want another patriotism because there is none better than the latter. Teach that by professing this patriotism and learning about the grandeur of a democratic citizen's duties, we can make our voices felt with more efficiency when the moment of demanding our rights might appear.[66]

Two years later, at the dedication of Prat's statue in Santiago, Luis Carriola hoped that the spirit of Prat might "contribute to keep safe and with all its strength and vigor, the feeling of patriotism, which miserable social elements are trying to undermine."[67]

Of course, Prat continued to be a popular theme in Chilean school books. Quite possibly the popularity was another product of the movement for civic education. School books, like education itself, had become more than a means of providing the student with factual knowledge. As Otto Schlott noted, the textbook was to "awaken and nourish in the child's soul the love of the motherland."[68]

Not all of the nation's textbooks were uniformly enthusiastic about the hero of Iquique. While the majority of these books described the Battle of Iquique, a few mentioned Prat only briefly.[69] Most of the texts, however, like the educational journals and public speeches, continued to emphasize Prat's virtuous life. Pedro Barrientos, for example, praised Prat for being a dutiful son, an excellent student, and a good family man.[70] Alejandro Silva emphasized Prat's obedience to his superiors, his discipline, and his love of work.[71] In a book written by Armando Pinto for the teaching of moral education to children, the only person cited was Arturo Prat, whose example was to inspire the children to be "studious, disciplined, just, polite, affectionate, and valiant."[72]

Prat's devotion to duty also remained a popular theme. Colección H. E. C. stressed this in a historical textbook they published.[73] Alejandro Silva and S. Gonzales underlined Prat's statement: "I will fulfill my duty."[74] One unknown author described the anguish Prat must have felt when faced with death and aware that he would never again see his family, but noted that even this deep emotion paled before his love for his motherland.[75] Walterio Millar alleged that Prat had a "religious respect for duty and showed an inflexible will to fulfill it."[76] Alejo Roa wrote a short play comparing Arturo Prat and Napoleon Bonaparte. The Frenchman was considered inferior to Prat because "he did little or nothing for his nation." As Roa noted, "If you want your motherland to honor you, first fulfill your duty and then enjoy yourself. . . . To fulfill your duty, that was Prat's last exhortation."[77] César Bunster told his young readers that Prat was sad when he sacrificed his life for Chile, but if they wanted to emulate him they too must be prepared to give all for their motherland.[78]

Unlike the articles and speeches, the school books tended to concentrate on Prat's academic performance. Perhaps this was because textbooks were designed for children while the articles or published speeches were often delivered to audiences composed of teachers and university students. Indeed, some of the speeches appeared to exhort the teachers to perform their duties.[79]

Generally the textbooks, while praising Prat, did not offer the reader much variety. It does appear—perhaps only to this author's jaundiced eye—that some school books were remarkably similar to one another.[80] This similarity may reflect the strong influence of one edition upon subsequent works, or simply a lack of originality. Nonetheless, textbooks, like the educational journals, stressed the importance of Prat as a symbol of national sacrifice and devotion to duty.[81]

IV Arturo Prat and the "Achieving Society"

In his essay, "Education, Values, and Entrepreneurship," Seymour Lipset stated that the United States and Latin America had different value systems: the North Americans were achievement oriented, strivers, aggressive; the Latins supposedly prized caste more than hard work and depreciated manual labor. Supposedly these cultural values influenced both educational systems: The Latins traditionally favored the humanities; the Americans, pragmatists par excellence, the sciences.[82]

There is some substance to the claim that North American education stressed the practical aspects. Ruth Miller Elson's study of nineteenth-century American school books concluded that education in the United States dispensed not only "useful knowledge to foster success in the material world but also to produce those qualities of character which we associate both with Puritanism and with the self-made man: thrift, hard work, and the rejection of frivolity."[83]

Professor Elson illustrated her thesis by citing the examples of George Washington and Benjamin Franklin. She noted that although Washington was an educated and cultured individual, American school books scarcely mentioned these attributes. The general impression was that Washington was a practical man of action and certainly not the intellectual. Franklin appears to have undergone a similar transformation. American texts did not mention his impressive scientific or diplomatic skills or his reputation as a *bon vivant*, only his industry and thrift. As Elson noted, the American hero-figure is "a practical, moral, hard-working man who needs 'useful knowledge' to get ahead in the world but finds scholarship unnecessary and even demeaning."[84]

The study of Prat's image in the Chilean school system indicates perhaps, that Professor's Lipset may not have been totally accurate when he wrote that the Latin-American school did not teach its students to achieve. On the contrary, there is an enormous similarity between the treatment of Washington, Franklin, and Prat. Like their North American counterparts, Chilean school books lauded Prat's industry, hard work, and thrift. The fact that Prat was a lawyer was rarely mentioned. Instead the fallen hero was depicted as a man of action whose skills permitted him to prolong a naval battle against all odds. Prat's devotion to his mother, wife, and children.is also important and certainly seem incongruous in a society that supposedly condones marital infidelity among its male members.

Prat's image changed in the public school much as it had in the popular press. Perhaps one of the few differences between the two was that Prat remained relatively apolitical in the school system. Although essentially Prat was a figure of morality to the teacher and the student as he was to the general public, it would be too simplistic to describe Prat merely as a Chilean puritan. Indeed, it is questionable if he would have enjoyed that dubious compliment. Prat's image was transformed from a parochial figure, used to stimulate children to study, to become almost a god-figure who stood above politics. Prat represented the personification of Chilean pedagogical ideals: a figure who combined a devotion to country with a need to succeed materially. Chile needed both virtues, the first to overcome the dry rot of the parliamentary regime, the second to break the foreign economic stranglehold and reject the alien social doctrines that threatened to replace the prevailing laissez-faire liberalism. The Chilean school, perhaps more than any other segment of society, sought to change the nation. To modernize the country, to create a sense of oneness, to unify— these were the goals of education. For this reason, it needed a figure of strength, of virtue, and of honor. Once again the nation called on Arturo Prat and once again he served as an example to his countrymen.

8 ✝ ARTURO PRAT AND THE MILITARY

You are entering the place which preserves the relics of those who, with their heroic acts in the war and wise and honorable directives in peace, made the name of our Navy great and respected.

Think a moment, and, elevating your grateful thoughts, remember that you are the descendant of those who had for their watchword: the glory of the motherland and the satisfaction of duty fulfilled.

You are obliged to continue their work and to make yourselves worthy of such fathers. Look with faith toward the future. Pray and, from the depths of your heart, make a solemn promise to work honorably for the motherland and that your simple prayer may be the beautiful sacrifice which directs your triumphal march to glory.

Viva Chile!

—Words on the entrance to the Naval Museum at Valparaíso

Quite naturally the Chilean navy remembered Prat. Almost every officer commanding a warship has his picture hanging in his office or cabin. Presently there is a cruiser that bears the name of Prat, the third ship of the fleet to do so, as well as another *Esmeralda*, which like the first, is a training vessel for midshipmen. But the fleet was not always so devoted to the fallen hero. An analysis of the *Revista de Marina*, the official journal of the Chilean navy, indicates that there were three discernible periods in Prat's development as a hero: Prat was popular from 1886 to 1888; neither he nor the Battle of Iquique received any special mention, however, during the second period from 1889–1901; while in the third period, 1901-1950, Prat regained his position of high esteem. Although subject to certain distinctions, the shifts in Prat's popularity are generally similar to those that occurred in civilian society and appear to have the same causes. In order to demonstrate this, however, it is necessary to survey Chile's naval development.

I

Following the War of the Pacific, many Chilean naval officers believed that their nation was Latin America's preeminent maritime power[1] and, not surprisingly, they wanted the fleet to maintain this newfound superiority. This desire was not solely motivated by self-interest. According to many naval officers, Chile's geographic position and "personality" made it a natural maritime power; therefore, it followed that the country's very survival depended upon a strong fleet and merchant marine.[2] The proponents of a strong navy received additional support from the works of Alfred Thayer Mahan, whose writings were popular in Chilean naval circles, as well as from the rise of strong maritime powers like Great Britain, the United States, and Japan.

As a result, Chilean naval authorities believed that a nation was respected in direct proportion to the power it commanded.[3] Having achieved this strength in the recent war, Chile either had to maintain its position of power or decline. It became almost axiomatic, according to certain naval authorities at least, that the nation's destiny was interwoven with the sea. As one naval officer noted:

> That Chile ought to have a fleet capable of making it the supreme Latin American maritime power, or giving it at least parity with the most powerful of them, is a need so evidently and obviously recognized by the entire nation, from the supreme government to the average citizen, that . . . it is superfluous to demonstrate this again in this article.[4]

Chile's main naval rival was Argentina, but in the early 1890s few considered it a threat. Vicente Zegers, for example, while noting that Argentina was spending twice as much money on naval armanents as Brazil and Chile combined, still claimed that it did not constitute a menace because

> this nation [Argentina] does not have its roots in the sea. Its interests there are not as important as ours, nor does it possess the material elements necessary for the creation and maintenance of a powerful navy. For this reason we believe that in the future the role of the Argentine fleet will be purely defensive.[5]

Another commentator, in 1898, while noting that the Argentine press was boasting about its fleet, remarked somewhat caustically that they "are not telling us the composition and displacement of so formidable a flotilla nor the number of its guns, nor the nationality of its crews."[6]

Despite the appearance of complacency, not all was well with the Chilean navy, in part perhaps as a result of the 1891 civil war. Although the majority of the fleet sided with the rebels, forces loyal to Balmaceda retained control of two torpedo boats, the *Lynch* and *Condell*, and a converted merchant ship, the *Imperial*. Doubtless some of the high command did not want to engage in a bloody civil war because of the enormous damage that would result, but after the rebels initiated hostilities the pro-Balmaceda forces ceased to be so reluctant. In the predawn hours of April 23, the *Lynch* and the *Condell* attacked and sank the flagship of the rebel fleet, the *Blanco Encalada*, as it lay at anchor in the harbor of Caldera.[7]

When the war ended the victors, ignoring the biblical injunctions about mortals taking vengeance on their fellowmen, punished those who had remained loyal to Balmaceda. This purge hit the navy hard. The new government penalized various officers depending upon the enormity of their offences. It only temporarily retired three rear admirals, for example, Juan Latorre, Juan Williams Rebolledo, and Oscar Viel, but permanently expelled the commander of the *Lynch*. Ironically many of the survivors of the Battle of Iquique were among those punished: Arturo Wilson, Francisco Sánchez of the *Esmeralda*, and Enrique Reynolds and Miguel Sanz of the *Covadonga* were all forced to leave the naval service.[8]

The dismissal of these heroes disturbed some of the press. *El Porvenir*, for example, complained about their exclusion from the navy, and asked the government to make an exception in their case by allowing them to return to active duty.[9] Eventually the government pardoned all the survivors of Iquique and readmitted them, as well as most of the other former rebels, into the fleet.

More than generosity motivated this act.[10] Too few officers were being graduated from the Naval Academy, while many on active duty retired from the fleet, attracted by the higher wages to be earned in civilian society. It was difficult to recruit enlisted men, many of whom either deserted or left the fleet after their first tour of duty. Government economies restricted maneuvers and forced the disarming of certain vessels.[11] Amid these problems some of the smugness disappeared.

> Not only does Chile not possess a navy which is equipped to defend its long coastline, but instead of becoming larger . . . day by day it continues to decrease in size. The few units which exist for the protection of the glorious flag, are in great part composed of ships whose officers are almost all foreigners.[12]

By the mid-1890s, the renewed Argentine-Chilean border problems increased the probability of war between the two nations. During their reappraisal of the Argentine fleet, some naval officers discovered that Chile was no longer the most powerful naval power. As P. N. Martínez observed, Chile's navy was "a heterogeneous conglomeration of vessels which cannot respond to the tactical or strategic needs of the nation" and inferior in quality and strength to the Argentine fleet.[13] A year later, a second naval expert stated, "Today we cannot deny that our neighbor's naval power is superior to our own, and that with the initiation of the regime of armed peace, if we simply seek to equal them, they will order new ships to preserve their sought after naval supremacy."[14]

The regime of armed peace was the *Pactos de Mayo*, a series of treaties signed in 1902 which ended the Chilean-Argentine arms race. The agreement established some degree of parity in naval forces, and both nations promised not to accept delivery of the capital ships they had previously ordered. From Chile's point of view the treaty was disastrous, because it ended the arms race when Argentina was materially superior and because it confined Chile's sphere of influence solely to the Pacific Coast. Thus 1902 was a pivotal year for the fleet. Henceforth Chile had to accept a secondary role in Latin-American affairs.

The *Pactos* apparently had a devastating effect on the navy's morale, at least according to one anonymous author writing in the *Revista de Marina*.

> Today, Chile's navy is the second strongest of all the Hispanic American Republics; within a short time, due to the recent Brazilian naval armaments program, it will drop to third place. It will not be surprising if much later it should fall

behind the Peruvian navy, which has begun the construction
of two modern cruisers and a powerful armoured ship. . . .[15]

Conditions did not change for the better. Five years later, another
naval officer wrote:

> One's face flushes with shame when comparing our naval
> forces of today with those naval units of other epochs, when,
> without being boastful, we were Latin America's preeminent
> power. . . . Unfortunately these times have passed. Today we
> are South America's third best naval power and this is only
> because there are only three nations which maintain fleets.
> . . . If there were one more, we would be fourth.[16]

The navy attempted to improve its position by lobbying for higher appropriations, citing possible threats to the nation. According
to the *Revista de Marina* Chile's enemies surrounded it on three
sides: to the north was Bolivia, demanding an outlet to the sea;
Peru had built a fleet anxious to avenge its earlier defeat and to
resolve, in its favor, the Tacna-Arica dispute; on the east was
Argentina. Worse yet, Chile stood in the shadow of the Monroe
Doctrine which, like the sword of Damocles, posed a constant
threat to Chilean destiny.[17]

The *Revista de Marina* pleaded for a standardization of ships
claiming that a revitalized fleet would allow the nation to rest
easier. It feared, however, and not incorrectly, that internal politics might well prevent the implementation of a naval expansion
program.[18] Sadly it noted the difference between the parliamentary
governments and that of the "wise patriarch" Federico Errázuriz,
who had armed Chile in 1874.[19] "Submarino," an anonymous
writer for the *Revista,* blamed the fleet's wretched condition on the
"lack of protection and support by the men of the government
who should readily lend it."[20]

The situation became critical in 1909, when both the Brazilian
and Argentine navies acquired some dreadnoughts—super vessels
that added a new dimension to the Latin-American naval arms
race. Some argued that Chile should purchase this type of ship as
well, claiming that without them, the country would be defenseless
and forced to accept the tutelage of other nations in international
affairs.[21] Eventually the Congress authorized a naval expansion
program: the fleet was to acquire two British dreadnoughts, six
destroyers, and two submarines. Fate, however, intervened. At

the outbreak of World War I, the British seized the two capital ships and four of the destroyers, incorporating them into their own fleet. By the time the war ended, so had Chile's prosperity, and the nation could only purchase one of the dreadnoughts. This acquisition was perhaps not very wise because the ship, a veteran of Jutland and four years of steaming in the North Atlantic, was no longer a modern vessel.[22]

Chile's postwar depression meant the curtailment of any naval expansion programs, ending any hopes of the fleet's competing with its wealthier Argentine and Brazilian rivals. By its own admission the navy had lost its former preeminence and had become one of the hemisphere's lesser naval powers. Its dreams of continental hegemony gone, the fleet could console itself only with the memories of better days.

II Prat's Usage by the Fleet

The Navy resurrected Prat at two different times, each of which had a distinctive theme. During the first period, the fleet aggressively used Prat to press for higher government appropriations. His sacrifice was emphasized to remind the nation that it was indebted to Prat for having saved the motherland at Iquique, and for having made Chile famous. This debt, it intimated, could be paid by supporting the needs of the fleet.

One of the first examples of this tactic was an open letter, written by an anonymous "Officer of the Navy" and published in *El Mercurio* on May 21, 1884. The officer, who some believe was Luis Uribe,[23] severely criticized the government's prewar naval policies and claimed that its lack of enthusiasm, false economies, and disorganization had forced the fleet to engage in a "crude" campaign in which Chile's sailors became mere cannon fodder. He specifically cited the example of the *Esmeralda* to substantiate his claim, stating that this ship should have been scrapped, not used to fight a war. When it sailed, he wrote, its crew knew full well that the only service they could render to the nation was the sacrifice of their lives.

The officer demanded that Chile purchase ships equal in power to those of Brazil and Argentina. He further suggested that the government revise the system of naval education and improve the

Naval Academy carefully noting that "Prat, Condell, and other officers who knew how to act with skill, valor, and nobility" were graduates of that institution. The unknown officer closed his article stating:

> The country has proved on various occasions that it has adequate resources to support its navy. This institution has already provided heroes who are remembered with admiration and respect, not only by the Chilean people, but by those who have the soul and heart to appreciate the great virtues. Let us not lose, then, what we have won, and let us rebuild our navy. We are sure that if we proceed without forgetting the past and with faith in the future, our navy will come to be as solid in its construction as it has been glorious in its acts. Prat's shadow guides us; let us go and try to accomplish as soon as it is possible what nature seems to have commanded: that Chile become the first naval power in the world.
> These are the wishes of an officer of the navy.[24]

Other officers made similar comments. The editor of the *Revista de Marina* in 1885 carefully stressed the need for Chile to remain a first-rate naval power and promised that Prat would always be the fleet's emblem of heroism and the symbol of Chile's purest glory.[25] A year later the same journal stated that the *Esmeralda's* resistance had saved the nation at a crucial moment, adding, "The recognition which is due to Prat, Uribe, and Condell, will never equal the homage which posterity owes to these selfless and valiant men."[26]

The *Revista de Marina* repeated this theme until 1888 and later, after 1901.[27] When requesting appropriations for the naval museum, for example, the naval journal mentioned Prat's name in connection with Chile's need to realize that its greatness depended exclusively upon the improvement of its naval power.[28] A critic of Gonzalo Bulnes's *La Guerra del Pacífico*, writing in the *Revista de Marina*, claimed that the author was incorrect when he stated that the politicians had won the war; on the contrary, according to the reviewer, it was because of men like Arturo Prat and the navy that Chile had triumphed.[29] In 1920, another editorial stressed that the fleet's personnel were ready to sacrifice their lives for Chile, but noted that there was also a "reciprocal duty of the government to modernize the fleet's materiel and to better the economic situation of its personnel."[30]

Another method of making the nation aware of its debt to Prat, and therefore the fleet, was to stress that Prat had made Chile famous. In 1887, for example, one naval officer claimed that Prat had shown "to the world that a nation with such citizens will always be great and respected."[31] This theme became more popular after 1900. E. T. Chauviedez alleged that both North Americans and Englishmen knew and respected Prat's name.[32] "Nauta," another anonymous officer, stated the following year that prior to the war Chile had neither an international reputation nor had it attracted the world's attention. After Iquique, however, Chile, because of the immortal actions of Prat, "reached the dais which the nations with illustrious histories occupy."[33] Eventually this theme became the most popular method of publicizing Prat the hero. It made the nation's grandeur depend upon the navy, thus making the fleet the nation's favorite.[34]

The navy's efforts were successful. The press began to echo its demands; and, like the fleet, the newspapers used the twenty-first of May as an occasion to laud Prat and to lament Chile's naval decline. *La Unión* in 1910 stated that:

> it cannot help comparing the naval power of Chile at that time [during the War of the Pacific] with the present and says: how little we have advanced! Worse still, how much we have lost since then!
> The fleet of those years represented to the nation, proportionately speaking, a much more efficient element than the present one, if one compares the one to the other with respect to the nation's economic capacity.

It noted, however, that if the nation no longer commanded the naval power it once did, at least "today's sailors have been formed in the tradition of those heroes, and although we have lost naval supremacy, we are still preserving the superior quality of our sailors."[35]

In 1912, *El Mercurio* of Valparaíso used the anniversary of Iquique to draw attention to the decline of the navy and the merchant marine:

> Surely the important lesson which a strong country learns from the immortal sacrifices of her children will not be forgotten: the program written with their blood imposes duties upon the future generation. Chile's naval triumphs obligates

her not to abandon these waters which are the way to riches,
to military, political, and mercantile superiority in a very
large section of the South Pacific. . . . Chile has to protect,
develop its merchant marine: this is the most important patriotic lesson of the 21st of May.[36]

The Maritime League of Chile was founded in 1914,[37] and it
was no coincidence that its first meeting took place on the twenty-
first of May, below a picture of Arturo Prat. According to Roberto
Pretot Freir, one of the speakers, this had been done deliberately:
"In order to give to this act a great splendor the 21st of May has
been chosen, a day in which the Chileans filled with noble pride,
commemorate the great epoch of the naval battle of Iquique."[38]
On the same occasion, Guillermo Subercaseaux stated:

> . . . I only wanted to take advantage of this opportunity . . .
> to protest against the negligence and lack of civic spirit of
> those who, until the present, have prevented the passage of
> laws for the protection of our merchant marine.
> . . . for years, our nation, our beloved country, which is
> doubtless the most well organized democracy in Latin Ameri-
> ca, has suffered from a serious illness: the sterility of its weak
> and incompetent parliamentary governments, which have
> shown themselves completely impotent to satisfy, with intel-
> ligence and foresight, the nation's need for progress in the
> area of economics and administration.
> But while . . . some of the top people sleep an indolent sleep
> or prove themselves incompetent to solve these pressing prob-
> lems, who oppose the approval of certain laws like the one
> concerning the national merchant marine; public opinion,
> the people at the bottom, that is the national feeling, is
> awakening and indicating that they are capable of imposing
> their own will.[39]

Roberto Hernández alleged that Chile could best honor Prat
by supporting the fleet:

> It would be ironic; indeed it would be a cruel joke that we
> should honor the immortal sailor . . . without having a navy
> worthy of the name. . . . With old ships, riddled with im-
> perfections, with disorganized services, with a discontented
> officer corps, with crews who are even more discontented
> with a navy, in essence, full of deficiencies, it is a profanity to
> evoke the heroes' names. It is like inviting their spirits to look
> upon the ruins of what they loved so much!
> If, on the annual anniversary of the 21st of May, the na-

tion's leaders would study thoroughly what is happening in the navy and would cure its problems and remedy its needs, then the hands of Prat, and of his companions would be shaking with gratitude on seeing that Chile still loves the institution which they so much honored!

This in truth would be the best homage to the heroes of Iquique.[40]

Increasingly, however, the *Revista de Marina* characterized Arturo Prat as the naval officer who fulfilled his responsibilities. In 1902, "Nauta" reminded the fleet that its hero should be for them "a symbol and a living and instinctive stimulus for the fulfillment of military duties."[41] Three years later the same author called Prat "the personification of duty," and wrote that his entire life demonstrated his adherence to this code, a standard of conduct "imperative for all men, but doubly so for the sailor. . . . On our navy weighs, consequently, a heavy heritage and an enormous responsibility. We are sure that, should the need arise, it would honor its predecessors, by faithfully imitating the conduct of its inspiring genius."[42] In 1914, Prat's death was called a "precious legacy . . . the emblem which the navy must follow,"[43] while in 1925 another officer declared that "the virtues of abnegation and patriotism revealed by them [the heroes of Iquique] will endure forever in our beloved institution."[44]

Not only do these remarks seem oriented more toward the navy than civilian society, they seem to have a certain educational purpose. The close identification of the navy with Prat could well have been used to instill a sense of discipline and inspire the officer corps. As the fleet declined, morale fell. Prat was an ideal example to buttress faltering spirits, especially since the circumstances of his death symbolized the navy's post–1901 dilemma; like Prat, the fleet was alone, alienated, and materially weak.

It is especially interesting to note a series of articles published in the *Revista de Marina* and written by Manfredo Becerra in 1926. In the first, "The Concept of Duty in the Armed Forces," Becerra, citing Prat as the example for the Chilean naval officer to follow, stressed that duty was as necessary in peacetime as in war.[45] In another article, "Esprit de Corps," Becerra admitted that the virtues of abnegation and loyalty might have decayed in the fleet,[46] and seemed to attribute that to the rise of political disputes within the naval service, no doubt caused by the Alessandri coup and the involvement of the military in politics. Becerra inquired, "Why . . . are we raising divisive political questions, when the nation needs the patriotism of her children?"[47] It is also interesting to note that Becerra stressed that professional advancement should only be the result of

> long preparation, of painstaking study and the practice of one's profession. One should advance because he cultivated loyalty to the service and his companions, which can only be perfected through practice.
>
> Whoever studies the life of our sublime hero, Prat, with determined and affectionate devotion, will conclude that what he did in the waters of Iquique was consistent with his past life, that pure life which will eternally illuminate our Navy.
>
> It is not possible to forget for an instant that the officer corps cannot remain tranquil and that there will be no progress in the service itself as long as the individuals' interests take precedence over those of the navy; as long as one regards *esprit de corps* as something unnecessary or merely ideological. On the contrary, it is the life or pulsating force which forms for us, the members of the naval profession, regardless of branch or rank, the tie which binds us together.
>
> Our navy is called to great destinies. It must follow the heroic and luminous tradition which was first established by Blanco Encalda and Cochrane, then much later by Latorre, and finally by that sublime hero, Arturo Prat. To accomplish this, however, it is imperative that we persevere in cultivating, with all our strength with special interest and devotion, the great virtues which these officers possessed. This must be done regardless of the subtle political differences which separate men in the area of thought: we must cease considering social and economic differences. The institution [the navy] now recognizes that the uniform honors whomever wears it: without distinction to specialty, nor to branch, now that all serve the motherland. It is necessary, I say, that we all unite and form to sacrifice for one supreme end: the good of the service, and one single fixed ideal, the advancement of the institution and Chile.
>
> We must cultivate, then, *esprit de corps*. If someone fears that his will might weaken in the performance of his duty . . . he should remember the traditions of our race, and the sublime patriotism which the navy's greatest hero demonstrated that day when he had to fight against such superior forces, when there was not the slightest possibility of victory.

> He [Prat] is telling us, from his place of glory, that at all
> times and at each instant of our life, in war as in peace, the
> only watchword of the naval officer is: to render his sacred
> tribute to the feeling of duty.[48]

These articles are important because they reveal that a malaise
permeated the fleet. Perhaps this decline was the result of the 1924
revolution and the consequent involvement of the military in
civilian affairs. Regardless, the articles indicate that the navy
was no longer a cohesive service and that, like civilian society, it
used Prat to unify its members.

The press noticed this decline in professionalism and chastised
the navy for it. The irony was that the newspapers used Prat as a
means of correcting the fleet. In 1917, *La Unión*, for example, reminded the officer corps that

> . . . duty is not fulfilled at the banquet table, nor in the ball-
> room, nor at splendid parties, but in work, in obedience to
> discipline, and in the care of their ships; and in addition to
> this [the concept of duty] there is the responsibility that all
> should prepare themselves for the hour in which the mother-
> land might ask for their services.

The newspaper concluded that private and professional lives were
inseparable, and that sacrifice was necessary to both.[49] While, in
1923, another paper noted that although Prat had been poor, "he
never climbed the stairs of the government palace nor did he wait
in the offices of the naval ministry to deliver a letter of introduction."[50]

This political activity not only split the officer corps, it seems
to have demoralized the fleet by undermining the close relationship that had formerly existed between officer and enlisted man.
In 1931, following the overthrow of Ibáñez, a provisional government had been appointed which attempted to solve Chile's
enormous economic problems by reducing the salaries of public
employees. This struck hard at the already underpaid sailors, especially the married men who had families ashore. Many of the
enlisted men begged their officers to intercede for them with the
government. The crews of various ships even presented petitions
against the pay cuts, requesting that they be forwarded to higher
authorities. Alberto Hozven, captain of the battleship *Latorre*, at-

tempted to end the unrest among the squadron's enlisted men. He assembled his crew, as well as representatives from other ships, for a lecture. After calling his audience cowardly for bickering about the impending reductions in salary and ordering them to cease complaining, he commanded them to shout "Viva Chile!" Not one of the enlisted men obeyed him.[51]

Within hours there were clandestine meetings of enlisted men aboard the *Latorre*, and by evening they had formulated a plan. During the predawn hours of September 1, 1931, the *Latorre*'s crew seized control of their ship after having locked their officers in their cabins. Within minutes the remainder of the squadron signaled the *Latorre* that the rebels also commanded the other vessels. The Chilean fleet had mutinied.[52]

Some have claimed that the Communists fomented the 1931 naval uprising. Petty Officer Ernesto González, one of the rebel leaders, vehemently denied that the Communists had played any part in the rebellion, noting that the *Latorre*'s crew had rejected an offer of support from FOCH, a Communist-dominated labor organization. Even Admiral von Schroeders, the navy's emissary to the mutineers, conceded that only a few of the rebels were Communists and that many of the crew had legitimate grievances.[53]

Regardless of its cause, the movement received widespread support from other military and naval units. The remainder of the fleet, as well as the naval arsenal and the Escuela de Artillería, Torpedos y Electricidad at Talcahuano, the Escuela de Communicaciones at Valparaíso, the air station at Quintero, the artillery regiment "Arica" at La Serena, and the Carabineros of Coquimbo, pledged support to the mutineers. Within days, the ships at the naval base at Talcahuano, including the entire submarine flotilla, had sailed north to join the rebels who were cruising off Coquimbo.[54]

The government was divided over what course of action to pursue.[55] Some advocated using force immediately. Others, perhaps remembering the material consequences of the 1891 civil war were willing to parley with the dissident sailors and sent Admiral Edgardo von Schroeders to Coquimbo to discuss the situation with the mutineers. The rebellion, quite naturally, produced a profound crisis within the naval high command. In their attempts to quell the mutiny peacefully, the authorities tried to appeal to the crew's sense of patriotism,[56] and it was not surprising that among the various symbols invoked was that of Arturo Prat. The fleet's patriarch, Admiral Wilson, begged the rebels to surrender and cease wounding the motherland and her fleet. "Permit me," he said, "to invoke the spirit of Prat, the glorious commander of the *Esmeralda*, who when sacrificing himself for the motherland, would never have dreamed that his beloved navy would one day be found in such a sad state. With all my heart this old admiral begs you to stop."[57]

When von Schroeders's mission failed, the government decided to take direct action. An assault force seized the naval arsenal at Talcahuano, while other units subdued the remainder of the rebels. The climax of the mutiny came on September 6, when the air force attacked the fleet as it lay at anchor at Coquimbo. Intense anti-aircraft fire rendered the mission less than a total success: the planes did not sink one ship and only slightly damaged a submarine. Although the rebels suffered few casualties, the attack perhaps demonstrated that the mutiny was foredoomed and within hours most of the ships surrendered, including the *Latorre*, the focus of the mutiny.[58]

Like the navy, some of the press also referred to Prat when writing about the naval mutiny. *El Mercurio*, for instance, said that the example of Prat had influenced a young officer who had refused to surrender his command to the rebel forces.[59] The paper also alleged that the naval officers fighting to regain the naval arsenal also had been inspired by Prat's actions at Iquique.[60] It is interesting to note that when a new government was formed, following the start of the naval mutiny, one of the men named to a ministerial post was Arturo Prat Carvajal, son of the dead hero. While his appointment might have been a coincidence, at least one historian believed that he was chosen to influence the rebels to stop fighting.[61]

After the mutiny the figure of Prat was invoked as a unifying force within the fleet. A naval chaplain, in 1933, warned his audience about the evils of those who sought to overthrow Chile's institutions and hoped that Prat's spirit would purify the hearts of those who had been lured from the path of patriotism.[62] Another naval officer used the twenty-first of May to speak out against "the unhealthy ideas of those preachers without God or Law, those pariahs without a motherland."[63]

Political remarks of this nature began fading from the pages of the *Revista de Marina* as the turbulent 1930s came to an end and the later issues of the magazine ceased becoming involved in contemporary events. Occasionally a few articles complained about conditions in the navy,[64] and mentioned Prat's name to chide the government into acquiring additional materiel for the fleet.[65]

Slowly Prat's image became divorced from mundane affairs, perhaps because the navy became less involved in politics and more reconciled to its fortunes. The fallen hero, however, continued to be revered in the fleet, the quitessence of Chile's naval tradition. Beyond that, the hero still remained a source of duty and dedication for the navy, a symbol to be imitated as well as admired, a standard of conduct for the navy which future generations of officers promised to emulate.[66]

At the beginning of this chapter it was noted that Prat's initial popularity, and his revival, were linked to pressing problems in which a symbol of leadership was needed. During the first period of Prat's popularity, the Chilean navy was anxious to maintain the supremacy it had achieved during the War of the Pacific. The fleet used Prat as a means of advancing a program of expansion; the hero's death underscored the collective debt owed to the institution which had both nurtured the hero and had saved the country in time of danger. Thus the navy cloaked itself in Prat's image in order to exert moral pressure on the government.

During the second period, the years of naval expansion, the *Revista de Marina* scarcely, if at all, mentioned Prat. This was, however, an epoch of good times for the navy. Numerous ships were either added to the fleet or modernized. The navy, perhaps self-confident, and receiving all that it wished from the government, relegated Prat to the background because it no longer needed him to achieve its objectives. This lack of attention might also have resulted from splits that developed within the fleet after the 1891 civil war. The purge of the heroes of Iquique must have made the naval high command feel quite uncomfortable. The fleet was placed in the bizarre position of commemorating the battle when many of its survivors had been expelled from the officer corps. This too might have contributed to the reluctance of the *Revista de Marina* to commemorate the twenty-first of May in the years immediately following the civil war.

The third period, the restoration of Prat as a hero in the navy, was one of decline for the fleet. This may well have triggered Prat's return: like the civilian society, the fleet needed a symbol to remind it of its happier past. In addition, the navy used Prat as a means of retaining the people's affection and the government's financial support. The fleet stressed that Prat had made Chile world famous, and reminded civilian society that its younger officers were the spiritual heirs of his heroic traditions. Finally the navy used Prat to maintain morale. In a period of decay and neglect, he was an example of sacrifice to officers and men. During the years of political squabbling, his example emphasized higher loyalties: the navy and the motherland.

It would be incorrect, however, to assume that Prat's popularity ceased to fluctuate after 1901. In the years 1908 to 1912, the amount of space devoted to the fallen hero in the *Revista de Marina* declined. The low point seemed to be 1916 and 1917 when there was no mention of the fallen hero in the naval journal. Although this fact contradicts earlier generalizations, this inconsistency can be explained.

The Chilean fleet had not accepted its decline gracefully, but with support from the press, continued to demand reforms, higher appropriations, and newer ships, demands that, to a certain extent, were successful. Naval expenditures were on the upswing from 1905 to 1910. The government, moreover, implemented some of the suggested reforms. And the Congress, in 1909, authorized the acquisition of additional ships for the navy. Although this program never came to fruition, because of World War I, some benefits were realized. The British transferred five submarines, which were in the process of construction, to the Chilean fleet. These, in addition to the one already in its possession, gave Chile the strongest undersea force in South America. In addition, the navy believed that the war would not last long, and so it would be allowed to take possession of the escort and capital ships the British had previously seized. Thus, although Chilean naval power had drastically declined, it could be argued that the navy still hoped to resurrect itself. If so, then the decline of Prat in these years can be understood in terms of the earlier period, when the navy did not believe that it needed Prat because it was strong enough to stand on its own.

III Arturo Prat and the Army

The Chilean military journals written before 1900 rarely mentioned Arturo Prat. Neither *El Ensayo Militar* nor *El Boletín Militar*, the principal journals of that period, commemorated the twenty-first of May.[67] The one journal which observed the anniversary of the Battle of Iquique, *La Revista Militar de Chile*, did so only twice in the six years that it was published.[68] This lack of attention is understandable for Arturo Prat was a naval officer and therefore unimportant to the army. The military journals quite naturally concentrated on publicizing their own heroes and not those of a sister service.[69] Besides, it would have been unusual for the army to pay much attention to Prat when the official naval journal rarely mentioned him.

The few times it recalled the Battle of Iquique, the military usually claimed that Prat had also inspired the army's conduct at the battles of Tacna, Arica, and Concepción.[70] Occasionally the military periodicals referred to Iquique for purely professional reasons. One author, for example, demanded that Chile fortify its coastal cities to avoid another debacle like the twenty-first of May.[71] Military journals were no more enthusiastic about Prat after the turn of the century. The *Memorial del Estado Mayor del Ejército de Chile*, first published in 1906, did not commemorate the Battle of Iquique until 1913.[72] Even after that date, there were often years when the magazine failed to note the anniversary of the battle.[73]

Despite this cavalier treatment, when the army did mention Iquique, it often described it in much the same way as the navy did, claiming that the battle had enhanced Chile's international reputation, comparing it to Trafalgar and Thermopylae, and likening Prat to Nelson and Leonidas.[74] A more curious similarity was that the army not only used Prat for political purposes but began doing this long before the navy, perhaps indicating either a lack of reverence or, more likely, that the army officers were more politicized than their naval brothers.

In 1915, for example, an article on Prat hoped that the spirit of May 21 would lift the nation from "the miseries and dejection of political life, in order to carry it on the wings of optimism."[75] The following year, Agustín Echavarría, wished that "Prat's patriotism might inspire our leaders."[76] Politics became a theme again in the 1930s. Then Prat's memory was invoked, for instance, to shame those Chilean Communists who, by supporting Russia, were profaning the memory of those who died for the motherland. No Communist nation, the author claimed, could produce a hero the equal of Arturo Prat.[77] Someone else wrote in 1935, that Chileans had but one motherland to which they were united by blood and a common history.[78]

Ironically, the popular press used Prat to chastise the army just as it used him to criticize the navy. The army attempted to overthrow the government on May 20, 1919. After the coup was suppressed, the press could not resist making comparisons between the unsuccessful rebels and Prat:

> Today, 24 hours after the revelation [the nation was told of a group within the army which wanted to overthrow the government], the country commemorates (what a contrast) the greatest act of discipline and the purest ideal of military duty ever commemorated by any nation, big or small.
>
> The military men of 1879 were too busy with their professional problems, to discuss the political regime; they were still wandering, like great visions of an epoch, on the somber and glorious fields of Arauco. And the men of the sea prepared for the War of the Pacific and for the commerce of the world. Soldiers and sailors fulfilled the great duty which belongs to men of arms in the days of peace: to strengthen the organization of the nation. . . .
>
> Man has the duty of defending his country; he acts like a father who preserves with benevolence and forgiveness the weakness of his blood. This was the way the heroes of 1879 were; this was the way of the young captain Prat; this will be the way Chileans are when they feel like Antaeus, drawing their strength from the soil. Let us not try new things. Let us live faithful to the tradition that made us respectable, without trying to change the legislative regime, in spite of its defects, for another one of conceptions with no traditions in the history of cultivated nations.[79]

Generally the military journals did not emphasize Prat's importance. At best the articles published were a perfunctory courtesy given to a sister service which is honored if not loved. There was, however, an enormous difference between those military journals written for officers and those for enlisted personnel. The latter

publications, *La Bandera, La Patria,* and *La Revista del Subo-*
ficial,[80] rarely if ever failed to commemorate the Battle of Iquique
and devoted far more space to Prat and his exploits than did the
magazines for officers. Pictures of Prat, as well as those of the other
participants in the battle, appeared on the cover of enlisted journals.[81] Many of the authors of the various articles and poems about
the battle were themselves enlisted men.[82]

It is interesting to speculate why should Prat have been more
popular among enlisted men than among his brother officers. One
explanation might be that the officer corps deliberately cultivated
Prat's popularity in order to inspire the enlisted men to become
obedient, moral, and dutiful soldiers. Officers, on the other hand,
were presumed to be patriotic, moral, and obedient. This attitude
is difficult to understand unless one realizes the enormous difference between the two military castes. In the United States, for
example, only enlisted personnel can be awarded a good conduct
medal. Officers cannot win this decoration because their behavior
is always perfect. If it were not, they would not and could not be
officers.

All officers in Chile, before being commissioned, study at the
Military Academy. During that time, they are carefully observed
and subjected to rigorous examination. Enlisted men, however,
are an unknown quantity. Because they can be drafted, there may
be a considerable difference not only in their level of education but
in their motivation as well. For this reason, the enlisted men's publications were more than professional military journals. They were
used to indoctrinate their readers and to encourage a certain morality. Enlisted magazines, for example, were filled with articles
warning about the evils of alcoholism, venereal disease, and Communism, and praising the virtues of thrift, temperance, and patriotism.[83] And, it is quite possible that Arturo Prat was one of the
tools used to teach enlisted men how to be virtuous and to fulfill
their duty.

One of the earliest examples of this new use of Prat was an article published in *El Círculo Militar.* Interestingly enough, the main
character in the article was not the dead officer, but Sergeant Juan
de Dios Aldea, one of the enlisted men who boarded the *Huáscar*
along with Prat. The article included a biography on Aldea, stressing that he had been rapidly promoted because of his devotion to

duty, his self-discipline, and his hard work. Emphasizing Aldea was a novel approach. Clearly it had been done to popularize Iquique and to give it a more democratic flavor. Prat was an officer, and therefore, as the author claimed, a member of "a select and educated class of the nation." Aldea, however, represented the "masses, that class of people from whose bosom comes the individual, the troops who fill the ranks of our battalions and regiments; the anonymous hero." The magazine encouraged the soldiers to imitate Aldea's "simple, plain, austere life." The author also emphasized Aldea's obedience to Prat, stating that valor alone was insufficient to make a hero. Obedience, the magazine stated, was the supreme military virtue. The periodical, as if to encourage its readers to imitate Aldea's obedient example, claimed that if the dead sergeant were alive, he would be saying: "Comrades: the love of the motherland was my emblem, my religion, my duty, obedience my watchword; imitate me!"[84]

Later enlisted men's magazines, *La Bandera, La Patria,* and *La Revista del Suboficial,* tended to concentrate on Arturo Prat. The dead hero was characterized as the epitome of duty and morality.[85] Unlike the officers' journals, the enlisted journals included more material about the hero's personal life.[86] Indeed, while many of the officers' publications merely described the battle in rather stark tones, *La Bandera* and its successors wrote in greater detail, emphasizing the role that Arturo Prat played in the naval struggle.[87] On occasion there was a political comment, but there were fewer such comments in enlisted journals than in their officer counterparts.[88]

From the evidence, one might not only conclude that Prat's popularity was more obvious among the enlisted ranks than among the officers, but that his example was deliberately invoked in an attempt to instill in the soldier respect for authority and the need to sacrifice. Thus, while the officer corps limited itself to an almost cursory salute in memory of the navy's preeminent hero, the enlisted men were taught to treat him with reverence and respect.

✝ CONCLUSION

Comrade Ogilvy, unimagined an hour ago, was now a fact. It struck him as curious that you could create dead men but not living ones. Comrade Ogilvy, who had never existed in the present, now existed in the past, and when once the act of forgery was forgotten, he would exist just as authentically, and upon the same evidence, as Charlemagne or Julius Caesar.
—GEORGE ORWELL

This work has traced the formation of Prat's heroic image. It shows how a young naval officer, so obscure that the press initially misspelled his name, evolved into his nation's preeminent hero. Chileans admired and revered Prat not because of his accomplishments but for what he represented: dedication and self sacrifice.

The Chileans used his act of abnegation to arouse themselves from their peaceful lethargy. Prat's death, like that of Portales in 1837, galvanized the nation. The hero of Iquique became a living symbol of the Chilean nation in a death struggle with its enemies, a voice pleading to be revenged. Such a usage is not uncommon for a nation embarking upon a war when normally esteemed civilian virtues must be shunted aside in order to prepare the people for the ordeal of conflict.

What distinguished Prat is that certain elements also sought to capitalize on his death for political purposes. The Conservatives and the Liberal Democrats averred that Pinto not only had failed to equip the fleet properly, but that he set into motion the events that resulted in Prat's death. Throughout the remainder of the war, the dissidents used Prat to attack Pinto and his government. Under these circumstances one might be tempted to claim that Pinto's opponents stimulated Prat's popularity as part of their program to disgrace the president. The widespread and emotional reaction to Prat, the fact that numerous individuals even named their children for the hero of Iquique, demonstrates how unfounded would be this assertion.

Following the successful conclusion of the War of the Pacific, Prat declined in popularity only to be resurrected as a consequence of the parliamentary government's incompetence and corruption. From a purely military figure, Prat evolved into the incarnation of dynamic leadership and spiritual superiority: the man who brought fame to Chile; the warrior who had equalled the feats of the Ancient Greeks. To a nation where venality was rife, where a small clique devalued the country's money and perverted its electoral system, Prat represented the incarnation of civic virtue, a man so dedicated that no personal motive prevented him from fulfilling his civic obligations.

Prat's revival was also directed against the decline in private morality. Critics believed that the Nitrate Age had ushered in a period of conspicuous consumption which had eroded the supposedly traditional value system. Many citizens, yearning to restore to Chile its lost virtue, launched a moral crusade with Prat as its spiritual figurehead. The hero emerged as the epitome of private virtue: he was prized as a student; honored as a good husband, father, and son; eulogized as a symbol of abnegation in an era of naked cupidity.

It should come as no surprise that Prat's image had changed so drastically. Before, in time of war, Chile required a martial figure. Now, the people needed an example of austerity in the struggle against internal dangers: corruption, nepotism, and greed. Unable to discover some paradigm in their present leaders, Chileans turned to their past and chose Arturo Prat, the personification of civic virtues and fulfillment of duty, to inspire them in peace as he had in war.

Although the theme of individual and national regeneration remained important, Prat increasingly became identified with the movement for national unity. The collapse of the parliamentary regime in 1924, the chaos that followed, and the advent of radical political ideologies—Socialism, National Socialism, and Communism—shattered the once static framework of Chilean political life. The new parties preached radical solutions to traditional problems. The elite ceased to dominate politics; the masses surged forward, struggling not only for political control but demanding significant social and economic reforms.

The traditional press discovered in Prat a means to defend the *status quo*. The newspapers encouraged obedience to the regime by invoking Prat's image. They implied that the present government was the rightful heir of that Chile for which Prat had sacrificed himself and that to accept alien doctrines would be tantamount to rejecting the fallen hero. Although the press occasionally chided the government, recommending that it labor for the betterment of society, it still encouraged the citizen to emulate Prat by obeying the nation's leaders, by repudiating the new ideologies, and by struggling for the motherland.

The National Socialists and the Socialists continued the tradition of utilizing the hero to bait the government for its political and economic backwardness. It should come as no surprise that the new parties incorporated Prat into their political mythology, for they were simply employing a tradition established by earlier reform movements. Prat still remains a staple of the Left. In the last presidential campaign, *Clarín* proclaimed that if Prat were alive he would vote either for Tomic or Allende.[1] While this statement is debatable, it does indicate the extent to which Prat has become a political icon.

The manipulation of a hero's life and acts is, of course, not uncommon. A similar transformation has occurred with Bolívar, recently rediscovered as a fighter for social justice; San Martín has been used by Rosas, the Liberals, the Catholic Right, and the *Peronistas*.[2] Latins are not the only ones given to these practices. But a few days after Pearl Harbor, President Roosevelt decorated Captain Colin Kelly posthumously for sinking a Japanese battleship by diving his bomber onto its deck. Thus the United States acquired its first hero whose death served as an inspiration to the nation. Following the war, however, the heroic legend underwent some revisions. The government disclosed that Kelly had perished trying to keep his burning plane aloft until his crew could parachute to safety. It admitted, moreover, that the hero had sunk not a battleship but an unarmed transport. Still, the distortion was not so strained: unlike Comrade Ogilvy, Kelly at least existed and had died trying to aid his comrades.

It might be argued, however, that it is immaterial whether the hero possessed the virtues ascribed to him or even performed the acts credited to his name. Did it matter that Kelly had not died in a certain way or that he destroyed only a transport and not a battleship? For years men have revered Saint Christopher. The fact that the Church now disclaims his very existence does not obviate the fact that people worshiped him and drew from his acts the inspiration to continue their own lives.

What is significant is that the hero represents the epitome of a group's desire. A nation, a society, a people seek someone who exemplifies that which they are not and wish to be. If there is no mortal who can satisfy them, they will invent one—a Comrade Ogilvy; if one exists, but is less than perfect, they will embellish his acts—Colin Kelly. If all else fails, they will resort to myth.

Arturo Prat provided an excellent example to study. His act was so simple and patently unproductive that no one could claim that his popularity had a basis in pragmatic achievement. Prat died immediately so that no personality trait could sully or enhance his heroic reputation. He was not, like Washington, San Martín, or Bolívar, the Father of his Country and therefore was not the subject of the excessive adulation which surrounds men who create nations.

The Chilean people, threatened and frightened, needed a hero, and Arturo Prat was the first to meet their qualifications. He was not an ephemeral phenomenon, an Oliver Hazard Perry, who succeeded in his assigned task and then lapsed into obscurity. Indeed, Prat remained popular because the virtues he exemplified and the acts he performed could be used to meet the needs of a changing society. The hero, then, can embody the quintessence of a nation's aspirations and desires and thus become a symbol not of an age but of man's eternal search for perfection.

APPENDIXES

APPENDIXES

✝ APPENDIX I
Columns of Newsprint Devoted to Arturo Prat by various Chilean Newspapers, 1880-1931

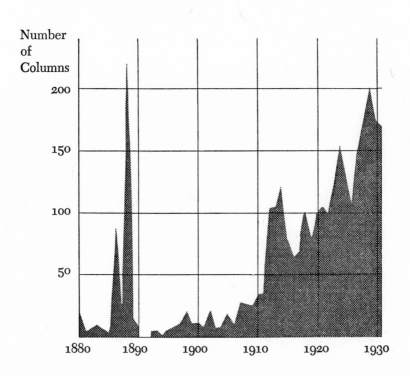

Number of Columns

Newspapers Used

1880–1900	1900–1931
El Estandarte Católico[1]	*El Diario Ilustrado*
El Ferrocarril	*El Mercurio de Santiago*
El Mercurio de Valparaíso	*El Mercurio de Valparaíso*

La Libertad Electoral[2]   *El Sur*
El Sur[3]   *La Unión*
La Unión[4]

[1] *El Estandarte Católico* became *El Porvenir* after 1890.
[2] *La Libertad Electoral* did not begin publication until 1886.
[3] *El Sur* did not begin publication until 1885.
[4] *La Unión* did not begin publication until 1885.

No newspapers were published during the 1891 revolution.

✝ APPENDIX II
Books and Materials about Arturo Prat Published between 1879 and 1950

1879   Ramon Guerrero Vergara y José Toribio Medina. *El Capitán de Fragata Arturo Prat. Estudio sobre su vida.*
Pedro Nolasco Préndez. *La Esmeralda.*
Bernardo Vicuña. *Biografía completa de Arturo Prat.*
Benjamín Vicuña Mackenna. *Las Dos Esmeraldas.*

1880   *Arturo Prat i el combate de Iquique.*
El 21 de Mayo de 1879, Homenaje de "La Patria" a los héroes de la "Esmeralda" y "Covadonga" en el primer anniversario del glorioso combate de Iquique.

1881   Fabio de Petris, *Sinfonía de la toma del Huáscar.*
Domingo Antonio Izquierdo. *Veintiuno de Mayo.*

1883   *Copia de la sesión solemne en la municipalidad de Santiago para honrar la memoria de Arturo Prat.*
Ramon Pachecho. *Episodios de la Guerra del Pacífico.*

1884   Francisco Valdés Vergara, *Justicia a un hombre de bien—Documentos relativso a la inhumación de los cadaveres del Capitán Arturo Prat y del Teniente Serrano.*

1885   Alfredo Irarrazaval Zañartu. *Veintiuno de Mayo de 1879—Los Mártires de Iquique.*

1886   *Homenaje a la marina nacional, 21 de Mayo de 1886.*

1887   Rubén Darío. *Canto épico de las glorias de Chile.*

1888   Justo Abel Rosales. *La apoteósis de Arturo Prat.*

1910   Vicente Grez. *El combate heroico.* (Reprint)

1912   *Partes oficiales del combate naval de Iquique.*

1914   Marfisa Muñoz Yurazeck. *Arturo Prat.*
        Miguel Rafael Urzúa. *Prat—Drama original en tres actos y en verso.*

1919   Luis Adan Molina. *La epopeya de Iquique.*

1925   Juan Simpson. *Algunos rasgos inéditos de la personalidad de Arturo Prat.*
        Lorenzo Villalón Madrid. *Combate navel de Iquique.*

1930   Pedro J. Muñoz Feliú. *El veintiuno de mayo de 1879.*

1933   Daniel Riquelme. *La toma del Huáscar. Cuento de la guerra y otras paginas.*
        Horacio Vio Valdivieso. *Reseño-historia de los nombres de las unidades de la armada de Chile.*

1934   Guillermo Izquierdo A. *Nelson y Prat.*

1936   Ramon Pacheco. *Episodios de la Guerra del Pacífico.* (Reprint)

1937   Emilio Rodríguez Mendoza. *La estrella sobre las mastiles.*

1940   *Defensa de la raza, 21 de mayo de 1879—21 de mayo de 1940.*

1943   Francisco Zapata Silva. *Homenaje a los héroes del combate de Iquique. 21 de mayo de 1879.*

1944   *Combate naval de Iquique. 21 de mayo de 1879.*
        Joaquín Díaz Garces. *Leyendas y episodios nacionales.*
        Voz de la patria. Combate naval de Iquique.

1947   Juan Peralta Peralta. *Arturo Prat Chacón. Heroe del mar.*

1948   Alejandro Fabres y Oscar Pereira H. *Arturo Prat. El heroe del mar.*

1950   Oscar Espinosa Moraga. "Arturo Prat, agente confidencial de Chile en Montevideo," *Boletín de la Academia Chilena de la Historia,* XVII (1950), 65–80.

✝ NOTES

✞ NOTES

Introduction

[1] Quoted from E. Bradford Burns, "The Blacks in Brazilian History," *West Georgia Studies in the Social Sciences*, VIII (1969), 53.

[2] Thomas Carlyle, *On Heroes, Hero-Worship, and the Heroic in History* (New York: Dolphin, n.d.), p. 9.

[3] Richard Hofstadter, *The Age of Reform* (New York: Vintage Books, 1955), p. 17.

[4] G. W. F. Hegel, *Lectures on the Philosophy of History*, trans. J. Sibree (London: George Bell, 1881), pp. 31–34.

[5] Herbert Spencer, *The Study of Sociology* (London: Kegan Paul, 1884), pp. 35, 37.

[6] Karl Marx, Preface to "A Contribution to the Critique of Political Economy," in Karl Marx and Frederick Engels, *Selected Works in Two Volumes* (Moscow: Foreign Languages Publishing House, 1955), I, 364–365.

[7] Leon Trotsky, *The History of the Russian Revolution*, trans. Max Eastman (Ann Arbor: University of Michigan Press, 1932), pp. 95–96.

[8] George Plekanov, *The Role of the Individual in History* (New York: International Publishers, 1967), pp. 41, 44, 48.

[9] Sidney Hook, *The Hero in History* (Boston: Beacon Press, 1955), pp. 154, 157, 166–168.

[10] Franz Alexander, "Psychoanalysis and Social Disorganization," *American Journal of Sociology*, XLII (1927), 810; Saul Scheidlinger, *Psychoanalysis and Group Behavior* (New York: W. W. Norton and Company, 1952), p. 136; Roger Money-Kyrle, "Varieties of Group Formation," in *Psychoanalysis and the Social Sciences*, ed. Geza Roheim (New York: International Universities Press, Inc., 1950), II, 314–315 (hereafter cited as *PASS*).

[11] Scheidlinger, *op. cit.*, pp. 30, 42; Otto Fenichel, *The Psychoanalytic Theory of Neurosis* (New York: W. W. Norton, 1945), p. 37; Roger Money-Kyrle, *The Meaning of Sacrifice* (London: The Hogarth Press, 1930), p. 68; Otto Rank, *The Myth of the Birth of the Hero* (New York: Vintage Books, 1964), p. 71; Raymond Saussure, "Psychoanalysis and History," in *PASS*, II, 34; Ernst Simmel, "Anti-Semitism and Mass Psychopathology," in *Anti-Semitism*, ed. Ernst Simmel (New York: International Universities Press, 1946), p. 52.

[12] Sigmund Freud, *Group Psychology and the Analysis of the Ego*, trans. James Strachey (New York: Bantam Books, 1960), pp. 47–53, 60–61; Nathan W. Ackerman, "Interaction Processes in a Group and the Role of the Leader," in *PASS*, IV, 112; Alexander, "Psychoanalysis," p. 786.

[13] Saussure, *op. cit.*, p. 34; Melitta Schmideberg, "The Role of the Psychotic Mechanism in Cultural Development," *The International Journal of Psychoanalysis*, XI (1930), 407; Money-Kyrle, "Varieties of Group Formation," *PASS*, II, 314, 328.

[14] Rank, *op. cit.*, pp. 69–71.
[15] Money-Kyrle, *The Meaning of Sacrifice*, pp. 55–56, 68; Freud, *op. cit.*, p. 76; Saussure, *op. cit.*, p. 34.
[16] Ackerman, *op. cit.*, p. 117.
[17] *Ibid.*, p. 117; Franz Alexander, "On the Psychodynamics of Regressive Phenomena in Panic States," in *PASS*, IV, 107–109.
[18] Money-Kyrle, *The Meaning of Sacrifice*, p. 54; Warner Muensterberger, "Observations on the Collapse of Leadership," in *PASS*, IV, 158; George Devereux, "Charismatic Leadership and Crisis," in *PASS*, IV, 147.
[19] Edith Weigert, "Conditions of Organized and Regressive Responses to Danger," in *PASS*, IV, 125; Devereux, *op. cit.*, p. 150.
[20] Simmel, *op. cit.*, p. 42; Weigert, *op. cit.*, pp. 125–126; Devereux, *op. cit.*, p. 147; C. G. Jung, *Essays on Contemporary Events* (London: Kegan Paul, 1947), pp. xiii, xvii.
[21] Weigert, *op. cit.*, pp. 123, 125; Alexander, "Psychology and Social Disᵬ organization," pp. 107, 109.
[22] Fritz Redl, "Phenomenon of Contagion and 'Shock Effect' in Group Therapy," in *Searchlights on Delinquency*, ed. K. R. Eissler (New York: International Universities Press, 1948), p. 317; Devereux, *op. cit.*, pp. 150–153; Simmel, *op. cit.*, p. 49; Saussure, *op. cit.*, p. 50.
[23] Neil J. Smelser, *Theory of Collective Behavior* (New York: The Free Press, 1962), pp. 120–127, 313–381, 417–427.

1. The Heroic Moment

[1] R. Nelson Boyd, *Chili: Sketches of Chili and the Chilians During the War 1879–1880* (London: Wm. H. Allen & Co., 1881), p. 180.
[2] *Chilian Times* (Valparaíso), March 30, 1878.
[3] Juan Williams Rebolledo, *Operaciones de la escuadra chilena mientras estuvo a las órdenes del contra-almirante Williams Rebolledo* (Valparaíso: Imprenta Progreso, 1882), pp. 50, 53–59, 61.
[4] Jorge Velarde, "El arca del marino," MS in the Biblioteca Nacional, Santiago, Chile; Letter of Miguel Grau to Señor General Director de la Guerra, May 23, 1879, *in* Geraldo Arosemena Garland, *El Contralmirante Miguel Grau* (Lima: San Martí y Cía., 1946), p. 83.
[5] Benjamín Vicuña Mackenna, *Las dos Esmeraldas* (Santiago: Imprenta del Centro Editorial, 1879), pp. 215–222.
[6] Although many of Prat's biographers describe his father as ill, none cite the cause of his infirmity. Arturo Prat's grandson, Dr. Arturo Prat Echaurren, himself a physician, believes that Prat's illness was the result of a cerebral thrombosis. Dr. Prat's diagnosis is based on conversations with his paternal grandmother, Prat's widow, who lived with Dr. Prat's family throughout his youth. Personal communication with Dr. Arturo Prat Echaurren, August 1966, Santiago.
[7] Bernardo Vicuña, *Biografía completa de Arturo Prat* (Valparaíso: Imprenta del Mercurio, 1879), p. 10.
[8] Juan M. Simpson, *Algunos rasgos inéditos de la personalidad de Arturo Prat* (Valparaíso: Imprenta Victoria, 1925), p. 9; Eliana Ceriani Bórquez, *Arturo Prat, abogado* (Santiago: Editorial Universitaria, 1964), pp. 21, 55–82; Ramón Guerrero Vergara y José Toribio Medina, *El Capitán de Fragata Arturo Prat, Estudios sobre su vida* (Valparaíso: Imprenta de la Armada, 1952), p. 97.

⁹ Letter of Carmela Carvajal de Prat to Jacinto Chacón, May 14, 1880, *in* Juan Peralta Peralta, *Arturo Prat Chacón, Héroe del Mar* (Valparaíso: Imprenta de Escuela Naval, 1953), p. 157.

¹⁰ Arturo Prat, "Libreta de gastos de entradas del año 1867 con escepción de su providencia de su empleo." In the possession of Dr. Arturo Prat Echaurren.

¹¹ Vicuña, *op. cit.*, p. 18.

¹² Peralta, *op. cit.*, p. 20.

¹³ Vicuña, *op. cit.*, p. 19. Prat suffered from erysipelas, an extremely painful skin disease; see letter of Carmela Carvajal de Prat to Jacinto Chacón, May 14, 1880, in Peralta, *op. cit.*, p. 157.

¹⁴ Simpson, *op. cit.*, p. 5; letter of Carmela Carvajal de Prat . . . , p. 157.

¹⁵ Letter of Arturo Prat to Carmela Carvajal de Prat, April 9, May 11, 1879, in Justo Abel Rosales, *La apoteósis de Arturo Prat i de sus compañeros de heroísmo muertos por la Patria el 21 de mayo de 1879* (Santiago: Imprenta de los Debates, 1888), pp. 109, 113.

¹⁶ Diario de Bitácora del Buque-Corbeta Esmeralda, Archivo Nacional, Biblioteca Nacional, Santiago, Chile; *El Mercurio* (Valparaíso), May 14, 1888. Although the article was not published until almost a decade after the war, its author had been with the fleet at the time of the battle.

¹⁷ There is substantial evidence to support the claim that the majority of the officers of both the *Esmeralda* and the *Covadonga* either were the victims of discrimination by the high command or were considered the least efficient officers of the fleet. Luis Uribe, for example, although a classmate of Prat's, was two ranks his junior and had retired from the navy when the war had begun. Ignacio Serrano had been in an administrative capacity at the outbreak of hostilities. Although one of six men commissioned in 1873, Serrano had the longest time in grade for his rank. The only officer who had been on sea duty when the war began was Francisco Sánchez who had been transferred, before the battle, from the more important *O'Higgins* to the less sought after *Esmeralda*. Although Sánchez had served in the navy for sixteen years, the majority of his classmates had been promoted to first lieutenant sooner than he.

In addition to these officers, there were also four midshipmen. One, Arturo Wilson, had been recalled from his civilian occupation; the remaining three had been transferred from either the ironclads or the corvettes prior to the attack on Callao. It should be noted that the midshipmen serving on foreign naval vessels were sent to the ironclads when they returned to Chile. Thus the *Esmeralda*'s midshipmen lost their berths on the more important ships to make room for perhaps the better trained naval cadets.

The same pattern manifests itself in the *Esmeralda*'s engineering staff. Vicente Mutilla, the most senior second engineer in the fleet, was transferred from the *Cochrane* to the *Esmeralda*. Dionisio Manterola, the ship's third engineer, was the most senior for his rank as well. His naval service dated from 1857. Three times he left the fleet, on the last occasion involuntarily. His shipmate, José Gutiérrez de la Fuente, had also entered the navy in 1857, and like Manterola, had resigned from the service twice before the outbreak of the war.

The allocation of officers to the *Covadonga* appears to parallel the example of the *Esmeralda*. Although Condell had been advanced rapidly, his naval career was chaotic. Twice he had resigned from the navy: the first time, for disciplinary reasons; the second, of his own accord. In 1879, Condell had

been the executive officer of the disarmed *Esmeralda*, and was considering leaving the navy when the war began.
Manuel Orella, Condell's second in command, had been commissioned in 1870. Of the six men who had been promoted to second lieutenant, three received their promotions earlier than he. Of the remaining two, one had almost five years less naval service. The *Covadonga's* two remaining officers, Demetrio Eusquiza and Estanislao Lynch, like Orella, were in administrative billets before the war. They were, in addition, the most junior officers for their rank.
The *Covadonga's* two naval cadets, Eduardo Valenzuela and Miguel Sanz, were both replacements. Before the war they had served on the corvettes. The same was true of the engineering staff. The original crew had been transferred prior to the battle, and their place was taken by Emilio Cuevas, who had earlier served on the *Esmeralda*, and Roberto Castillo, who may have been promoted from the ranks or contracted for after the outbreak of the war since there is no mention of him on the naval officer's rolls of 1878.
In this regard, see *Memoria de Guerra i Marina presentada al Congreso Nacional de 1877* (Santiago: Imprenta Nacional, 1877); *Memoria de Guerra i Marina presentada al Congreso Nacional de 1878* (Santiago: Imprenta Nacional, 1878); *Arturo Prat i el combate de Iquique* (Santiago: Imprenta Gutenberg, 1879), pp. 342–343; *El Mercurio* (Santiago), May 23, 1925.

[18] Letter of Rafael Sotomayor to Aníbal Pinto, June 1879, in *Correspondencia de Pinto*, Vol. I.

[19] Arturo Wilson, "Recuerdos del combate naval de Iquique el 21 de Mayo de 1879," *Revista de Marina*, LXXI (1926), 475.

[20] Luis Uribe, "Parte pasado por el segundo comandante de la 'Esmeralda,'" in Pascual Ahumada Moreno, *Guerra del Pacífico* (Valparaíso: Imprenta del Progreso, 1884), I, 295; Vicente Zegers Recasens, "Cartas del Guardia Marina don Vicente Zegers Recasens," in Ahumada, *op. cit.*, I, 302–304. There is a difference in the reports of the two men. Uribe claimed that Prat stated it was the Chilean flag that had never been surrendered while Zegers alleged that Prat stated no Chilean naval vessel had ever struck its colors. Both versions were used until the early 1900s. Thereafter, the official version was based on Uribe's report which the Navy subsequently adopted as its official version.

[21] Miguel Grau, "Partes peruanos," in Ahumada, *op. cit.*, I, 298.

[22] "Jeneral en jefe de Antofagasta a Ministro de la Guerra," in Ahumada, *op. cit.*, I, 286.

[23] "El corresponsal a Editor del El Mercurio," in Ahumada, *op. cit.*, I, 286.

[24] Letter of E. Altamirano a A. Pinto, in Ahumada, *op. cit.*, I, 286.

[25] "Jeneral en jefe a Ministro de Guerra," in Ahumada, *op. cit.*, I, 286–287.

[26] Arturo Benavides Santos, *Seis años de vacaciones. Recuerdos de la Guerra del Pacífico* (Santiago: Imprenta Universo, 1929), pp. 15–16; *La Revista del Sur* (Concepción), May 27, 1879.

[27] Mauricio Cristi, *Lectura patriótica. Crónica de la última guerra* (Santiago: Imprenta de El Correo, 1888), p. 15.

[28] *Ibid.*, p. 17.

[29] *La Revista del Sur*, June 3, 1879; *El Constituyente* (Copiapó), May 29, 1879; *La Discusión* (Chillán), May 28, 1879; *La Libertad* (Valdivia), June 7, 21, 28, 1879.

[30] Eulogio Altamirano, "Proclama," in Ahumada, *op. cit.*, I, 288.

[31] "Al pueblo de Santiago," *in* Ahumada, *op. cit.*, Vol. I, p. 293.

[32] Roberto Hernández C., "Estudio y prólogo de Roberto Hernández C.," in *El Capitán de Fragata Arturo Prat: El Vice Almirante Patricio Lynch* (Commandancia en Jefe de la Armada, 1952), p. 7.

[33] *El Nuevo Ferrocarril* (Santiago), June 30, 1879.

[34] *El Diario de la Guerra* (Santiago), September 4, 1879; Benjamín Vicuña Mackenna also listed cases of parents naming their children for Prat or the Battle of Iquique. See his *Las Dos Esmeraldas*, pp. cxxvi-cxxvii.

2. Chile, 1876–1879: The Crisis Society

[1] Letter of J. de V. Drummond Hay to Marquis of Salisbury, August 10, 1878.

[2] *El Diario de Avisos* (Santiago), January 17, 1879; *La Patria* (Valparaíso), March 26, 1879.

[3] *Discurso de S. E. el Presidente de la República en la apertura del Congreso Constituyente de 1891* (Santiago: Imprenta Nacional, 1891), pp. 7–8.

[4] Justo Arteaga Alemparte i José A. 2⁰ Espinosa, *Excelentísimo señor Aníbal Pinto* (Santiago: Imprenta del Mercurio, 1876), p. 9.

[5] [Benjamín Vicuña Mackenna], *La asamblea de los notables por un liberal sin nota* (Santiago: Imprenta de El Independiente, 1875), pp. 23–24; Justo Arteaga Alemparte, *Historia del año 75* (Santiago: Imprenta de El Ferrocarril, 1876), pp. 56, 58; Félix Garmendia, *Las elecciones infames* (Santiago: Imprenta de El Independiente, 1876), pp. 5–7.

[6] *The Chilian Times*, February 19, 1876.

[7] *El Chicote* (Valparaíso), March 9, 1876, printed a cartoon showing Pinto addressing a political meeting, all of whose members were asleep; letter of Aníbal Pinto to F. Helquera, August 7, 1875, *Fondos Varios*, vol. 414.

[8] *El Estandarte Católico* (Santiago), February 11, 1876; *El Pueblo* (Santiago), February 14, 1876; see also Ramón 2⁰ Harriet, *La verdad de hoi* (Valparaíso: Imprenta de La Patria, 1875), pp. 9, 11; *De un nuevo partido político en Chile* (Talca: Imprenta de La Opinión, 1875), pp. 26, 33, 37, 42.

[9] *El Padre Cobos* (Santiago), March 31, 1877.

[10] *La Revista del Sur*, January 6, 1876; *La República* (Santiago), January 12, 1876; *The Chilian Times*, January 15, 1876.

[11] *El Ferrocarril* (Santiago), March 2, 1876.

[12] *Guía del elector liberal para las elecciones jenerales de 1876* (Imprenta de la Librería del Mercurio, 1875), pp. 5–7; *Representación a la Excma. Comisión Conservadora* (Santiago: Imprenta de la República de J. Núñez, 1876); *Reclamo de nulidad de las elecciones del departamento de Quillota* (Santiago: Imprenta del Mercurio, 1876); *Reclamo de nulidad de las elecciones del departamento de Putaendo* (Santiago: Imprenta del Mercurio, 1876); *Reclamo de nulidad de las eleciones del departamento de Casablanca* (Santiago: Imprenta del Mercurio, 1876).

[13] *The Chilian Times*, January 15, April 22, 1876; *La Revista del Sur*, January 25, April 6, 1876.

[14] *El Pueblo*, February 21, April 24, 1876; *El Chicote*, March 23, 1876.

[15] Williamson to William Hunter, July 19, 1876, *United States Diplomatic Reports—Chile*, in United States of America, State Department, *Dispatches from U.S. Ministers to Chile, 1876–1879*.

[16] *El Mercurio* (Valparaíso), February 26, 1879.

[17] *El Independiente* (Santiago), January 14, 1879; *La Patria*, January 28, 1879; *Manifiesto de los secretarios del directorio jeneral del partido conservador dirijen a sus amigos i correlijionarios políticos* (Santiago: Imprenta de El Independiente, 1878), p. 5.

[18] *El Obrero* (Chillán), March 16, 1879.

[19] Hilda Jofré Ramírez, *Las primeras sociedades anónimas* (Santiago: Editorial Universitaria, 1964), pp. 14–15, 22.

[20] *Resumen de la hacienda pública desde 1833 hasta 1914* (London: Spottiswoode & Co., 1914), p. 93.

[21] Frank W. Fetter, *Monetary Inflation in Chile* (Princeton, N.J.: Princeton University Press, 1931), p. 26.

[22] Benjamín Vicuña Mackenna quoted in Guillermo Subsercaseaux *El sistema monetario i la organización bancaria de Chile* (Santiago: Sociedad, Imprenta y Litografía Universo, 1920), p. 149.

[23] Fetter, *op. cit.*, p. 17; *Sinópsis estadística de la República de Chile* (Santiago: Imprenta Nacional, 1917), p. 139.

[24] *El Constituyente*, May 26, September 7, 1876; *The Chilian Times*, June 10, 1876.

[25] Francisco Antonio Encina, *Historia de Chile desde la prehistoria hasta 1891* (Santiago: Editorial Nascimento, 1949–1952), XVI, 65.

[26] *El Constituyente*, June 9, September 7, December 28, 1876.

[27] *La Revista del Sur*, September 30, October 17, 28, November 2, 1876.

[28] *El Deber* (Valparaíso), March 26, 1877.

[29] *La Discusión*, March 15, 1877.

[30] *La Revista del Sur*, August 14, 18, October 2, 1877.

[31] *La Discusión*, October 13, 16, December 16, 19, 1877; *La Libertad*, October 13, 20, 1877.

[32] *El Mensajero del Pueblo* (Santiago), September 1, 29, November 10, 1877.

[33] *El Estandarte Católico*, November 17, 1877.

[34] *El Deber*, August 1, 1877.

[35] *La Revista del Sur*, September 2, October 12, 1876; *La Libertad*, September 8, 1877; *La Discusión*, December 16, 1877.

[36] *El Constituyente*, October 11, 22, 31, 1878.

[37] *Boletín de la Sociedad Nacional de Agricultura*, IX (1877), 90 (hereafter cited as *BSNA*).

[38] *La Libertad*, October 20, 1877; *La Discusión*, September 6, 1878; *La Revista del Sur*, January 3, 1878.

[39] *Mefistófeles* (Santiago), April 20, 1878.

[40] *The Chilian Times*, June 17, 1876; *La Discusión*, September 14, 1876; *La Libertad*, November 4, 1876; *La Aurora* (Curicó), July 29, 1879; Cámara de Diputados, *Proyectos sobre creación de policía rural sometidos a su consideración* (Santiago: Imprenta Nacional, 1878).

[41] *The Chilian Times*, January 29, March 18, 1876.

[42] *La Discusión*, May 4, 1878; *La Revista del Sur*, February 8, 1878.

[43] *The Chilian Times*, June 10, 1876; *La Revista del Sur*, August 26, 1876, July 16, 1878.

[44] *El Constituyente*, August 2, October 24, 1876, February 7, 1878; *La Revista del Sur*, April 20, 27, May 11, 1876, March 27, 1877; *La Libertad*, November 18, 1876; *La Discusión*, January 4, September 5, 1877, January 8, 1878.

[45] *El Ferrcarril*, October 26, 1877; *La República*, April 23, May 5, August

23, 1876, February 2, 1877; *La Revista del Sur*, February 8, 1876; *La Discusión*, January 5, August 19, 1878; *La Libertad*, December 23, 1876, February 2, 1878.

46 *El Independiente*, September 5, 1877.

47 *El Mensajero del Pueblo*, June 29, 1878; *El Constituyente*, March 23, April 16, August 2, 1876, January 18, 1878; *La Libertad*, March 29, 1876; *La Revista del Sur*, March 29, June 30, 1876; *La Discusión*, August 9, 1878.

48 *Discurso de su excelencia el Presidente de la República en la apertura del Congreso Nacional en 1877* (Santiago: Imprenta Nacional, 1877), pp. 7–9.

49 *Memoria de Ministerio de Hacienda presentada al Congreso Nacional en 1877* (Santiago: Imprenta Nacional, 1877), pp. v, xiv, lxv, lxvi.

50 *El Pueblo*, July 30, 1876.

51 *BSNA*, VIII (1876), 4; Adolfo Carrasco Albano, *La cuestión financiera para 1877* (Santiago: Imprenta de la Librería del Mercurio, 1876), p. 10.

52 *Estadística comercial de la República de Chile correspondiente al año 1877* (Valparaíso: Imprenta del Universo de G. Helfmann, 1878), p. xiv.

53 *The Chilian Times*, January 27, 1877; Marcial González [Ignotus] "El meeting de los obreros en Santiago," *Revista Chilena*, VII (1877), 281.

54 Ignotus, *op. cit.*, pp. 282–283, 287–288; Marcial González, "La situación fiscal," *Estudios económicos* (Santiago: Imprenta Gutenberg, 1889), pp. 267–302.

55 *Estadística comercial de la República de Chile correspondiente al año 1877*, pp. xxv, xxvi, xxvii; *BSNA*, IX (1877), 47; *BSNA*, X (1878), 89.

56 Letter of Alberto Blest Gana to Aníbal Pinto, March 3, 16, October 18, November 19, 29, 1878; *Fondos Varios*, vol. 413.

57 *BSNA*, IX (1878), 341–342.

58 *Cámara de Diputados, sesiones ordinarias*, June 6, 1878, pp. 24, 26.

59 *Cámara de Diputados, sesiones estraordinarias*, October 30, 1878, pp. 35–36.

60 *Cámara de Diputados, sesiones ordinarias*, June 6, 1878, p. 16.

61 *Cámara de Diputados, sesiones secretas*, July 22, 1878, pp. 366–379.

62 Aníbal Pinto, "Apuntes," *Revista Chilena*, XIII (1921), 339–342; Fetter, *op. cit.*, pp. 30–31; Agustín Ross, *Chile 1851–1910* (Santiago: Litografía y Encuadernación Barcelona, 1911), pp. 33–34.

63 *El Ferrocarril*, January 29, 31, 1879; *El Independiente*, February 12, 1879.

64 *El Ferrocarril*, January 7, 1879.

65 *Ibid.*, January 7, 9, 1879.

66 *El Obrero*, March 16, 1879.

67 *Las Novedades* (Santiago), January 20, 1879.

68 *El Estandarte Católico*, January 11, 1876, January 4, September 19, October 6, 13, 1877; Abdón Cifuentes, *Memorias* (Santiago: Editorial Universitaria, 1936), II, 145.

69 *El Estandarte Católico*, July 28, 1876, May 22, July 5, 1877; *El Mensajero del Pueblo*, July 15, 1876, April 7, July 15, 1877.

70 *El Estandarte Católico*, July 10, 13, August 6, 1877; *El Mensajero del Pueblo*, August 25, 1877; *A nuestros amigos i correlijionarios políticos* (1879); *Cámara de Diputados, sesiones ordinarias*, November 2, 1877, p. 78; Rafael Valetín Valdivieso, "Proyectos de lei de cementerios," *Boletín Eclesiástico*, VI (1880), 548–549.

71 *La República*, December 12, 1876, March 8, 1877; *La Libertad*, August 25, October 13, 1877; *La Discusión*, July 7, 1877.

72 *Espocisión a nuestros conciudadanos* (1878), p. 5.
73 *La Revista del Sur*, June 18, July 11, 1878.
74 *El Independiente*, June 16, 18, 1878.
75 Miguel Guzmán Rosales y Octavio Vió Henríquez, *Don Francisco de Taforó y la vacancia arzobispal de Santiago, 1878–1887* (Santiago: Editorial Católica, 1964), pp. 39, 60, 67, 76; Crescente Errázuriz, *Algo de lo que he visto. Memorias de don Crescente Errázuriz* (Santiago: Editorial Nascimento, 1934), pp. 265–268, 273.
76 Letter of Alberto Blest Gana to Aníbal Pinto, September 15, 1878; *Fondos Varios*, vol. 413.
77 *El Estandarte Católico*, January 16, 21, February 3, 1879; *El Independiente*, January 21, 1879.
78 Robert N. Burr, *By Reason or Force* (Berkeley and Los Angeles: University of California Press, 1965), pp. 125, 133–134.
79 *Senado, sesiones secretas*, December 11, 1878, p. 47; see also Adolfo Ibáñez, *La diplomacia chileno-arjentina. Una contestación* (Santiago: Imprenta de "Los Tiempos," 1879).
80 *La Patria*, January 9, 13, 15, 25, 27, 1879; *El Independiente*, January 14, 15, 1879; *El Mercurio*, December 9, 13, 14, 19, 1878; *Los Tiempos* (Santiago), January 29, 1879.
81 *¡Al pueblo de Santiago!* (Santiago: Imprenta del Independiente, 1879).
82 *La Patria*, January 27, 1879; *El Fígaro*, January 18, February 1, 1879; *El Mercurio*, January 17, 1879.
83 *The Chilian Times*, February 22, 1879.

3. The War of the Pacific: The Heroic Medium

1 *El Ferrocarril*, March 15, 1879; *El Mercurio*, February 15, 25, 1879; *Los Tiempos*, February 18, 1879; *El Independiente*, February 14, 1879.
2 *El Ferrocarril*, January 21, March 22, 1879; *Los Tiempos*, January 16, February 16, 1879; *La Patria*, January 21, February 11, 1879; *El Independiente*, February 11, 14, 1879.
3 *El Ferrocarril*, February 12, 1879; *El Mensajero del Pueblo*, March 8, 1879; *Los Tiempos*, January 22, 1879; *La Discusión*, February 9, 1879.
4 *El Ferrocarril*, February 14, 1879.
5 *El Mercurio*, February 25, 1879; *Los Tiempos*, February 18, 1879; *El Diario de Avisos*, February 13, 1879; *La Revista del Sur*, February 20, 1879.
6 *Los Tiempos*, February 9, 1879; *Las Novedades*, February 10, 1879; *La Patria*, February 26, 27, March 1, 1879; *El Diario de Avisos*, February 20, 22, 1879.
7 *El Ferrocarril*, February 23, 1879; *El Independiente*, March 11, 12, 1879; *La Patria*, February 28, 1879.
8 *El Independiente*, March 4, 1879.
9 *Los Tiempos*, February 19, 1879.
10 *El Estandarte Católico*, March 1, 4, 1879; *El Ferrocarril*, March 1, 1879; *El Independiente*, March 6, 1879.
11 *El Ferrocarril*, March 8, 9, 1879; *El Independiente*, March 8, 1879.
12 *El Independiente*, March 13, 18, 1879; *El Ferrocarril*, March 18, 1879; *La Patria*, March 12, 1879; *Senado, sesiones secretas*, March 24, 1879, p. 7.
13 *Los Tiempos*, March 11, 1879; *La Patria*, February 28, 1879.

[14] *El Mercurio*, February 28, March 1, 1879; *El Estandarte Católico*, March 11, 1879; *Las Noticias* (Talca), March 14, 1879.

[15] *El Estandarte Católico*, March 1, 1879; *La Patria*, February 28, March 4, 1879; *El Mercurio*, February 25, March 1, 1879; *El Independiente*, March 13, 23, 1879; *El Ferrocarril*, March 20, 1879; *Las Noticias*, March 7, 1879; *Diputados, sesiones estraordinarias*, March 27, 1879, p. 716; *Diputados, sesiones secretas*, March 29,1879, p. 113; *Senado, sesiones secretas*, March 24, 1879, pp. 7–9.

[16] *El Mensajero del Pueblo*, March 22, 1879; *El Ferrocarril*, March 26, 27, 28, 1879; *El Independiente*, April 4, 1879; *El Estandarte Católico*, March 29, 31, 1879.

[17] *Resumen de la hacienda pública desde 1833 hasta 1914*, p. 47; *Memoria de Guerra i Marina presentada al Congreso Nacional de 1876* (Santiago: Imprenta Nacional, 1876), pp. ix, xxi; *Memoria de Guerra de 1877*, pp. xi, xvii; *Memoria de Guerra de 1878*, pp. xii, 100.

[18] Carlos Grez, "La supuesta preparación de Chile para la Guerra del Pacífico," *Boletín de la Academia Chilena de la Historia*, III (1935), 138–139; Emilio Körner y J. Boonen Rivera, *Estudios sobre historia militar* (Santiago: Imprenta Cervantes, 1887), II, 292; *Memoria de Guerra de 1878*, Anexo no. 3, pp. 101–102.

[19] Mariano Paz Soldán, *Narración histórica de la guerra de Chile contra Perú y Bolivia* (Buenos Aires: Imprenta y Librería de Mayo, 1884), pp. 106–115; Carlos Dellepiane, *Historia militar del Perú* (Buenos Aires: Círculo Militar, 1941), II, 66, 75; M. Fernando Wilde Cavero, *Historia militar de Bolivia* (La Paz, 1963), pp. 137–142, 145–146; J. C. Clavero, "Perú, Bolivia i Chile sus departamentos, población, . . . en 1879," *in* Pascual Ahumada Moreno, *Guerra del Pacífico* (Valparaíso: Imprenta del Progreso, 1884), I, 146; Körner y Rivera, *op. cit.*, II, 294–295; Francisco A. Machuca, *Las cuatro campañas de la Guerra del Pacífico* (Valparaíso: Imprenta Victoria, 1926), I, 95.

[20] Clavero, *op. cit.*, p. 146; Paz Soldán, *op. cit.*, p. 109; Dellepiane, *op. cit.*, II, 66, 75, 79; Körner y Rivera, *op. cit.*, II, 294–295; Perú, *Memoria del ramo de guerra presentado al Congreso ordinario de 1878 por el Ministerio de Guerra y Marina* (Lima: Imprenta del Estado, 1878), I, 3–6.

[21] Clavero, *op. cit.*, p. 146; Wilde, *op. cit.*, pp. 145–146; Edmundo H. Civiti Bernasconi, *Guerra del Pacífico* (1879–1883) (Buenos Aires: Círculo Militar, 1946), I, 119, 121; Machuca, *op. cit.*, I, 37.

[22] Agustín Blanco to Ministerio, May 1, 1879; Quiñones to Ministerio, April 17, 1879, *in* Ahumada, *op. cit.*, II, 16–18.

[23] Körner y Rivera, *op. cit.*, II, 290, 294–295; Indalicio Téllez, *Historia de Chile—Historia militar* (Balcells i Cía., 1925), I, 151–154.

[24] *El Estandarte Católico*, March 8, 20, 1879; *El Mercurio*, March 1, 21, 1879; *The Chilian Times*, May 3, 1879; *El Constituyente*, March 7, 1879; *El Independiente*, March 5, 19, 20, 1879; *El Correo de La Serena* (La Serena), February 22, 25, March 20, 1879; *El Ferrocarril*, February 25, March 5, 1879.

[25] *El Correo de Quillota* (Quillota), April 14, May 1, 1879; *The Chilian Times*, March 10, 1879; *El Mercurio*, April 6, 1879; *Las Noticias*, April 3, 1879; *El Independiente*, March 19, 20, 1879.

[26] Alejandro García Castelblanco, *Estudio crítico de las operaciones navales de Chile* (Santiago: Imprenta de la Armada, 1929), p. 154; Ramón Vidal Gormaz, "Memoria del comandante de arsenales," *Memoria de Guerra*, 1878, p. 241; *Memoria de Guerra*, 1878, pp. 221, 232–233; Luis Uribe Orrego, *Los*

combates navales en la Guerra del Pacífico (Valparaíso: Imprenta de "La Patria," 1886), p. 11.

27 Uribe, *op. cit.*, pp. 9–11.

28 Manuel Vegas G., *Historia de la marina de guerra del Perú* (Lima: Imprenta "Lux" de E. L. Castro, 1929), pp. 179–180; Geraldo Arosemena Garland, *El contralmirante Miguel Grau* (Lima: San Martí y Compañía, 1946), p. 72.

29 Paz Soldán, *op. cit.*, pp. 107–108.

30 "La Perou en 1878. Notice historique et statistique (publicación final hecha con motivo de la esposición universal de París)," quoted in Diego Barros Arana, *Obras Completas*, Vol. XVI, *La Guerra del Pacífico* (Santiago: Imprenta, Litografía, Encuadernación Barcelona, 1914), p. 72.

31 Perú, *Memoria . . . de marina*, II, 8–9, 13.

32 *La Opinión Nacional* (Lima), March 14, 1879; *El Comercio* (Lima), March 14, 1879, *in* Ahumada, *op. cit.*, I, 548.

33 Rafael Sotomayor to Aníbal Pinto, April 7, 1879, "Correspondondencia de don Rafael Sotomayor a don Aníbal Pinto sobre la Guerra del Pacífico," *Revista Chilena*, XV (1922), 182 (hereafter cited as *CRS*); Rafael Vial to Antonio Varas, March 15, 1879, *Correspondencia de don Antonio Varas sobre la Guerra del Pacífico* (Santiago: Imprenta Universitaria, 1918), pp. 18–19 (hereafter cited as Varas).

34 Alberto Blest Gana to Marquis of Salisbury, June 28, 1879; Marquis of Salisbury to Alberto Blest Gana, July 6, 1879; Treasury Chambers—Draft Treasury, July 14, 1879, in Great Britain, Public Record Office, *Foreign Office 16 (Chile)*, vol. 204.

35 Domingo Santa María to José Victorino Lastarria, May 20, 1879, "Cartas de don Domingo Santa María a José Victorina Lastarria," *Revista Chilena*, VI (1918), 250; Rafael Sotomayor to Aníbal Pinto, May 12, 1879, *Correspondencia de Pinto*, Vol. I.

Peru attempted to obtain aid from Argentina. See the letters of the Peruvian Minister to Argentina and Irigoyen, March 26, 1879, and May 7, 1879, in José M. Echeñique Gandarillas, "La declaración de guerra del 5 de abril de 1879," *Revista Chilena*, XI (1927), 76.

36 Letter of Rafael Sotomayor to Aníbal Pinto, May 5, 12, 1879, *Correspondencia de Pinto*, Vol. I; Gonzalo Bulnes, *Guerra del Pacífico* (Valparaíso: Sociedad Imprenta y Litografía Universo, 1911), I, 180, 191–197.

37 Juan Williams Rebolledo, *Operaciones de la escuadra chilena mientras estuvo a las órdenes del contra-almirante Williams Rebolledo* (Valparaíso: Imprenta Progreso, 1882), pp. 20–21; letter of Rafael Sotomayor to Antonio Varas, April 21, 1879, *in* Varas, pp. 49–50; letter of Rafael Sotomayor to Aníbal Pinto, May 5, 1879, in *Correspondencia de Pinto*, Vol. I.

38 Arturo Cuevas, *Estudio estratéjico sobre la campaña marítima de la Guerra del Pacífico* (Valparaíso: Talleres tipográficos de la Armada, 1901), pp. 17–21; García, *op. cit.*, pp. 163–164.

39 *El Ferrocarril*, April 27, 1879; *El Independiente*, April 19, 1879; letter of Rafael Sotomayor to Aníbal Pinto, April 27, 1879, *CRS*, 192.

40 Letter of Rafael Vial to Antonio Varas, May 9, 1879, *in* Varas, p. 76; Williams Rebolledo, *op. cit.*, p. 33.

41 Cuevas, *op. cit.*, p. 43; García, *op. cit.*, 160.

42 For the campaign of the Huáscar see M. Melitón Carvajal, "Reseña de la campaña del Huáscar contra Chile en 1879," *Revista Chilena*, XV (1922), 87.

[43] Letter of Domingo Santa María to Antonio Varas, July 20, 1879, *in* Varas, p. 191.

[44] Domingo Santa María to Aníbal Pinto, June 25, 1879, *Fondos Varios*, vol. 416; letter of Rafael Sotomayor to Antonio Varas, June 16, 1879, *in* Varas, p. 148.

[45] Letter of Rafael Sotomayor to Aníbal Pinto, June 7, 1879, *Correspondencia de Pinto*, Vol. I; Letter of José Alfonso to Aníbal Pinto, May 23, 1879, *Fondos Varios*, vol. 414; letter of Rafael Sotomayor to Antonio Varas, June 5, 1879, *in* Varas, p. 129.

[46] Letter of Domingo Santa María to Aníbal Pinto, June 25, July 26, 1879, *Fondos Varios*, vol. 416.

[47] Letter of Domingo Santa María to Antonio Varas, July 20, 1879, *in* Varas, p. 190; letter of José Alfonso to Aníbal Pinto, August 1, 1879, *Fondos Varios*, vol. 414.

[48] Letters of Rafael Sotomayor to Aníbal Pinto, May 12, June 4, 1879, *Correspondencia de Pinto*, Vol. I.

[49] Letter of Domingo Santa María to Aníbal Pinto, June 25, 1879, *Fondos Varios*, vol. 416.

[50] Letter of Justo Arteaga A. to Aníbal Pinto, May 16, 24, June 6, 1879, *Fondos Varios*, vol. 415; letter of José Alfonso to Aníbal Pinto, June 13, 1879, *Fondos Varios*, vol. 414; letter of Domingo Santa María to Aníbal Pinto, June 25, 1879, *Fondos Varios*, vol. 416; letter of Roberto Souper to Cornelio Saavedra, June 4, 1879, *Fondos Varios*, vol. 559.

[51] Letter of Domingo Santa María to Aníbal Pinto, June 25, 1879, *Fondos Varios*, vol. 416; letter of Rafael Sotomayor to Aníbal Pinto, June 4, 1879, *Correspondencia de Pinto*, Vol. I.

[52] *El Ferrocarril*, April 15, 1879; *La Patria*, April 23, 1879; *El Independiente*, April 15, 1879.

[53] *El Ferrocarril*, April 9, 1879.

[54] Pastoral del Ilustrísimo Obispo de la Concepción José Hipólito Salas, *Boletín de la Guerra del Pacífico*, May 2, 1879.

[55] Pastoral del Ilustrísimo Obispo de La Serena, José Manuel Orrego, *Boletín de la Guerra del Pacífico*, May 2, 1879.

[56] *El Estandarte Católico*, March 28, 1879; *La Patria*, March 22, April 4, 1879.

[57] *El Independiente*, March 2, 1879.

[58] *Ibid.*, April 9, 1879.

[59] *La Patria*, April 5, 9, 1879.

[60] *Ibid.*, April 16, 1879.

[61] *El Independiente*, June 12, 1879.

[62] *El Centinela* (San Carlos), June 19, 1879.

[63] *El Mensajero del Pueblo*, July 26, 1879.

[64] *El Independiente*, July 22, 1879.

[65] *La Patria*, July 19, 1879.

[66] *El Nuevo Ferrocarril*, July 21, 1879.

[67] *El Independiente*, June 7, July 11, 1879; *La Patria*, July 26, 1879.

[68] *El Independiente*, July 11, 1879.

[69] *LaPatria*, August 1, 1879.

[70] *El Nuevo Ferrocarril*, July 21, 1879.

[71] *El Centinela*, July 12, 1879; *La Patria*, August 12, 23, 1879; *El Mercurio*, June 20, 1879.

[72] *La Patria*, July 10, 1879.

73 *El Correo de Quillota*, June 29, July 24, 1879; *El Mercurio*, July 15, 1879.
74 X. [pseud.], *La patria está en peligro* (1879), pp. 4–5.
75 *Las Novedades*, May 28, 1879; *La Opinión* (Talca), July 31, 1879.
76 *Los Tiempos*, July 31, August 1, 1879.
77 *El Independiente*, July 31, 1879.
78 *El Mercurio*, July 31, August 1, 1879; *El Nuevo Ferrocarril*, August 11, 18, September 15, 1879; *La Patria*, August 1, 1879; *El Independiente*, August 2, 1879; *La Discusión*, September 4, 1879.
79 *La Revista del Sur*, August 7, 1879; *El Mercurio*, August 1, 13, 1879.
80 *El Mercurio*, July 31, 1879; *Las Noticias*, August 1, 1879.
81 *El Mercurio*, August 22, 1879; *El Independiente*, August 1, 1879; *La Patria*, August 2, 1879; *La Discusión*, September 4, 1879.
82 *La Patria*, August 2, 1879.

4. The Hero and His Time

1 Letter of Domingo Santa María to Antonio Varas, June 27, 1879, *in* Varas, p. 155; letter of Rafael Sotomayor to Aníbal Pinto, April 7, 1879, *CRS*, p. 180.
2 Letter of Domingo Santa María to Aníbal Pinto, June 25, 1879, *Fondos Varios*, vol. 416.
3 Letter of Rafael Sotomayor to Antonio Varas, June 13, 1879, *in* Varas, p. 142; letter of Domingo Santa María to Aníbal Pinto, June 25, 1879, *Fondos Varios*, vol. 416; letter of Rafael Sotomayor to Aníbal Pinto, June, 1879, "Correspondencia de don Rafael Sotomayor con el general don Justo Arteaga y don Aníbal Pinto sobre la Guerra del Pacífico," *Revista Chilena*, XVII (1924), 415 (hereafter cited as *CRSJA*).
4 Letter of Domingo Santa María to Antonio Varas, June 24, 1879, *in* Varas, pp. 155–156.
5 Letter of José Alfonso to Aníbal Pinto, June 13, 1879, *Fondos Varios*, vol. 414: "Simpson told me a very important and unusual fact. The evening before the fleet sailed north, a mail ship arrived in Iquique. Simpson spoke with its captain as did Salamanca, the Fleet Chief of Staff, and a little later, Williams, who was on board incognito. The mailboat's captain told Simpson and Salamanca that Prado [the President of Peru] was due to leave Callao soon, on the *Chalaco*, for Arica. Simpson added that he presumed, with good reason, that this information would have been passed on to Williams, first by the captain of the mail ship and then by Salamanca. . . ."
In his book, *Operaciones de la escuadra chilena mientras estuvo a las órdenes del contra almirante Williams Rebolledo*, the admiral stated, on page 44, that on the night in question, a ship did arrive from the north. This vessel, the *Lontué*, was under the command of one N. Potts. Williams claimed that Potts had told him that the Peruvian fleet was still in port because the *Independencia* was undergoing repairs.

The *Lontué* may well have been the ship referred to by Simpson because it arrived on the morning of May 16, at 3:00 A.M. The issue, therefore, seemingly becomes a question of whom to believe: Williams or Simpson.

Still, there is additional evidence that appears to support the allegation of Simpson. Others, for example, also reported that Williams knew that the Peruvian fleet was ready to sail (letters of Rafael Sotomayor to Aníbal Pinto, April 24, 27, 1879, in *CRS*, pp. 188, 191). Indeed, according to a letter of

Sotomayor, various government officials in Santiago expected the Peruvians to leave Callao (see his letter to Antonio Varas, June 5, 1879, *in* Varas, p. 132).

It does appear, then, that the Peruvian sortie from Callao was not only not unexpected but that Williams was forewarned. It is interesting to note that Williams went to enormous lengths to demonstrate that Potts had told him that the Peruvians were still in Callao, even writing this in italics. The vehemence of his denials does seem excessive.

[6] *El Mercurio* of Santiago, May 21, 1929.

[7] Arturo Wilson, "Recuerdos del combate naval de Iquique el 21 de mayo de 1879," *Revista de Marina*, LXXI (1926), 478.

[8] Arturo Wilson, "Recuerdos del combate naval de Iquique," *Revista de Marina*, LXXVI (1931), 322.

[9] "An hour had passed in this unequal battle, when I observed that the *Huáscar* was steaming toward the *Esmeralda*, passing by the *Independencia*'s bow. The latter had been ordered, quite correctly, to attack us. In this moment we were fifty meters from the reefs of the shallows, running the risk of being run aground on the shore; from the shore there was rifle fire directed against us and the *Independencia* was approaching to ram us. I considered that our position was not desirable; from this location we could not help the *Esmeralda*, which was fighting desperately. A shot from the *Huáscar*'s 300 mm gun had pierced my ship, shattering the wooden foresail at its base. I managed to leave the port, directing all my fire at the *Independencia*, which at a distance of 200 meters was firing its own guns" (Carlos Condell, *Memoria de Guerra i Marina presentada al Congreso Nacional de 1879* [Santiago: Imprenta de la República de Jacinto Núñez, 1879], pp. 31–32).

[10] Carlos Condell, "Comandancia de la cañonera 'Covadonga,'" *in* Pascual Ahumada Moreno, *Guerra del Pacífico* (Valparaíso: Imprenta del Progreso, 1884), I, 296.

[11] Letter of Eulogio Altamirano to Aníbal Pinto, May 27, 1879, *in* "Cartas a don Aníbal Pinto," *Revista Chilena*, XIII (1921), 230.

[12] Luis Uribe, quoted in Arturo Wilson, "Recuerdos . . . 21 de mayo," p. 487.

[13] Letter of Domingo Santa María to Aníbal Pinto, June 25, 1879, *Fondos Varios*, vol. 416.

[14] *Cámara de diputados, sesiones ordinarias*, August 27, 1879, p. 458.

[15] *La Patria*, July 17, 1879.

[16] *El Ferrocarril*, May 28, 1879.

[17] *El Independiente*, June 5, 1879.

[18] *La Patria*, May 26, 1879.

[19] *El Maipo* (San Bernardo), June 6, 1879.

[20] Benjamín Vicuña Mackenna, "Pájinas de una leyenda del mar," *in* Ahumada, *op. cit.*, I, 317; *El Independiente*, May 31, 1879.

[21] Esteban Muñoz Donoso, "Oración fúnebre pronunciada por el presbítero don Esteban Muñoz Donoso," *in Arturo Prat i el combate de Iquique*, p. 159.

[22] *The Chilian Times*, October 11, 1879.

[23] José Manuel Orrego, "Pastoral del Ilustrísimo Obispo de La Serena," *Boletín de la Guerra del Pacífico*, May 2, 1879.

[24] José Hipólito Salas, "Pastoral del Ilustrísimo Obispo de la Concepción," *Boletín de la Guerra del Pacífico*, May 2, 1879.

[25] Francisco S. Belmar, *Manual del soldado en defensa de Chile contra Bolivia* (Santiago: Imprenta de "Los Tiempos," 1879), p. 20.

[26] Muñoz, Donoso, *Arturo Prat i el combate de Iquique*, pp. 151, 153.

27 *El Independiente*, June 20, 1879.
28 Belmar, *op. cit.*, p. 23.
29 *Ibid.*, p. 14.
30 *El Estandarte Católico*, May 26, 1879.
31 Esteban Muñoz Donoso, "A Prat," in Pedro Nolasco Préndez, *La Esmeralda* (Santiago: Imprenta de la República de Jacinto Núñez, 1879), p. 31.
32 *El Mercurio*, May 28, July 11, 1879.
33 Wilson, "Recuerdos . . . Iquique," pp. 325–326.
34 Salvador Donoso, "Oración fúnebre pronunciada por el presbítero don Salvador Donoso," in *Arturo Prat i el combate de Iquique*, pp. 168, 179–180; poem by Mercedes I. Rojas, "El 21 de Mayo," in *El Ferrocarril*, June 17, 1879; *El Nuevo Ferrocarril*, July 21, 1879.
35 *El Independiente*, June 20, 1879.
36 Salas, *Boletín de la Guerra del Pacífico*, May 2, 1879.
37 Ramón Menéndez Pidal, *The Spaniards in Their History*, trans. Walter Starkie (New York: W. W. Norton, 1966), pp. 36–37.
38 *El Nuevo Ferrocarril*, September 22, 1879.
39 *El Ferrocarril*, May 29, 1879.
40 Máximo del Campo, "El héroe del 21 de mayo de 1879," in Préndez, *op. cit.*, p. 68; Domingo Izquierdo, "Prat," in *ibid.*, p. 53; *El Independiente*, July 3, 1879.
41 Izquierdo, *in* Préndez, *op. cit.*, p. 53.
42 *El Independiente*, June 5, 1879.
43 *El Ferrocarril*, June 1, 1879.
44 *Ibid.*, August 9, 1879.
45 *La Patria*, May 24, 1879.
46 *El Diario Oficial de Chile*, May 26, 1879.
47 *La Patria*, May 26, 1879.
48 *Ibid.*
49 *El Ferrocarril*, May 28, 1879.
50 *El Mercurio*, May 30, 1879; *La Patria*, September 9, 1879; *El Ferrocarril*, June 28, 1879.
51 Muñoz Donoso, *Arturo Prat i el combate de Iquique*, p. 161.
52 *El Ferrocarril*, June 28, 1879.
53 *Ibid.*, May 28, 1879.
54 *El Ferrocarril*, May 31, 1879; *El Independiente*, July 13, 1879; Víctor Cueto, "El 21 de mayo," *in* Préndez, *op. cit.*, p. 15; Donoso, in *Arturo Prat i el combate de Iquique*, p. 174.
55 Eduardo de la Bara, "Arturo Prat," *in* Ahumada, *op. cit.*, I, 349.
56 *El Mercurio*, May 28, July 18, 1879.
57 *Revista del Sur*, June 17, 1879.
58 *Los Tiempos*, May 27, 1879.
59 *El Mercurio*, May 26, 28, 1879.
60 *El Ferrocarril*, June 10, 1879.
61 *El Diario Oficial de Chile*, May 26, 1879.
62 *Los Tiempos*, May 25, 1879.
63 *El Mercurio*, May 28, 1879.
64 *Ibid.*, May 26, 1879.
65 *El Independiente*, May 29, 1879.
66 *La Patria*, May 30, 1879; *El Estandarte Católico*, May 24, 1879; *El Mercurio*, May 24, 1879.
67 *Los Tiempos*, May 25, 29, 1879.

[68] *El Diario de la Guerra*, May 24, 1879; *Los Tiempos*, May 29, 1879.
[69] *El Diario de la Guerra*, May 24, 1879.
[70] *El Estandarte Católico*, May 23, 1879; *La Patria*, May 24, 1879.
[71] *El Estandarte Católico*, May 23, 24, 1879.
[72] *El Diario de la Guerra*, May 24, 1879.
[73] *El Independiente*, May 27, 1879.
[74] *Cámara de Diputados, sesiones ordinarias*, July 29, 1879, p. 330.
[75] *El Centinela*, July 26, 1879.
[76] *El Independiente*, July 18, August 3, 1879.
[77] *El Mercurio*, July 19, 1879.
[78] *El Independiente*, September 30, 1879.
[79] *El Centinela*, August 9, 1879; *Revista del Sur*, July 31, 1879.
[80] *La Patria*, July 30, 1879.
[81] *El Independiente*, July 30, 1879.
[82] *El Ferrocarril*, June 30, 1879; see also *El Mercurio*, July 15, 1879; *El Centinela*, August 9, 1879.
[83] *Boletín de la Guerra del Pacífico*, June 1, 1879.
[84] *Cámara de Diputados, sesiones ordinarias*, June 7, 1879, p. 35.
[85] *El Nuevo Ferrocarril*, July 21, 1879, January 1, 1880.
[86] *La Patria*, April 5, 1879.
[87] *El Ferrocarril*, June 1, 1879.
[88] *El Mercurio*, May 28, 29, 31, June 19, July 21, 24, August 1, 1879.
[89] *La Patria*, August 1, 1879.
[90] *El Independiente*, May 27, 1879, for example, noted that "certain men have . . . used the sacrifices of the valiant men of the *Esmeralda* for their own benefit."
[91] *El Independiente*, June 20, 1879.
[92] Benjamín Vicuña Mackenna, "Los héroes de Iquique," *in* Pedro J. Muñoz Feliú, ed., *El veintiuno de mayo de 1879* (Santiago: Imprenta del Ministerio de Guerra, 1930), pp. 17–18. See also Arturo Prat Chacón, *Observaciones a la lei electoral vijente* (Valparaíso: Imprenta del Mercurio, 1876).
[93] Letter from the Cámara de Diputados to doña Rosario Chacón de Prat, in *Arturo Prat i el combate de Iquique*, pp. 297–299.
[94] Letter from the Municipalidad de Santiago to doña Carmela Carvajal de Prat, in *Arturo Prat i el combate de Iquique*, pp. 308–309.
[95] "Convocatoria a un mítin al pueblo de Santiago; discursos y conclusiones," in *Arturo Prat i el combate de Iquique*, p. 126.
[96] *El Diario Oficial de Chile*, May 26, 1879.
[97] *Cámara de Diputados, sesiones ordinarias*, June 3, 1879, pp. 9–10.
[98] *Ibid.*, June 10, 1879, p. 52.
[99] *Ibid.*, July 12, 1879, p. 238.
[100] *Ibid.*, p. 237.
[101] *Senado, sesiones ordinarias*, July 11, 1879, pp. 59–60.
[102] *Los Tiempos*, August 7, 1879.
[103] *Cámara de Diputados, sesiones ordinarias*, August 27, 1879, p. 458.
[104] *Ibid.*, June 10, 1879, p. 53.
[105] *Ibid.*, June 3, 1879, pp. 9–10.
[106] *Ibid.*, June 10, 1879, p. 52.
[107] *Ibid.*, July 12, 1879, p. 238.
[108] *Senado, sesiones ordinarias*, July 11, 28, August 8, 1879, pp. 59–60, 121, 129.

[109] El Centinela, June 12, 1879.
[110] La Patria, April 29, 1879.
[111] Los Tiempos, May 29, 1879.
[112] La Patria, August 14, 1879.
[113] El Mercurio, June 14, 1879; La Patria, June 6, 1879.
[114] El Nuevo Ferrocarril, August 18, October 20, 1879.
[115] El Estandarte Católico, May 23, 1879.
[116] El Independiente, June 17, 1879.
[117] El Nuevo Ferrocarril, July 14, August 18, September 1, 15, 1879.
[118] El Independiente, June 17, 1879; El Ferrocarril, June 5, 1879.
[119] El Independiente, July 3, 1879.
[120] Cámara de Diputados, sesiones estraordinarias (sesiones secretas), June 19, 1879, p. 131; El Nuevo Ferrocarril, August 18, 1879.
[121] El Independiente, June 25, 1879; La Patria, June 23, 1879.
[122] Benjamín Vicuña Mackenna, "Discurso en la recepción, en Santiago, de los marinos de la 'Covadonga,'" in Feliú, op. cit., p. 100.

5. Prat and the Parliamentary Regime: 1880–1920

[1] El Estandarte Católico, May 19, 1886.
[2] Ibid., May 21, 1889.
[3] El Mercurio, May 21, 1890.
[4] El Estandarte Católico, May 21, 1890.
[5] El Ferrocarril, May 22, 1892.
[6] El Mercurio, May 22, 1893.
[7] El Sur (Concepción), May 21, 1893.
[8] El Mercurio, May 22, 1895.
[9] El Estandarte Católico, May 21, 1884.
[10] El Mercurio, May 21, 1885; see also La Unión (Valparaíso), May 17, 1885.
[11] El Estandarte Católico, May 21, 1885.
[12] El Mercurio, May 21, 1890.
[13] Ibid., May 21, 1894.
[14] Ibid., May 21, 1895. See also La Libertad Electoral (Santiago), May 21, 1900; La Unión, May 21, 1890; May 21, 1892.
[15] El Ferrocarril, May 21, 1885. In 1886, La Unión also complained about the lack of public enthusiasm (May 21, 1886).
[16] El Estandarte Católico, May 21, 1885.
[17] El Mercurio, May 22, 1890. On May 22, 1893, the same paper claimed that the people went to the celebration, not to pay homage to Prat but to look at the troops parading in their equipment.
[18] El Estandarte Católico, May 21, 1890.
[19] There is no more telling proof that the public's interest in Prat had waned than two editorials. On May 21, 1900, La Libertad Electoral noted: "It was not twenty one years ago that . . . Prat and his companions in sacrifice provided Chile with one of its finest and surely most glorious days, and it now appears that everyone has forgotten this memorable event." And one reads in the May 21, 1909, issue of La Unión: "In the past years, it appeared that patriotism had fallen asleep and that the memory of that day [the 21st of May] would be erased from our history; the 21st of May was a day like any other and passed unnoticed, without any more celebration than the opening

of the crypt which contained the remains of the fallen heroes of that epic battle."

20 *Recopilación de leyes por orden numérico arreglada por la secretaría del consejo de estado* (Santiago: Imprenta, Litografía y Encuadernación Fiscal de la Penitenciaría, 1917), VIII, 163. See also *Senado, sesiones estraordinarias,* January 16, 1913, pp. 1307–1308; January 6, 1914, pp. 428–429; *Senado, sesiones ordinarias,* July 27, 1914, pp. 374–376.

21 *El Mercurio,* May 21, 1886, May 21, 1888.

22 *Ibid.,* May 21, 1897.

23 *El Estandarte Católico,* May 21, 1888; *La Unión,* which was not a Catholic paper, did the same on May 21, 1916.

24 *El Sur,* May 21, 1889, May 21, 1890, May 21, 1903; *El Estandarte Católico,* May 19, 1886; *El Mercurio,* May 21, 1888, May 21, 1896; *El Ferrocarril,* May 21, 1902.

25 *La Unión,* May 21, 1907: "Through our veins flows the passionate blood of the Spanish; from them we inherited fearless courage; from the Araucanian, the love of the soil . . . from both, patriotism." *El Mercurio* of Valparaíso, May 21, 1911, wrote that Iquique "subsumes all the qualities of our race." *El Diario Ilustrado* (Santiago), May 21, 1912, noted: "The battle . . . erects a perpetual monument of glory, of the purest and most sublime kind, to the patriotism and the valor of the 'Raza Chilena.'"

26 *El Mercurio* of Valparaíso, May 21, 1914, May 21, 1920, May 21, 1923; *El Mercurio* of Santiago, May 21, 1905, May 21, 1921; *El Diario Ilustrado,* May 21, 1914; *La Unión,* May 21, 1914.

27 *El Porvenir* (Santiago), May 21, 1905, observed: "The patriots, the men who dream of the enrichment of Chile, will find in the perfection of the modest and valiant Captain [Prat] an example to follow and a lesson worthy of repeating endlessly to their fellow citizens. Civics ought to be taught with facts, and there is no better example than the sacrifice of the crewmen of the corvette which Prat . . . commanded." *El Mercurio* of Santiago, on May 21, 1908, stated: "The history of the events which occurred 29 years ago should be told in every possible way, in the schools and the factories, in the countryside and the cities, in every home as an example of past times whose memory should always be emulated by every Chilean to remind him to fulfill his civic duties." *El Diario Ilustrado,* on May 21, 1914, explained that Prat's final act had more than mere military significance, for it was "above all a sublime act of obedience which is . . . the most eloquent example of civic spirit to be found in our history."

28 *El Mercurio* of Santiago, May 21, 1905, May 21, 1921; *El Mercurio* of Valparaíso, May 21, 1925.

29 For alternative views on the overthrow of Balmaceda, see Harold Blakemore, "The Chilean Revolution of 1891 and its Historiography," *Hispanic American Historical Review,* XLV (1965), 393–422.

30 Frank W. Fetter, *Monetary Inflation in Chile* (Princeton, N. J.: Princeton University Press, 1931), pp. 47–49, 52–53, 77, 84–85, 101, 104, 107, 109, 112, 119, 125, 189. For an alternative interpretation, see Albert O. Hirschman, *Journeys Toward Progress* (New York: Doubleday, 1965), pp. 215–235.

31 *Resumen de la hacienda pública,* pp. 86, 89, 90; Semper and Michels, *La industria del salitre en Chile,* trans. Javier Gandarillas and Orlando Ghigliotto Salas (Santiago: Imprenta Barcelona, 1908), p. 291.

32 Luis Barros Borgoño, *Caja de crédito hipotecario* (Santiago: Librería y Imprenta Artes y Letras, 1930), p. 151.

[33] Fetter, *op. cit.*, p. 120.

[34] Francisco Antonio Encina, *Nuestra inferioridad económica* (Santiago: Editorial Universitaria, 1912), p. 296.

[35] Alejandro Bertrand, *La crisis salitrera* (Paris: Louis Michaud, 1910), p. 14.

[36] *Ibid.*, p. 22.

[37] Ibid., p. 13; Semper and Michels, *op. cit.*, pp. 140–147.

[38] *Resumen de la hacienda pública*, pp. 29–40; "The Chilean Treasury, without doubt, rests essentially on the nitrate industry" (Semper and Michels, pp. 118–119).

[39] Luis Aldunate quoted in Aníbal Pinto Santa Cruz, *Chile un caso de desarrollo frustrado* (Santiago: Editorial Universitaria, 1962), pp. 55–56.

[40] F. Javier Cotapos Aldunate, *El aporte del capital extranjero en la industria minera de Chile* (Santiago: Talleres Gráficos "Simiente," 1947), pp. 13, 37.

[41] Sergio Sepúlveda, *El trigo chileno en el mercado mundial* (Santiago: Universidad de Chile, 1959), pp. 62, 72, 75–76, 80.

[42] *Ibid.*, pp. 96–97; Marto Ballesteros, "Desarrollo agrícola chileno, 1910–1955," *Cuadernos de Economía*, II (1965), 28–30.

[43] Teodoro Schneider quoted in Pinto Santa Cruz, *op. cit.*, p. 91.

[44] Samuel Valdés Vicuña, *La solución del gran problema del día* (Santiago: Imprenta i Encuadernación Roma, 1895), p. 35.

[45] Fetter, *op. cit.*, p. 117.

[46] Adolfo Murillo, *La mortalidad urbana en Chile* (Santiago: Imprenta y Encuadernación Roma, 1896), pp. 9, 11.

[47] Luis Galdames, "Los movimientos obreros en Chile," in *Ciencias Económicas y Sociales*, Volumen VIII de los *Trabajos del Cuarto Congreso Científico (1⁰ Pan-Americano)*, ed. Julio Philippi (Santiago: Imprenta, Litografía y Encuadernación Barcelona, 1911), VIII, 375–376; Arturo Contreras, *El derecho de los pobres* (Santiago: Imprenta Aurora, 1904), p. 16; Marcelo Segal, "Biografía de la ficha salario," *Mapocho*, II (1963), 17–31; Semper and Michels, *op. cit.*, pp. 106–107; Enrique Oyarzún, *Discursos parlamentarios* (Concepción: Tipografía i Litografía José V. Sonlodre, 1913), pp. 132–174; Eduardo Vergara Ruiz, *El pago del salario en Chile* (Santiago: Litografía y Encuadernación Barcelona, 1914), pp. 24–25.

[48] Efraím Vásquez, *El trabajador ante la lei i ante la sociedad* (Santiago: Imprenta y Litografía Universo, 1908), pp. 40–44; Monseñor Edwards, "Por Bascuñán, "El proletariado rural en Chile," *Contribución del Centro Industrial y Agrícola al IV Congreso Científico y 1⁰ Pan Americano* (Santiago: Imprenta y Litografía Universo, 1908), pp. 40–44; Monseñor Edwards, "Por la salvación de la raza," *Revista de Educación Nacional*, XIII (1917), 448; Armeliano Bobadilla Sáenz, *Habitaciones para obreros* (Santiago: Imprenta Barcelona, 1907), p. 18.

[49] Galdames, *op. cit.*, 376–377; Murillo, *op cit.*, pp. 12–15.

[50] Burr, *op. cit.*, pp. 196–197, 238, 252–259.

[51] *El Sur*, May 20, 1902.

[52] Anjel Vicuña, *La convención liberal democrática celebrada en Santiago el 28 de noviembre de 1896* (Santiago: Imprenta y Encuadernación Roma, 1896), p. 42.

[53] *El Porvenir*, May 21, 1896.

[54] *El Mercurio* of Santiago, May 21, 1904.

[55] José Maza, *Sistemas de sufragio i cuestión electoral* (2d ed.; Santiago: Imprenta "La Ilustración," 1913), pp. 28–29, 43–44; *El Mercurio* of Santiago, May 21, 1901; Luis Castro Donoso, *De actualidad* (Santiago: Imprenta Turín, 1901), p. 8.

[56] Ana Johnson, "Educación cívica en Chile," *Revista Pedagójica*, III (1907), 213; Julio Saavedra, "La educación cívica en Chile," *Revista Pedagójica*, III (1907), 67.

[57] Saavedra (*op. cit.*, p. 69) called this phenomenon "exotismo." Emilio Rodriguez Mendoza, *Ante la decadencia* (Santiago: Imprenta Moderna, 1899); Tancredo Pinochet Le-Brun, *La conquista de Chile en el siglo XX* (Santiago: Imprenta "La Ilustración," 1901), pp. 82–93; Encina, *op. cit.*, pp. 202–203.

[58] *La Unión*, May 20, 1908; X. X. [pseud.], *La crisis económica* (La Serena: Imprenta, Encuadernación y Litografía Americana, 1913), p. 14; Nicolás Palacios, *Nacionalización de la industria salitrera* and *Decadencia del espíritu de nacionalidad* (Santiago: Salón Central de la Universidad, 1908).

[59] Máximo del Campo, *Liga de acción cívica, Su fundación en Santiago de Chile* (Santiago: Imprenta A. Hinojosa P., 1912), p. 35.

[60] Julio Valdés Cange, *Cartas al excelentísimo Señor don Pedro Montt* (2d ed.; Valparaíso: Imprenta Universo, 1909), p. 33.

[61] Enrique Mac-Iver, *Crisis moral de la República* (Santiago: Imprenta Moderna, 1900), pp. 16, 18.

[62] Ismael Tocornal, *Liga de acción cívica*, p. 18; Roberto Mario [Carlos Pnto Durán], *Como se hunde el país! Desgobierno, clericalismo, oligarquía, corrupción, decadencia* (Santiago: Imprenta San Francisco, 1917), pp. 9–12; Abraham König, *La constitución de 1833 en 1913* (Santiago: Imprenta Santiago, 1913), pp. 58–59; Castro Donoso, *op. cit.*, pp. 8–9.

[63] Vicuña, *op. cit.*, p. 5.

[64] König, *op. cit.*, pp. 51, 64.

[65] Máximo Hertel, *Los dirigentes y la ruina de Chile* (Santiago: Imprenta Universitaria, 1915), p. 15.

[66] *El Ferrocarril*, May 22, 1904.

[67] Maximiliano Ibáñez, *El régimen parlamentario en Chile* (Santiago: Imprenta Cervantes, 1908), pp. 16–17.

[68] Ernesto E. Lefevre M., *Arqueo* (Santiago: Imprenta y Encuadernación "El Globo," 1907), pp. 24, 30.

[69] Ismael Tocornal, *op. cit.*, p. 18.

[70] Alberto Valdivieso Araoz, *Oportunistas y doctrinarios ante la opinión pública* (Santiago: Imprenta de "El Correo," 1896), p. 5.

[71] Eliodoro Yáñez y Anjel Guarello, *Cámara de Diputados, sesiones ordinarias*, August 30, 1899, pp. 816–818, 821.

[72] *El Mercurio* of Santiago, May 22, 1913.

[73] *El Diario Ilustrado*, June 3, 1902; *El Mercurio* of Santiago, May 22, 1913.

[74] L. Sierra M. and Eduardo Moore, *La mortalidad de los niños en Chile* (Valparaíso: Imprenta Central, 1895), p. 25; Murillo, *op. cit.*, p. 6.

[75] *El Mercurio* of Valparaíso, May 20, 1917.

[76] Javier Díaz Lira, *Observaciones sobre la cuestión social en Chile* (Santiago: Imprenta Chile, 1904), pp. 10–11, 20–21.

[77] Lefevre, *op. cit.*, p. 6.

[78] König, *op. cit.*, p. 43; Lefevre, *op. cit.*, p. 23.

[79] *El Porvenir*, May 21, 1896.

[80] Aníbal Sanfuentes, *Discurso en la convención celebrada en Santiago el 15 de octubre de 1899* (Santiago: Imprenta de la Alianza Liberal, 1899), p. 8; Mario, *op. cit.*, pp. 57–58.

[81] José Alfonso, *El parlamentario i la reforma política en Chile* (Santiago: Cabeza i Cía., 1909), p. 20; *El Mercurio* of Santiago, May 21, 1901.

[82] Máximo del Campo, *Liga de acción cívica*, p. 35.

[83] Alfonso, *op. cit.*, p. 36.

[84] Miguel Echenique Gandarillas, *La liga de acción cívica*, pp. 31–33.

[85] *El Porvenir*, May 22, 1892: "Dates like the one which has just passed, or like that of the 7th of January, raise and sooth the spirit in moments like these in which we are now living, when the nation's character is depressed and in a state of moral decay; they bring to mind the civic and heroic virtues of the Chilean people and encourage us to hope that its glories and liberties will always be preserved, its traditions respected. . . .

"A sailor, a companion of the great heroes who on this day wrote the most splendid page in our history, who sealed with the blood of heroes and martyrs the destiny of the motherland in a foreign war, today has in his hands these same destines, after a sad and prolonged internal war.

"If today, in the silence of his meditations, he [Montt] might invoke the memory of those glorious companions who have passed on to the inmortality of history, he also might find, in one of those solemn moments, that, together with deciding his own fate, he can compromise the fate of the motherland. And in such a case, reasonable propositions are not enough, nor are good intentions; manly acts are needed. What is great and admirable in the action of Prat is that he did not hesitate or weaken for a single instant; what will assure the glory of a leader is to plan for the good of the nation and to realize it.

"We are rapidly moving away from the 21st of May . . . from all those great historic moments in which the citizens had but one heart, a single will and one desire to save the motherland. Divisions continue to split the Chilean family with the same characteristic acrimony which the epochs of bad governments have displayed; there are bastard ambitions and crooked maneuvering above and profound discontent below; we do not have citizens as in the good days of patriotism; the same guiding light and the same compass; we are not all moving behind the same ideal; . . . all is seen to be muddy, stirred up, and irritated. The wishes and needs of the country, nevertheless, are so evident and tangible that he who might wish resolutely to attend to them should not vacillate in achieving his goal.

"Well then, the sailor [Montt] who today guides the great rudder [of state] . . . can take definite resolution from the 21st of May which might save his name and save the nation from the dangers which audacious hands are heaping above him. . . . In the immensities of the ocean are whirlpools which insensibly attract ships; those who think they can navigate in tranquil waters [will discover that] the government is lost; the ship, like a wounded bird, begins to fly in circles which grow narrower each time around. The clamor of the shipwrecked rises, and now all is lost. Be careful of the maelstrom."

[86] *El Sur*, May 21, 1893: "In our times such different problems . . . emerge like terrifying hosts; when . . . the many republican virtues—the jewels and pride of our administration—have disappeared. Now that the horizon grows dark and threatening, and the course uncertain and menacing, it is imperative that all our leaders—indeed, anyone who might be involved in public life— model themselves on the sublimely abnegating Arturo Prat and his heroic

companions. That serene and calm sacrifice is one of man's most precious possessions for the life, the honor, the glory and the greatness of the country!

"At the present time the nation is beset by economic, political, and social problems whose solutions require the patriotism, prudence, abnegation, and the sacrifice of all personal interests to one supreme goal: the motherland. Everyone, each in his own sphere—be it in the government, the parliament, or a political party—must follow the shining path marked in the waters of Iquique by the sword of that invincible captain who was inspired by only one ideal: the nation, symbolized by that flag which was floating at the mast head of his ship. . . . "

[87] *El Porvenir*, May 21, 1893: "The memories of past injuries should neither be nutured nor should they engender long-lasting hatreds; . . . we must try to reconcile the members of the Chilean family; political parties do not exist simply to fight each other to the last breath or to tear each other apart without mercy. They should be pleased when they can do something to benefit the motherland. . . . They should seek peaceful solutions to their disputes, to try to resolve the reasons for discord and soothe the harshness of future and, unfortunately, inevitable political battles. When we commemorate common glories, the partisan interests are forgotten and political passions are cooled, in order to attend only to the good of the nation." See also *El Ferrocarril*, May 21, 1893.

[88] *La Libertad Electoral*, May 21, 1901.

[89] *El Mercurio* of Valparaíso, May 21, 1903.

[90] *El Porvenir*, May 21, 1904: "They [the heroes of Iquique]—those echoes of sacrifice, those glorious lights which in a day of undying memory illuminated the motherland's flag—seem to materialize from a beautiful world, which unfortunately, now appears very distant.

"Our eyes widen [when we compare] the figures of the martyrs of Iquique, united only by the generous desire to die in defense of the flag entrusted to their valor, with the currishness of today!

"This constant memory . . . is especially important . . . now that it is necessary to search for a means of teaching ideals which are now belittled and degraded by an atmosphere not suitable either to patriotism or to hope.

"There is no source more pure, ample, or fertile, than the heroic sacrifice of the martyrs of Iquique. For these men the motherland was the epitome of their desires; the sublime objective of their efforts.

"Oh that these inmortal memories might inspire feelings of abnegation and patriotism in our men and that they could exorcise from them the pettiness which divides them and wastes their efforts.

"This would be the best offering which we could dedicate to the memory of the heroes of Iquique."

[91] *El Mercurio* of Santiago, May 21, 1915.

[92] *Ibid.*, May 21, 1912.

[93] *La Unión*, May 21, 1913. Two years later, May 21, 1915, the same paper carried the following editorial: "We were poor but honest and sober. The spirit of sacrifice and of abnegation dwelt in our souls and, above all, . . . we loved the motherland.

"Now look at the present picture.

"The people, the old people, who once responded with daring . . . today cry out, poor and hopeless, because above all they see corruption and incompetence.

"The old sobriety has died. We are now living in a complete scandal which pollutes all things, from finance and economics to politics; the spirit of abnegation and sacrifice has been replaced by a fierce selfishness and unbridled greed.

"Although we might wish to forget [these things], a recent example . . . springs to mind, demonstrating how enormous has been the greed of those who are chosen to be the leaders of the people.

"Compare Prat, dying on the deck of an enemy ship . . . with the leaders of the present regime! Look how . . . the motherland today is simply an orator's empty mouthings.

"One sees a sad and somber picture, then, when comparing the present situation with the anniversary of that date. Can the picture of our old glories awaken in our souls the lost patriotic love . . . the inexhaustible fountain of all the good supreme loves and the national glories?

"The sound of trumpets still vibrates in our ears. . . . We should listen attentively and prepare ourselves for the battle. There are victories to be won in the enemy's country; there are even greater ones on our soil.

"And we salute the descendants of those martyrs and those who followed their example."

94 *El Mercurio* of Santiago, May 21, 1907. On May 21, 1904, a reporter for the same paper questioned: "Who believes in that [sacrifice] today? The sense of duty carried to the point of sacrifice of one's life seems now so strange. . . . How much time has passed? Some people say approximately twenty years. It seems like so much more. . . .

"His [Prat's] sacrificing spirit conquered land, wealth, and power for us. Do not let him find out what we have done with all of that: Do not allow him to learn how the country has misused that power and wealth."

95 *El Mercurio* of Santiago, May 21, 1909, felt that the anniversary of Iquique was important for the children of Chile because "we can remind them that there is a loftier goal than mere material interests: an ideal for the children which is like a religion; a higher and sacred impulse which is the distinctive characteristic of those born on this soil. That spirit, that ideal, that force, which urges them to live always ready to give their lives for the country, to fulfill their duty to the point of sacrifice, to be loyal to this concept at every moment, regardless of force or the most painful conditions."

96 *El Diario Ilustrado*, May 21, 1907.

97 *El Mercurio* of Santiago, May 21, 1908; *El Mercurio* of Valparaíso, May 21, 1908.

98 *La Unión*, May 21, 1912, May 21, 1907: "Now let us ask ourselves, we who live in this present generation, from the highest to the most humble: what have we done today to imitate this man? When have we put the comfort of the nation before our personal interests?"

99 *El Diario Ilustrado*, May 21, 1914: "Here is the most important lesson which should be imprinted not simply on the memories of our children but on the consciences of all our citizens.

"The basis of society rests on its member's order, honor, and fulfillment of duty. If we were to take away respect for legislation and the natural laws . . . all of the institutions would fall apart, endangering the individual's security and even his life.

"Today more than ever, this great lesson of valor and of civic spirit needs to be propagated throughout the nation. We are losing our respect for the laws; we are losing our public and private morality; we are losing the sense of civic valor needed to act against the machinations of the political merchants; we are, finally, losing the concept of solidarity and commonality. What is left . . . is this cruel selfishness which is becoming rooted with an absolute disdain for the rights of the rest.

"If we do not wish our society to disintegrate, we have to follow the example of the hero who was valiant in war because he had been virtuous in peace."

[100] *El Diario Ilustrado,* May 21, 1915: "In order to educate our nation in the civic and heroic examples of our race, so that we will be completely and eternally Chilean, we need only turn to the past—to the names of the heroes of Iquique—who did not need foreign examples in order to die.

"We see in our national industries, in our factories and parks, the cloth for our women, the finery for their daughters, the machines which can work and cultivate our rich country, the equipment and armaments with which we will fight. . . .

"We should beg the wise and severe teachers of our youth to inculcate in their students the sacred love of our land and its flag; and, of the abnegating Chilean, from the mothers of our children, from the most beautiful half of the motherland, from them we beg that they will suckle, raise, and educate their children, from the cradle onward, with the delicious nectar of patriotism. We hope that they will teach their infants—those pieces of their souls— to include, together with the sacred name of God, a blessing for the Republic; that these children will understand that we are an independent and sovereign race, that they were born Chileans.

"On the day that the people forsake all the evil which has recently been imported, when the industries are reborn, and a severe austerity again reigns —then Chile will return to its former splendor. Our race will raise up Chile to the same level of strength and sovereignty as Prat, Condell, and their companions of glory of the 21st of May."

[101] *El Mercurio* of Santiago, May 21, 1912: "When we see that it [Iquique] is such a recent event, one still within our living memory, and we realize what one man can do in the service of his country, desolation overcomes us, because it is seen that those days of glory are now so distant."

El Mercurio of Valparaíso, May 21, 1914, noted: "Everyone understands in Chile, thanks to that example [Prat], that it is necessary, like Prat, to be honest, hard working, a good head of the family and a good citizen, in order to be able to be truly patriotic and capable of heroism." *El Diario Ilustrado,* May 21, 1918, wrote: "It is necessary to benefit from their lessons, and for this it is not required that the motherland be in a moment of danger in order to ask for the blood and the lives of her children. History shows us that those men who knew how to be an example in battle were also those who, in peace, fulfilled their duty, accepting . . . the sacrifices of daily work which, although not always as brilliant, is still as meritorious as the former."

6. Prat and the Established and Radical Press: The Hero 1920–1950

[1] Enrique Mac-Iver, *Crisis moral de la República* (Santiago: Imprenta Moderna, 1900), p. 5.

[2] José Maza, *Sistemas de sufragio i cuestión electoral* (2d ed.; Santiago: Imprenta "La Ilustración," 1913), pp. 218–219.

[3] *El Mercurio* of Santiago, May 22, 1913; *El Diario Ilustrado,* June 3, 1902.

[4] Joaquín Edwards Bello, quoted in Frederick Pike, *Chile and the United*

States, *1880–1962* (Notre Dame, Ind.: University of Notre Dame Press, 1965), p. 176.

5 *El Mercurio* of Santiago, May 21, 1920. An article in *El Diario Ilustrado*, May 21, 1924, observed: "They [the heroes of Iquique] serve as a standard of comparison with the present selfishness. They gave their blood and their lives because they would not see the honor of the motherland threatened, and we sadly note that now it is the motherland which is being sacrificed; there is no higher concept of duty than that which inspired Prat and his companions of glory. They, who should serve as an example for the rest, rule the nation for their own benefit, desires, and aspirations. They use their power, and even the nation's dignity, for the benefit of their own [interests] or for that of a clique."

6 *El Mercurio* of Santiago, May 21, 1920. In the same issue, another commentator wrote: "It is not enough to venerate Prat's memory with words: it is necessary . . . to honor it with acts, which means, if necessary, the unconditional postponement of the most sought-after goals for the general welfare of all the sons of Chile."

7 *El Diario Ilustrado*, May 21, 1922.

8 *El Mercurio* of Valparaíso, May 21, 1924; *El Mercurio* of Santiago, May 21, 1924, May 21, 1926.

9 *El Mercurio* of Valparaíso, May 21, 1924.

10 *Ibid.*, May 22, 1925: "In these hours of anxiety and even of doubt, the event which we alluded to [the Battle of Iquique], takes on an enormous importance. A nation whose sons are united by these latent traditions, whose people render homage to the genuine representative of their virtues—the men who gave up their lives for the honor and advancement of the Republic—cannot become the victim of disorder and anarchy. They must accept, unconditionally, the great needs of the nation. Then, the small divisions will disappear, doubtless due to the intensity of national unity. . . . The innate patriotism of the children of this land resists the attacks of the worker. While the latter, if he is . . . more aware, is very appreciative of the efforts of his predecessors to make this country great and respected. He is aware of the unavoidable duty of the new generation to preserve this precious legacy, achieved through enormous sacrifices for the enrichment of the Republic.

11 John Reese Stevenson, *The Chilean Popular Front* (Philadelphia: University of Pennsylvania Press, 1942), pp. 43–47; Frederick M. Nunn, *Chilean Politics, 1920–1931* (Albuquerque: University of New Mexico Press, 1970), pp. 117–133, 142–159.

12 *La Unión*, May 21, 1929.

13 *Ibid.*, May 22, 1927. In an article entitled, "Porteños a votar," Ibáñez was described as follows: "He has purged the administration of those who were stealing from the public treasury; he has reformed and purified the judiciary and has given assurances that in the future there will be justice for the rich and the poor; he has made economies, cutting out useless employees, and balancing the budget; he has established norms in the pending international question [the Tacna-Arica dispute]; he has swept the Communists from the nation and has restored peace to labor and has imposed respect on the bureaucracy. . . ."

14 *El Mercurio* of Valparaíso, May 22, 1928; *La Unión*, May 22, 1928.

15 *El Diario Ilustrado*, May 21, 1926: "What beautiful lessons are to be found in the 21st of May! We are reaching a point where few are encouraged

to fulfill their duty loyally. On the contrary, almost all try to elude it, especially if it involves troubles, problems, and dangers to their personal interests. "The situation has become worse. Through a series of truly criminally complacent acts, it has been even proper to strike the word 'duty' from the popular language, substituting for it the word 'right' . . . as a result, we have many people who do not wish to subject themselves to any discipline, who do not respect any institution or law, who claim that they are being persecuted and repressed when the authorities, obligated to maintain the internal peace between diverse social forces, dare to call on them to fulfill their duty."

La Unión, May 21, 1931: "Today, apart from its intrinsic significance, it [the battle] has a deeper significance, which revives the spirit of the present generation: it is a sense of responsibility toward the motherland.

"If in each area of the nation, each citizen felt this sense of duty, we are sure that very beneficial results would materialize.

"One does not serve the motherland only on the field of battle; one also serves her, and with particular efficiency, in civil life as well, in whatever endeavor the individual undertakes.

"The son who considers and respects parental counsel; the student, in the simple but important act of learning a lesson; a worker at his labor in the shop or in the factory; the man supporting his way through life, of learning and vigor, in short, all of us who form the great family of the nation, can dignify the motherland and honor the heroes each moment of our existence."

16 *La Unión*, May 21, 1927.

17 *El Diario Ilustrado*, May 21, 1928; *El Mercurio* of Santiago, May 21, 1929.

18 *La Unión*, May 21, 1918.

19 *El Mercurio* of Valparaíso, May 21, 1929.

20 Aníbal Pinto Santa Cruz, *Chíle un caso de desarrollo frustrado* (Santiago: Editorial Universitaria, 1962), p. 110; Nunn, *op. cit.*, pp. 160–161.

21 Leonardo Guzmán, *Un episodio olvidado de la historia nacional* (Santiago: Editorial Andrés Bello, 1966), pp. 15–24.

22 Stevenson, *op. cit.*, pp. 51–52.

23 Germán Urzúa Valenzuela, *Los partidos políticos chilenos* (Santiago: Editorial Jurídica de Chile, 1968), pp. 71–73, 76–78; Stevenson, *op. cit.*, pp. 61–62.

24 Julio César Jobet, *Ensayo crítico del desarrollo económic-social de Chile* (Santiago: Editorial Universitaria, 1955), pp. 190–194, 202–205.

25 Stevenson, *op. cit.*, pp. 64, 69, 73–80, 86–88.

26 *La Unión*, May 21, 1932.

27 *El Mercurio* of Santiago, May 21, 1932; *El Mercurio* of Valparaíso, May 21, 1932.

28 *El Mercurio* of Santiago, May 21, 1934; *La Unión*, May 21, 1934.

29 *El Diario Ilustrado*, May 21, 1938.

30 *La Unión*, May 21, 1939.

31 *El Mercurio* of Santiago, May 21, 1941.

32 *Ibid.*, May 21, 1932.

33 *El Diario Ilustrado*, May 21, 1936; see also *El Diario Ilustrado*, May 21, 1938.

34 *La Unión*, May 21, 1937; see also *La Unión*, May 21, 1939.

35 *El Mercurio* of Santiago, May 21, 1938.

36 *Ibid.*, May 21, 1933.

[37] *El Mercurio* of Valparaíso, May 21, 1934, May 21, 1935; *El Mercurio* of Santiago, May 21, 1935, May 21, 1937; *El Diario Ilustrado*, May 21, 1934; *La Unión*, May 21, 1937.

[38] *El Mercurio* of Santiago, May 21, 1934.

[39] *Ibid.*, May 21, 1935.

[40] *El Diario Ilustrado*, May 21, 1937.

[41] *Ibid.*, May 21, 1938.

[42] *La Unión*, May 21, 1936.

[43] *El Mercurio* of Valparaíso, May 21, 1935. For other examples of the dedication of the Milicia Republicana, see *Milicia Republicana*, I (October 1933), 5, 22; I (November 1933), 27; I (December 1933), 9–10; I (June 1934), 27, 30–36; II (May 1935), 1, 7, 9, 11–15.

[44] *El Diario Ilustrado*, May 21, 1938.

[45] *Ibid.*, May 21, 1941.

[46] *Ibid.*, May 21, 1939.

[47] *La Unión*, May 21, 1940; *El Diario Ilustrado*, May 21, 1938.

[48] *La Unión*, May 21, 1941.

[49] Pinto Santa Cruz, *op. cit.*, pp. 107–114; Albert O. Hirschman, *Journeys Toward Progress* (New York: Doubleday, 1965), pp. 216, 246–247.

[50] Pinto Santa Cruz, *op. cit.*, p. 137; Hirschman, *op. cit.*, p. 216.

[51] *El Mercurio* of Valparaíso, May 21, 1942.

[52] *La Unión*, May 21, 1944: "The love of the motherland, according to the lesson of the hero, translates itself into the fulfillment of duty. It might be during the cruel disasters of the war or in the peaceful exercise of industry, the arts, professional work or in commerce, but he who fulfills his duty serves his motherland in the best manner in which he is capable. He is not a patriot, nor does he love his nation, nor has he understood the lesson of the heroes, if he considers that he has fulfilled his obligation by visiting the crypt of Prat, . . . or by being lazy or indifferent to his books and his duties. Nor is the worker [patriotic] if he considers his work an intolerable hardship, if he believes that his employer is an enemy who it is necessary to oppose at each moment by means of sabotage, hatred, and fraud.

"The employee [is not patriotic] if he fails in his duty of being enterprising, who neither studies nor perfects himself, in order to offer to the nation a product improved by his effort.

"The nation is passing through crucial moments, which demand more than they ask, an extraordinary dedication, a responsible and conscious dedication to the fulfillment of duty." See also *La Unión*, May 21, 1945, May 21, 1949; *El Mercurio* of Valparaíso, May 21, 1947, May 21, 1948, May 21, 1949; *El Diario Ilustrado*, May 21, 1950.

[53] *La Unión*, May 21, 1942, May 21, 1944, May 21, 1945; *El Mercurio* of Valparaíso, May 21, 1942, May 21, 1946, May 21, 1948, May 21, 1949; *El Mercurio* of Santiago, May 21, 1943, May 21, 1946, May 21, 1949.

[54] *El Mercurio* of Valparaíso, May 21, 1947.

[55] In 1938 the MNS changed its name to the *Vanguardia Popular Socialista* and operated under this new title until 1941.

[56] Jorge González von Marées, *El Mal de Chile* (Santiago: Talleres Gráficos "Portales," 1940), p. 9.

[57] *Ibid.*, pp. 18–21, 26, 28–30, 33, 35, 41, 78; see also his *El problema del hambre* (Santiago: Ediciones Ercilla, 1937).

[58] *Ibid.*, pp. 71, 89–90; *El Trabajo* (Santiago), May 17, 24, 1934.

[59] González von Marées, *El problema del hambre*, pp. 86–87.

60 *Trabajo* (Santiago), May 17, 24, 1934, May 18, 1935. One headline, published on May 20, 1936, read: "The International Sanhedrin Inspiration of the Economic Policies of Ross."
61 *Ibid.*, May 22, 1936.
62 *Ibid.*, May 17, 24, 1934, May 18, 1935, May 22, 1936.
63 *Ibid.*, May 24, 1934.
64 *Ibid.*, May 18, 1935.
65 *Ibid.*, May 18, 1935.
66 *Ibid.*, May 20, 1936.
67 *Ibid.*, May 21, 1937.
68 *Ibid.*, May 18, 1935.
69 *Ibid.*, May 20, 1937.
70 *Ibid.*, May 22, 1936.
71 *Ibid.*, May 20, 21, 1937.
72 *Ibid.*, May 20, 1937.
73 *Ibid.*, May 21, 1937.
74 *Ibid.*
75 *Ibid.*, May 21, 1938.
76 *Ibid.*, May 21, 1939.
77 Hernán Ramírez Necochea, *Origen y formación del partido comunista de Chile* (Santiago: Editorial Austral, 1965), pp. 51–62; Sergio Guilisasti, *Partidos políticos chilenos* (2d ed.; Santiago: Editorial Nascimento, 1964), pp. 309–312; Lía Cortés y Jorge Fuentes, *Diccionario político de Chile* (Santiago: Editorial Orbe, 1967), p. 99.
78 Eudocio Ravinés, *The Yenan Way* (New York: Scribner, 1951), pp. 179, 183–184.
79 *Frente Popular*, May 21, 1937. Traditionally the Communist journals did not seem to favor Arturo Prat. Only once, on May 23, 1922, did *La Federación Obrera* grudgingly admit the existence of the Battle of Iquique. Even then, the editorial depreciated the event and its principal hero. In 1923 and 1924, the newspaper failed to commemorate the 21 of May. In 1925, the journal changed its name to *La Justicia*. The editorial policy, at least vis-à-vis Prat, remained the same, and no mention was made of the hero or his death in 1925 or 1926. *La Bandera Roja* (1931–1934) and *El Frente Único* (1934–1936), which were sporadically published following the overthrow of Ibáñez, followed the same tradition of ignoring the Battle of Iquique and its principal hero.
80 *Ibid.*, May 20, 1938.
81 *Ibid.*, May 21, 1937, May 21, 1938.
82 *Ibid.*
83 Federico Gil, *The Genesis and Modernization of Political Parties in Chile* (Gainesville: The University of Florida Press, 1962), p. 36.
84 *El Siglo*, May 21, 1941. Although Prat was not mentioned, there was a substantial amount of material devoted to Earl Browder, the head of the Communist party in the United States.
85 *Ibid.*, May 21, 1942.
86 *Ibid.*, May 21, 1941.
87 *Ibid.*, May 21, 1943. See also *El Siglo* for May 21, 1944, and May 21, 1945.
88 *Ibid.*, May 21, 1942.
89 *Ibid.*, May 21, 1943.
90 *Ibid.*, May 21, 1944.

91 *Ibid.*, May 21, 1945.
92 In all the editorials published on Navy Day, both O'Higgins and Lord Cochrane were mentioned as many times, if not more, than Prat.
93 *El Siglo*, May 21, 1946.
94 *Ibid.*, May 21, 1947.
95 *Ibid.*, May 21, 1948.
96 When the newspaper resumed publication, it continued its traditional editorial policy. In an article entitled "Chile y su mar" (May 21, 1953), the author, Orlando Millas, concentrated on an economic interpretation of Chilean history. The article did mention Prat but said that the battle in which he died "is like a projection of the former battles fought together by the Chileans, Peruvians, and Bolivians on these same seas against Spanish imperialism." The remainder of the article was an attack on British and American economic imperialism. The United States was especially attacked for building the Panama Canal and for preventing Chile from trading with other nations. The last remark was doubtless a reference to the embargo on trade with Iron Curtain countries.
97 Marcelo Segal, *Desarrollo del capitalismo en Chile* (n. p., 1953), pp. 301, 304, 309. Some of the predecessors were *Centro Social Obrero, La Unión Socialista,* and *El Partido Obrero Francisco Bilbao.* See also Guiliassti, *op. cit.,* p. 256.
98 The founders of *La Opinión* were Juan Bautista Rossetti and Juan Luis Mery. Raul Silva Castro, *Prensa y periodismo en Chile (1812–1956)* (Santiago: Ediciones de la Universidad de Chile, 1958), p. 386.
99 *La Opinión*, May 21, 1935, May 21, 1936, May 21, 1937, May 21, 1939. Not all the Socialist press was equally enthusiastic about Prat as was *La Opinión, La Consigna* (1934–1941), the official journal of the Socialist party, never mentioned either Prat or the Battle of Iquique. *La Crítica* (1939–1942), however, always published an editorial commemorating the Battle of Iquique, Arturo Prat was rarely mentioned. See *La Crítica*, May 21, 1940, May 21, 1941, May 21, 1942.
100 *Ibid.*, May 21, 1933, May 21, 1935, May 21, 1936, May 21, 1939, May 21, 1942.
101 *Ibid.*, May 21, 1933.
102 *Ibid.*, May 21, 1935, May 21, 1936.
103 *Ibid.*, May 21, 1936, May 21, 1937.
104 *Ibid.*, May 21, 1935.
105 *Ibid.*, May 21, 1933, May 21, 1936, May 21, 1937.
106 *Ibid.*, May 21, 1935.
107 *Ibid.*
108 *Ibid.*, May 21, 1936.
109 *Ibid.*, May 21, 1938.
110 *Ibid.*, May 21, 1933.
111 "Prat is the highest personfication of the Chilean people. From this heroic group, which lives subjugated to caste but which knows how to act gloriously for the Republic. The hero of Iquique did not belong to the oligarchy governing the nation. But he was an authentic son of the people, silent, resigned, and profound . . ." (*La Opinión*, May 21, 1938, May 21, 1941).
112 *La Opinión*, May 21, 1942.
113 *Ibid.*, May 21, 1944.
114 *Ibid.*, May 21, 1946.
115 *Ibid.*, May 21, 1947.
116 *Ibid.*, May 21, 1949.

7. Arturo Prat and Education

1 *El Ferrocarril*, May 23, 1881.

2 *Ibid.*

3 *Ibid.*, May 22, 1884.

4 *Ibid.*

5 Orestes Tornero L., *Compendio de la historia de Chile* (3d ed.; Santiago: Librerías del Mercurio, 1880), p. 70. For later editions of the same work, see the bibliography.

6 Miguel Luis Amunátegui, *Compendio de la historia política i eclesiástica de Chile* (11th ed.; Santiago: Librería Europea de Nicasio Ezquerra, 1881), p. 127. For later editions, see the bibliography.

7 Esteban Muñoz Donoso, *Compendio de historia de América i Chile* (2d ed.; Santiago: Imprenta de R. Varela, 1881), p. 439; Gaspar Toro, *Compendio de historia de América i especialmente de Chile* (Santiago: Imprenta Nacional, 1881), p. 181; Gaspar Toro, *Compendio de historia de Chile (1492–1884)* (2d ed.; n.p., n.d.), pp. 182–185. For subsequent editions of these books, see the bibliography.

8 Toro, *Compendio de historia de Chile*, p. 182.

9 *Lecciones de historia de Chile para el uso en las escuelas públicas* (Santiago: Imprenta Cervantes, 1887), p. 69.

10 José M. Muñoz, "El patriotismo en la escuela," *Revista de Instrucción Primaria*, VIII (1893), 210 (hereafter cited as *RIP*); see, by the same author, "La enseñanza de la historia i la formación del carácter," *RIP*, VIII (1893), 66.

11 Ana Johnson, "Educación cívica," *Revista Pedagógica*, III (1907), 213 (hereafter cited as *RP*); Julio Saavedra, "La educación cívica en Chile," *RP*, III (1907), 67.

12 "Solicitud de la Asociación de Educación Nacional a S. E. el Presidente de la República. Octubre 31, 1907," *La Revista de Asociación de Educación Nacional*, III (1907), 251 (hereafter cited as *RAEN*).

13 "Memoria del Presidente de la Asociación de Educación Nacional, correspondiente a 1911," *Revista de Educación Nacional*, VIII (1912), 67–107 (hereafter cited as *REN*); "Memoria del Presidente de la Asociación de Educación Nacional," *REN*, IX (1913), 76; "Memoria del Presidente de la Asociación inicial al Gobierno sobre la reforma de la enseñanza pública de la Asociación de Educación Nacional," *REN*, XVI (1920), 58–96.

14 Tancredo Pinochet Le-Brun, *La conquista de Chile durante el siglo XX* (Santiago: Imprenta, Litografía y Encuadernación "La Ilustración," 1909); Alejandro Venegas [Julio Valdés Cange], *Sinceridad: Chile íntimo de 1910* (2d ed.; Santiago: Imprenta Universitaria, 1910); see also his *Cartas al excelentísimo don Pedro Montt* (2d ed.; Valparaíso: Imprenta Universo, 1909).

15 Luis Galdames, "El nacionalismo en la educación," *RIP*, XXXI (1912), 125; see also J. Albornoz G., "La educación del carácter," *La Educación Nacional*, IV (1908), 153 (hereafter cited as *LEN*).

16 Domingo Amunátegui Solar, *El progreso intelectual y político de Chile* (Santiago: Editorial Nascimento, 1936), p. 127; Domingo Amunátegui Solar, *La democracia en Chile* (Santiago: Universidad de Chile, 1946), p. 223; Fernando Campos Harriet, *Desarrollo educacional 1810–1960* (Santiago: Editorial Andrés Bello, 1960), p. 35; Amanda Labarca Hubertson, *Historia de la enseñanza en Chile* (Santiago: Imprenta Universitaria, 1939), pp. 184, 195, 199–200.

[17] Labarca, *op. cit.*, pp. 185–186; "Carta de David Montt a Sr. Dr. Carlos Fernández Peña," *RP*, VI (1910), 162.

[18] Amanda Labarca H., "Educación nacional," *RAEN*, III (1907), 121.

[19] Saavedra, *op. cit.*, p. 69.

[20] "Crónica pedagógica: La conquista de Chile en el siglo XX," *RP*, V (1909), 180.

[21] Galdames, *op. cit.*, p. 130.

[22] Julio Saavedra, "Nuestro idioma patrio," *RAEN*, III (1907), 194–196.

[23] Rodolfo Lenz, "Memoria sobre las tendencias de la enseñanza del idioma patrio en Chile," *El Educador*, X (1900), 67.

[24] Ruperto Oroz, "El amor patrio," *La Enseñanza*, I (1902), 133.

[25] Antonio Bórquez Solar, "La epopeya olvidada," *RP*, V (1909), 161–163; Víctor Domingo Silva, "El himno de la raza," *REN*, XVI (1920), 198; Anjel A. Arías Lillo, "Programa de instrucción cívica, economía política, i social para la Escuela Normal de Preceptores de Curicó," *LEN*, IV (1908), 324–325.

[26] Pinochet Le-Brun, pp. 73–76.

[27] Jermán Muñoz, "Necesidades de fundar una sociedad que se ocupe de proteger a la Raza Chilena," *RP*, VI (1910), 201–206; "Pensamientos de el libro 'La raza chilena,'" *REN*, VIII (1912), 292; "Por la salvación de la raza," *REN*, XIII (1917), 436–453; "Un gran movimiento chileno para salvar la raza i proteger el hogar," *REN*, XVI (1920), 391–417; "Crónica pedagógica," *RP*, V (1909), 175–177; "La guerra al alcohol," *RIP*, XIV (1900), 449–456; Rodolfo Méndez, "Enseñanza anti alcohólica," *La Enseñanza*, I (1902), 58–60; "El patriotismo i las virtudes cívicas en la educación, *RP*, VII (1911), 185.

[28] Luis Galdames, *Educación económica e intelectual* (Santiago: Imprenta Universitaria, 1912), pp. 55, 224, 238–239.

[29] Francisco Antonio Encina, *La educación y el Liceo* (Santiago: Editorial Universitaria, 1962), pp. 120–160; Carlos Fernández Peña, "Defensa de la Escuela de Artes i Oficios," *REN*, X (1914), 354; "Se impone la acción," *REN*, XII (1916), 3–4; "La decadencia de la raza," *REN*, XII (1916), 146; Arcadio Alvarez Barboza, "Los nuevos libertadores de Chile," *REN*, XII (1916), 177–178.

[30] Francisco Antonio Encina, *Nuestra inferioridad económica* (Santiago: Imprenta Universitaria, 1912). The Association of National Education also published his *La educación y el Liceo* in 1912. Other publications of the same association of a related nature: Nicolás Palacios, *Decadencia del Espíritu Nacional* and *Nacionalización de la industria salitrera* (Santiago: Estensión Universitaria de la Asociación de la Educación Nacional, 1908).

[31] "Un año nuevo," *RP*, VII (1911), 2; Francisco Antonio Encina, "Reforma de nuestra educación nacional," *RP*, VII (1911), 5–6; "Se impone la acción," *REN*, XII (1916), 3–4.

[32] Galdames, "El nacionalismo en la educación," p. 131; "Educación económica del país," *REN*, VII (1911), 402; Arcadio Álvarez B. "Nuestra independencia económica," *LEN*, VIII (1912), 24; "Petición para establecer la educación cívica i la continuidad de nuestra Educación Nacional, de acuerdo en la Memoria de Instrucción Pública en 1907," *REN*, VIII (1912), 407.

[33] Guillermo Subercaseaux, "Política nacionalista," *REN*, IX (1913), 271–273; Enrique Cannobbio, "Defensa de la Escuela de Artes i Oficios," *REN*, X (1914), 414; "Programa de acción cívica de la Asociación de Educación

Nacional del Departamento de Extensión Universitaria Secundaria en 1915,"
REN, XI (1915), 48–49.

[34] "El patriotismo i las virtudes en la educación," *RP*, VII (1911), 185–186; "Petición para establecer la Educación Cívica i la continuidad de nuestra educación nacional, de acuerdo con la memoria de instrucción pública de 1907," *REN*, VIII (1912), 407; Rafael Luis Daza Lira, "Necesidades de la instrucción primaria," *REN*, IX (1913), 313–316; Julio Maza, "El sistema de elección presidencial," *REN*, XI (1915), 173; "Educación cívica," *REN*, XI (1915), 187–188; "Petición inicial al gobierno sobre reforma de la enseñanza pública de la Asociación de Educación Nacional," *REN*, XVII (1921), 12.

[35] Ruperto Oroz, "La enseñanza educativa," *RIP*, XIII (1899), 16; Muñoz, "La enseñanza de historia," pp. 65–66.

[36] This was clearly demonstrated in an article by Ruperto Oroz, "La enseñanza educativa." The article noted that since 1885, the purpose of education had changed. Prior to that time, at least according to Oroz, the school only sought to transmit knowledge. This did not, however, benefit society. Schools now taught their students to resist evil and to contribute more to the nation. See also José Muñoz, "Observaciones sobre la enseñanza de la instrucción cívica, la economía política i la economía doméstica." *RIP*, VIII (1894), 577–578; Juan Madrid, "La instrucción cívica debe figurar en el programa de estudios de las escuelas elementales i superiores," *RIP*, V (1891), 705–709; P. O. Morales Vera, "La instrucción cívica en la escuela primaria," *RIP*, IX (1895), 558–561.

[37] Madrid, *op. cit.*, p. 706; Morales Vera, *op. cit.*, p. 559; Gutenberg C. Lagos, "Estudios sobre la educación moral," *RIP*, XVIII (1904), 22; Muñoz, "Observaciones . . . ," p. 578; E. Arellano, "La Patria," *El Educador*, V (1895), 97; José 2⁰ Varela, "De la eduación en jeneral," *RIP*, XV (1901), 65; Carlos Robinet, "Los deberes cívicos," *El Educador*, VIII (1898), 102–103; José María Muñoz, "El deber," *RIP*, XXIII (1909), 327; José S. Enlufe, "Programas," *LEN*, V (1909), 119.

[38] Ramón López Pinto, "Memoria del alumno normalista pensionista en los Estados Unidos," *RIP*, III (1888), 354; Muñoz, "Enseñanza . . . ," pp. 66–68; Domingo Villalobos B., "La enseñanza de historia en la escuela pública," *El Educador*, II (1890), 20–21; Muñoz, "El patriotismo . . . ," pp. 211, 214; Albornoz, *op. cit.*, pp. 153–156; Manuel Ortiz, "La enseñanza de historia," *RIP*, IV (1890), 289; "Programa de historia," *RIP*, XXVII (1913), 22; M. Rodríguez Mendoza, "La enseñanza de la historia en las escuelas públicas," *RIP*, I (1887), 697.

[39] López, *op. cit.*, p. 354.

[40] *Ibid.*; Ortiz, *op. cit.*, p. 289; Muñoz, "La enseñanza . . . ," p. 66.

[41] Ortiz, *op. cit.*, p. 289.

[42] Muñoz, "La enseñanza . . . ," p. 66; López, *op. cit.*, p. 354; Arías Lillo, *op. cit.*, p. 325; Enrique Cannobbio, "Discursos," *REN*, XI (1915), 187–189.

[43] Francisco Valdés Vergara, *Lecturas infantiles preparadas para niños de ocho a doce años de edad* (Santiago: Imprenta Cervantes, 1888).

[44] Francisco Valdés Vergara, *Historia de Chile para la enseñanza primaria* (2d ed.; Valparaíso: Imprenta del Universo de Gmo. Helfman, 1898), pp. 316–327. For later editions of this same work, see the bibliography.

[45] Domingo Villalobos, *Lecciones de historia de Chile* (Santiago: Imprenta Cervantes, 1893), pp. 192–194; Domingo Villalobos, *Tratado elemental de historia de Chile* (Santiago: Imprenta y Encuadernación Barcelona, 1896), p. 165. For later editions of these same works, see the bibliography.

46 "Miscelánea: Escuela Normal de Preceptores de Santiago," *El Educador*, VII (1897), 27.

47 *El Mercurio*, May 21, 1897.

48 Daniel Aeta Astorga, "Paseos escolares," *RIP*, XV (1901), 193; "El 18 de Setiembre i el 21 de Mayo," *La Enseñanza*, VIII (1909), 175.

49 Francisco 2⁰ Alarcón S., "Clase de historia de Chile," *RIP*, XIV (1900), 484; Adela Lira G., "Sección práctica," *LEN*, IV (1907), 22. In the latter article the teacher wrote a lesson outline on a ship and managed to weave into this theme the story of Prat.

50 Samuel Zenteno Araya, "Lo que significa la bandera chilena," *REN*, VIII (1912), 253.

51 "Fallecimiento de don José Bernardo Suárez," *La Enseñanza*, XI (1912), 45; Carlos Fernández Peña, "Necrolojía a don José Bernardo Suárez," *REN*, VIII (1912), 167.

52 R. O., "El 21 de Mayo i la educación cívica de los niños en las escuelas públicas," *RIP*, XXVIII (1914), 238; see also R. O. "Crónica escolar," *RIP*, XXVII (1913), 362.

53 Víctor Hernández, "El 21 de Mayo en la Escuela Normal de Preceptores de Santiago," *RIP*, IV (1890), 622.

54 F. J. Morales, "Iquique en la Escuela Normal de Preceptores de Santiago," *RIP*, VI (1892), 634–635.

55 I. D. Romildo Colombo, "Discurso patriótico pronunciado el 21 de Mayo," *La Enseñanza*, I (1902), 109–110, 113.

56 Luis Galdames, *Temas pedagójicos* (Santiago: Imprenta Universitaria, 1913), 129–130; "El Congreso Nacional de enseñanza secundaria," *REN*, VIII (1912), 467; José Pinochet Le-Brun, "La evolución de nuestro régimen político y la educación nacional," *REN*, XXI (1925), 4; Maximiliano Salas Marchan y José Pinochet Le-Brun, "La reforma de la enseñanza pública en la asamblea de la Asociación de Educación Nacional," *REN*, XVII (1921), 55; Guillermo Subercaseaux, "Educación moral i relijiosa en la enseñanza del estado," *REN*, XIII (1917), 228; Rómulo Peña, "La reforma de la educación nacional," *Revista de Educación Primaria*, XXXII (1922), 218, 220 (hereafter cited as *REP*).

57 Darío Salas, *El problema nacional* (Santiago: Imprenta i Litografía Universo, 1917), p. 311.

58 Marfisa Muñoz Yurazeck, *Arturo Prat* (Santiago: Imprenta Universitaria, 1914), pp. 3, 7; also published in *REN*, X (1914), 188–193.

59 Félix González Rocuant, "¿Qué es la Patria?" *REN*, XII (1916), 181.

60 A. Bórquez Solar, "Prat i su pléyade," *REP*, XXXI (1921), 206–207.

61 Ruperto Oroz, "El amor a la patria," *El Educador*, XII (1902), 41.

62 José María Muñoz Hermosilla, "La Patria," *RIP*, XXIII (1909), 423.

63 "La patria i la familia," *La Enseñanza*, XI (1912), 108; Francisco A. Machuca, "Principios de instrucción cívica," *RIP*, XX (1906), 94–95.

64 "El 21 de Mayo," *RIP*, (1892), 633; "El aniversario del combate de Iquique en la Escuela Normal de Preceptores en Santiago," *El Educador*, VI (1896), 26; "Aniversario patrio," *RP*, VII (1911), 149.

65 R. O., "Crónica escolar," *RIP*, XXVII (1913), 364, 368.

66 Luis Berríos, "El maestro i el momento nacional," *REN*, XV (1919), 143.

67 Luis Carriola, "El 21 de Mayo en crónicas," *REP*, XXXI (1921), 188.

68 Otto Schlott, "El libro de lectura," *RIP*, III (1888), 177.

69 Esteban Muñoz Donoso, *Compendio de la historia de Chile* (Santiago:

Imprenta Emilio Pérez L., 1893), p. 103; Daniel Riquelme, *Compendio de historia de Chile* (Valparaíso: Librería e Imprenta Sud Americana de Barra i Cía, 1899), p. 468; Javier Méndez M., *Lecciones históricas de Chile* (Santiago: Imprenta y Encuadernación Chile, 1906), pp. 103–104; Luis Galdames, *Estudio de la historia de Chile* (2d ed.; Santiago: Imprenta Universitaria, 1911), pp. 424–426. For later editions of these works, see the bibliography.

[70] Pedro J. Barrientos Díaz, *Compendio de historia de Chile* (Santiago: Imprenta i Encuadernación Lourdes, 1911), pp. 96–97.

[71] Alejandro Silva, *Historia de Chile* (Santiago: Librería de la Federación de Obras Católicas, 1915), p. 91.

[72] Armando Pinto, *Enseñanza de la moral, Dedicada a los niños, 1, 2, y 3 años de las escuelas primarias* (Santiago: Imprenta y Encuadernación "Claret," 1923), pp. 58–59; see also Armando Pinto, *Historia de Chile* (4th ed.; Santiago: Editorial Nascimento, 1925), pp. 120–123.

[73] Colección H. E. C., *Historia de Chile* (Santiago: Imprenta Franco Chilena, 1925), p. 245; see also Aurelio Díaz Meza, *Historia de Chile* (Santiago: Imprenta y Litografía Barcelona, 1915), pp. 308–309; Colegio de los SS. CC., *Historia de Chile* (Santiago: Imprenta Universo, 1926), pp. 256–257, 261.

[74] Silva, *op. cit.*, p. 91; S. Gonzales F., *Pequeña reseña histórica de Chile* (2d ed.; Antofagasta: Imprenta Castellana, 1921), p. 64.

[75] *Historia de Chile* (5th ed.; Santiago: Librería y Editorial Escolar, n.d.), II, 150–151.

[76] Walterio Millar, *Historia de Chile ilustrada* (Concepción: Imprenta Hispano-Chilena, 1930), p. 182.

[77] Alejo Roa R., *Sexto libro de lectura* (2d ed.; Santiago: Editorial Salesiana, n.d.), p. 93.

[78] César Bunster, *El niño chileno* (Santiago: Imprenta Universitaria, 1944), I, 78–79. There are numerous other examples of influence of Prat in children's primers. See, for example, José Manuel Borgoño, *Silabario* (Santiago: Imprenta y Encuadernación Fiscal de la Penitenciaria, 1918), p. 42; Luis Baltra Olivares y E. Muñoz Yevenes, *Libro de lectura y redacción* (Santiago: Imprenta Universitaria, 1924), Vol. II; Manuel Guzmán Maturana, *Libro de lectura* (8th ed.; Santiago: Editorial Minerva, 1948), II, 176.

[79] Pío Cid, "La boya de la Esmeralda," *RIP*, XXV (1911), 259.

[80] Compare Francisco Frías V., *Historia de Chile* (Santiago: Editorial Nascimento, 1949), pp. 277–279 with Galdames, *op. cit.*, pp. 348–350.

[81] Anjel T. Vásquez, *Nuestra historia nacional al alcance del pueblo* (Santiago: Imprenta La Tracción, 1926), pp. 120–122; Luis Pérez P., *Lecciones de historia de Chile* (2d ed.; Santiago: Editorial Minerva, 1921), pp. 83–85; Manuel Rozas, *Diccionario cívico chileno* (Talleres Gráficos "Cóndor," 1928), pp. 186–187; Domingo Amunátegui Solar, *Historia de Chile* (Santiago: Editorial Nascimento, 1933), II, 84–86; J. T. Ramírez, *Historia de Chile* (2d ed.; Santiago: Editorial Nascimento, 1937), pp. 271–272; Walterio Millar, *Historia de Chile ilustrada* (Santiago: Ediciones Orbe, 1938), pp. 294–299; Elías Almeyda Arroyo, *Lecciones de historia, geografía y educación cívica* (Santiago: Imprenta Universo, 1932), pp. 132–135; Colección H. E. C., *Historia de Chile* (18th ed.; Santiago: Editorial La Salle, 1944), pp. 89–90; Pedro J. Alvarez Bórquez, *Recopilaciones históricas* (2d ed.; Santiago: Imprenta América, 1945), pp. 76–79; Benjamín Claro Velaso, "La lección del héroe. Mayo de 1943," *Mensajes a los niños de Chile* (Santiago: Imprenta de la Universidad de Chile, 1945), pp. 27–37; Vicente Bustos Pérez, *Historia de Chile* (26th ed.; Santiago: Imprenta y Litografía Universo, 1944), pp. 164–

168; Silva Campos, *Episodios nacionales* (Santiago: Editorial O'Higgins, 1945), pp. 274–284; Ramón Pérez Yánez, *Forjadores de Chile* (Santiago: Editorial Zig-Zag, 1953), pp. 279–282. For subsequent editions, see the bibliography.

[82] Seymour Martin Lipset, "Values, Education, and Entrepreneurship," in *Elites in Latin America*, ed. Seymour Martin Lipset and Aldo Solari (New York: Oxford University Press, 1967), pp. 4, 8, 10–11; see also David Mc-Clelland, *The Achieving Society* (Princeton, N.J.: D. Van Nostrand Company, Inc., 1961).

[83] Ruth Miller Elson, "American Schoolboks and 'Culture' in the Nineteenth Century," in *The National Temper*, ed. Lawrence W. Levine and Robert Middlekauff (New York: Harcourt, Brace & World, Inc.), p. 119.

[84] Ruth Miller Elson, *Guardians of Tradition* (Lincoln: University of Nebraska Press, 1964), pp. 192–203, 228.

8. Arturo Prat and the Military

[1] Robert N. Burr, *By Reason or Force* (Berkeley and Los Angeles, University of California Press, 1965), p. 167.

[2] Carlos Condell, "Defensa de nuestro litoral," *Revista de Marina*, I (1885), 135–136 (hereafter cited as *RM*); Luis A. Goñi, "Comparitivo de los tipos de blindados que pertenecen a la República Arjentina y a Chile," *RM*, I (1885), 500; see also J. F. C., "Protección a la marina mercante nacional," *RM*, XXVIII (1900), 447–451; P. N. M., "La marina de guerra es indespensable a la defensa militar del país," *RM*, XLVI (1909), 90.

[3] José María Santa Cruz, "Reseña de defensa," *RM*, I (1885), 429.

[4] W. Frías, "Economías de nuestra escuadra con relación a su disciplina e instrucción," *RM*, I (1885), 452.

[5] Vicente Zegers, "Organización del personal naval en las distintas potencias del globo," *RM*, XIII (1892), 544.

[6] P. N. M., "Crónica," *RM*, XXV (1898), 1909.

[7] Encina, XX, 115; Aníbal Bravo Kendrick, *La revolución de 1891* (n.p., 1946), pp. 56–59; Maurice Hervey, *Dark Days in Chile* (London: Edward Arnold, 1891–92), pp. 132, 135, 178–181; *La Revolución de 1891, Memorias de Don Fanor Velasco* (2d ed.; Santiago: Dirección General de Talleres, 1925), pp. 291–295.

[8] *Memoria del Ministerio de Marina presentada al Congreso Nacional* (Santiago: Imprenta Nacional, 1892), pp. 62–64A; *Memoria del Ministerio de Marina presentada al Congreso Nacional* (Santiago: Imprenta Nacional, 1893), pp. 110–114.

[9] *El Porvenir*, May 21, 1892; see also Anselmo Blanlot Holley, *Perfiles de la situación* (Santiago: Imprenta Franco Chilena, 1893), pp. 15–16. Apparently there was a provision in the amnesty law which exempted anyone who had served in the War of the Pacific. This could only be implemented, however, at the pleasure of the president. The fact that Montt himself was a naval officer might explain why he was so hostile toward those officers who had participated in the sinking of the *Blanco Encalada*.

[10] *Memoria del Ministerio de Marina presentada al Congreso Nacional* (Santiago: Imprenta Nacional, 1894), pp. xxiv, xxvi, 27, 29, 48–49, 59, 61; *Memoria del Ministerio de Marina presentada al Congreso Nacional* (Santiago: Imprenta Nacional, 1895), pp. 43–55; *Memoria del Ministerio de Marina presentada al Congreso Nacional* (Santiago: Imprenta Nacional, 1896),

p. 52; *Memoria del Ministerio de Marina presentada al Congreso* (Santiago: Imprenta Nacional, 1897), p. 127.

[11] R. Beaugancy A., "Oficiales para la armada," *RM*, VIII (1889), 276–279; Orompello, "Los sueldos en la armada," *RM*, XXXVIII (1905), 131–136; "Reformas prácticas de actualidad en la marina," *RM*, XXXVIII (1905), 218; Laboremus, "Reclutamiento," *RM*, XXII (1897), 507; Lindor Pérez G., "Un programa," *RM*, XXV (1898), 1725–1727; Matías López V., "La falta de personal en nuestra armada," *RM*, XLIV (1908), 298; Arturo Fernández V., "Parte del jefe de la escuadrilla de evoluciones," *RM*, XIII (1892), 304–305; J. Federico Chaigneux, "Medida económica para el armamento o desarme de nuestra escuadra," *RM*, XIV (1893), 134; La Redacción, "Economías en los presupuestos de guerra y marina," *RM*, XXVIII (1899), 387.

[12] Manuel Cabrinety y G., "La marina mercante en Chile," *RM*, XXIV (1898), 1004–1005.

[13] P. N. Martínez, "Composición de nuestro material naval," *RM*, XXXI (1901), 143; see also E. A. S., "Los armamentos navales en Sud América," *RM*, XLI (1906), 339; J. F. C., "La protección de nuestras costas," *RM*, XXVIII (1900), 449–451.

[14] A. Brown, "Nuestras futuras construcciones navales," *RM*, XXX (1902), 347.

[15] E. A. S., *op. cit.*, pp. 337–338.

[16] "Las neuvas construcciones navales," *RM*, L (1911), 86–87.

[17] "¿Porqué alarmarse?" *RM*, L (1911), 1–2; Nauta, "La renovación de la escuadra," *RM*, XXXI (1906), 1063; Submarino, "¿En qué ha quedado la proyectada reconstrucción de nuestra armada?" *RM*, XXXX (1906), 988.

[18] "La reconstrucción de la escuadra," *RM*, XXXIX (1905), 4.

[19] *Ibid.*; see also "La renovación de nuestra escuadra y la campaña contra los Dreadnoughts," *RM*, XLIX (1910), 447.

[20] Submarino, *op. cit.*, p. 987; see also "Deberes de la hora presente," *RM*, XLVI (1909), 459.

[21] S. Valdés C., "La renovación de nuestra escuadra: Los 'Dreadnoughts' i el ABC Sud Americano," *RM*, XLIX (1910), 446–447; "La renovación . . . Dreadnoughts," 441–444.

[22] Francisco Rojas M., *Administración naval en Chile comparada* (Santiago: Imprenta Chile, 1934), pp. 94–95, 120; Carlos López U., *La historia de la marina de Chile* (Santiago: Editorial Andrés Bello, 1969), pp. 336–360.

[23] Letter of Carlos López U. to William F. Sater, November 2, 1969.

[24] *El Mercurio*, May 21, 1884.

[25] E. Chouteau, "A nuestros lectores, *RM*, I (1885), 4, 6.

[26] E. Chouteau, "Arturo Prat," *RM*, II (1886), 713.

[27] Eusebio Porto Carrero, "21 de mayo," *RM*, IV (1887), 597; Nauta, "El 21 de mayo," *RM*, XXXII (1902), 458–460; "La fecha gloriosa," *RM*, XXXVI (1904), 489–491; "El 21 de mayo," *RM*, XXXVII (1905), 455–458; "El aniversario glorioso, 21 de mayo," *RM*, XLII (1907), 449–450; "21 de mayo," *RM*, L (1911), 337–338; "21 de mayo," *RM*, LII (1912), 411–413.

[28] "El museo naval," *RM*, XLVI (1909), 610.

[29] Mario Vergara Z., "Comentarios sobre la historia de la Guerra del Pacífico," *RM*, LXIV (1919), 339.

[30] M. V. Z., "El problema de los sueldos en la armada," *RM*, LXV (1920), 212.

[31] Porto Carrero, *op. cit.*, p. 597.

[32] E. T. Chauiedez, "El 21 de mayo," *RM*, XXXI (1901), 33.

[33] Nauta, "21 de mayo," *RM*, XXXII (1902), 459.

[34] Nauta, "El 21 de mayo," *RM*, XXXVIII (1905), 455–456; "21 de mayo," *RM*, L (1911), 337–338; "21 de mayo," *RM*, LIII (1913), 420–421; "21 de mayo," *RM*, LXV (1920), 351–352; "El combate de Iquique," *RM*, LXVI (1921), 353–354.

[35] *La Unión*, May 21, 1910.

[36] *El Mercurio* of Valparaíso, May 21, 1912.

[37] Prat became almost a permanent fixture to the merchant marine. Indeed, the Liga Marítima de Chile admitted that the twenty-first of May had been deliberately chosen as its founding date because "it wanted to place itself under the shelter of the glorious spirit of the dead of that brilliant event" ("Nuestro saludo al 21 de Mayo de 1879," *Liga Marítima de Chile*, II [1916], hereafter cited as *LMC*). See also "21 de mayo," *LMC*, I (1915), 1–4. The *LMC* was published from 1914 to 1921, but I could only locate the issues from 1915 to 1916. Subsequent maritime journals, *Nautilus* and *Mar*, continued to commemorate the anniversary of Iquique and the heroism of Prat. In 1929, for example, *Nautilus* devoted almost its entire May issue to Iquique. See *Nautilus*, II (1929).

The merchant marine publications, perhaps seeking to further their own development, stressed the close relationship between the naval and merchant fleets. Celebrating the Battle of Iquique was one way of reminding the nation of the role of the merchant marine in time of war. Furthermore, these celebrations demonstrated how interdependent was Chile's growth and its fleet of merchantmen. See E. C. S., "21 de Mayo de 1879," *Nautilus*, II (1929), 1–2; E. C. S., "La marina mercante como arma auxiliar de la Armada," *Nautilus*, II (1924); Nautilus, "La marina mercante y la marina de guerra de Chile," *Nautilus*, VI (1934).

Arturo Prat and the Battle of Iquique received widespread attention in these journals: "Los héroes del Pacífico," *Nautilus*, II (1930); Edmundo González Lynch, "Prat, modelo de civismo," *Nautilus*, IV (1932); "La glorias de Chile," *Nautilus*, V (1934); "21 de mayo," *Nautilus*, VIII (1937); "La epopeya naval de Iquique," *Nautilus*, VIII (1938), 3; Enrique Bunster, "Arturo Prat, abogado," *Mar*, XX (1949), 53–58.

Nautilus was pleased to note that one of the survivors of Iquique, Admiral Arturo Wilson, was an honorary member of the Merchant Marine Association and that he was on the board of directors of one of its charitable organizations. See "Visita de honor," *Nautilus*, V (1933); Las glorias de Chile," *Nautilus*, VI (1934); Pierre Chile, "El almirante Arturo Wilson y el hogar del marinero mercante," *Nautilus*, VIII (1937), 3–5.

There was a striking difference in the way that the *Revista de Marina* and the merchant marine journals described Prat. The civilian magazines were more cosmopolitan and less nationalistic. They were, for example, among the first to honor Grau and Bolognesi, Peru's heroes of the War of the Pacific: "1879–1931," *Nautilus*, III (1931); "Los héroes del Pacífico," *Nautilus*, II (1930).

Unlike the naval journal, the merchant marine appeared to be more political. There were laudatory articles on Ibañez, for instance, including a poem which likened him to such luminaries as Spain's Primo de Rivera and Italy's Mussolini. See "Los héroes del Pacífico," *Nautilus*, II (1930), and E. C. S., "Rendención," *Nautilus*, II (1929).

The merchant marine also emphasized Prat's civilian virtues far more than their naval counterparts. See, for instance, "La epopeya naval de

Iquique," *Nautilus*, VIII (1938); "El otro Arturo Prat," *Nautilus*, XXII (1950); "Responsabilidad histórica," *Mar*, XV (1944), 35; "Significado del 21 de mayo," *Mar*, XX (1949), 51–52. Despite these differences, there were some similarities. Both the navy and the merchant marine prized Prat's sense of duty and his devotion. See, for example, "21 de Mayo de 1879," *Nautilus*, XII (1941), and "Otro 21 de Mayo," *Nautilus*, XIV (1942).

Toward the end of the 1940s, the merchant marine journal's dedication to Prat appeared to wane. *Nautilus* wrote no articles on Prat in 1943 or in 1948–1949; *Mar* made no mention of Prat from 1945 to 1948. It is quite possible that there were articles on the hero of Iquique in *Nautilus* between 1945 and 1958; however, I could not locate the issues for those years.

In summation, it appears that the merchant marine, for some of the same reasons as the navy, paid an enormous amount of attention to Arturo Prat. The hero was used, in part, to remind the public of the need for a strong merchant marine whenever possible.

38 *El Mercurio* of Valparaíso, May 21, 1914.

39 *Ibid.*

40 *La Unión*, May 21, 1917.

41 Nauta, "El 21 de mayo," *RM*, XXXII (1902), 460.

42 Nauta, "El 21 de mayo," *RM*, XXXVIII (1905), 456–457.

43 "Crónica Nacional 21 de mayo," *RM*, LVI (1914), 423.

44 Alejo Marfán, "El 21 de mayo," *RM*, LXX (1925), 486.

45 Manfredo Becerra, "El concepto del deber en las instituciones armadas," *RM*, LXXI (1926), 646.

46 Manfredo Becerra, "Espíritu de cuerpo," *RM*, LXXI (1926), 632.

47 Becerra, "El concepto . . . armadas," p. 643.

48 Manfredo Becerra, "Espíritu," *RM*, LXXII (1927), 7, 14–16.

49 *La Unión*, May 21, 1917.

50 *El Mercurio* of Santiago, May 21, 1923.

51 Ernesto González B., *El parto de los montes o la sublevación de la marinería* (Santiago: Talleres Gráficos, "Cóndor," 1932), pp. 4–7, 9–10; Edgardo von Schroeders, *El delegado del gobierno y el motín de la escuadra* (Santiago: Sociedad Imprenta y Litografía Universo, 1933), pp. 110–112.

52 González, *op. cit.*, pp. 16–17.

53 For a discussion of the various influences that may have precipitated the naval mutiny, see González, *op. cit.*, pp. 32–34; von Schroeders, *op. cit.*, pp. 9, 44, 114–115; Carlos Sáez M., *Recuerdos de un soldado* (Santiago: Biblioteca Ercilla, 1934), III, 38; Ricardo Donoso, *Alessandri Agitador y Demoledor* (México: Fondo de Cultura Económica, 1954), II, 54–55, 68; *El Mercurio* of Santiago, September 8, 9, 1931.

54 Sáez, *op. cit.*, III, 41, Leonardo Guzmán, *Un episodio olvidado de La historia nacional* (Santiago: Editorial Andrés Bello, 1966), p. 78; González, *op. cit.*, pp. 19–20.

55 von Schroeders, *op. cit.*, pp. 12–13, 106; Sáez, *op. cit.*, III, 41,; Guzmán, *op. cit.*, p. 47; González, *op. cit.*, p. 36.

56 von Schroeders, *op. cit.*, p. 5.

57 *El Mercurio* of Santiago, September 3, 1931.

58 Sáez, *op. cit.*, III, 43; González, *op. cit.*, pp. 44–58.

59 *El Mercurio* of Santiago, September 8, 1931. It is interesting to note that the editorial was entitled "The Battle is Unequal," a quotation from Prat's last speech.

60 *Ibid.*, September 8, 9, 1931.

61 Donoso, *op. cit.*, II, 58.

62 "Crónica nacional: Capellán de la Armada don Julio Ramírez," *RM*, XLIX (1933), 475.

63 Capitán de Fragata Edgardo Streeter, "Crónica," *RM*, L (1936), 391.

64 Juan Stream, "Tomando el nivel," *RM*, LXXVIII (1932), 121–124; J. Claro, "Chile en el mar," *RM*, LIII (1939), 613–615; Luis Andrade L., "Nuestro problema económico," *RM*, LIV (1940), 693–707.

65 "Iquique y Punta Gruesa," *RM*, L (1936), 293–294.

66 Edgardo von Schroeders, "Crónica," *RM*, LXXVI (1931), 647; "El día de la gloria," *RM*, XLIX (1933), 175; J. A. Ramírez, "Tradiciones navales," *RM*, XLIX (1933), 178; Capitán de Fragata Rafael Santibañez, "Crónica nacional," *RM*, L (1935), 415–416; "21 de mayo de 1879," *RM*, LI (1935), 297–300; "21 de mayo de 1879," *RM*, LI (1937), 261; "21 de mayo!!!," *RM*, LII (1938), 295–297; "21 de mayo!!!," *RM*, LIII (1939), 254; "21 de mayo," *RM*, LIV (1940), 289; "Tradición," *RM*, LV (1941), 281; "Un año más," *RM*, LVI (1942) 263; Santiago Zavala, "Crónica Nacional," *RM*, LVI (1942), 429; "21 de mayo," *RM*, LVII (1943), 2; "La gran fecha de la Armada," *RM*, LVII (1944), 352; "La gloria inmeresible de Iquique," *RM*, LIX (1945), 407; "La conmemoración del 66° aniversario de la epopeya del 21 de mayo de 1879," *RM*, LIX (1945), 559–560; "Crónica Nacional," *RM*, LIX (1945), 562; "La gesta heroica," *RM*, LXII (1948), 529; "La conmemoración del aniversario del combate naval de Iquique," *RM*, LXIV (1950), 365–366.

67 *El Boletín Militar*, published from 1894 to 1900, contained no articles commemorating the Battle of Iquique. *El Ensayo Militar*, published from 1889 to 1890, did not publish any articles on Iquique. It did, however, celebrate the anniversaries of the Battle of Arica ("Crónica Militar," *El Ensayo Militar*, I (1889), 138–140 and of San Francisco ("Monumento commemorativo de la batalla de San Francisco," *El Ensayo Militar*, I (1889), 302–305).

68 *La Revista Militar de Chile*, hereafter cited as *RMIL*, appeared from 1885 to 1890. Its issues included two articles on Arturo Prat: "24 de mayo de 1885," *RMIL*, I (1885), 117–118; and U. A. F., "Correspondencia especial para La Revista Militar, La apoteósis de los héroes," *RMIL*, V (1888), 452–472.

69 Examples of the various military battles that were commemorated: "Crónica Miliar," *El Ensayo Militar*, I (1889), 138–140; F. Pérez, "Aniversario de la Batalla de Buin," *RMIL*, II (1887), 307–311.

70 "24 de mayo de 1885," *RMIL*, I (1885), 118; Nicanor de la Sotta, "El ejército de Chile," *El Ensayo Militar*, II (1890), 306.

71 Alfredo Vial Solar," Necesidad de fortificar nuestros puertos," *Boletín Militar*, I (1894), 360 (hereafter cited as *BMIL*).

72 Until 1915 the magazine was called *Memorial del Estado Mayor del Ejército de Chile*. After that date it was entitled *Memorial del Ejército de Chile* (hereafter cited as *MEC*), regardless of when it was published. Its first article on Prat appeared in 1913: "21 de mayo de 1879," *MEC*, VIII (1913), 551–552.

73 This journal did not mention Prat in 1906–1912, 1917–1918, 1922–1923, 1926–1927, 1930, 1936, 1939–1940, 1942–1943, or 1945.

74 "21 de mayo de 1879," *MEC*, VIII (1913), 551; La Dirección, "21 de mayo de 1879," *MEC*, IX (1914), II; "21 de mayo de 1879," *MEC*, XXII (1928), 7–9; Capitán Chávez, "El 21 de mayo," *MEC*, XXVI (1933), viii.

75 La Dirección, "Iquique," *MEC*, X (1915), II.

76 Agustín Echavarría, "El 21 de mayo de 1879," *MEC*, XI (1916), III.

77 Capitán Marcial Vergara M., "El 21 de mayo," *MEC*, XXVII (1934), 401–402.

78 "Coronel Enrique Caballero ante la tumba del soldado desconocido durante la ceremonia conmemorativa del combate naval de Iquique," *MEC*, XXVIII (1935), 339.

79 *El Mercurio* of Santiago, May 21, 1919.

80 *La Bandera* appeared from 1921–1933. *La Revista del Suboficial* (hereafter cited as *RS*) was published from 1933 to 1937. *La Patria* was available from 1937 to 1944.

81 "El combate de Iquique," *La Bandera*, I (1921); *La Bandera*, II (1922); *La Bandera*, III (1923).

82 L. E. C. A., "A los héroes de Iquique," *La Bandera*, II (1922), 135–136; F. Fuenzalida A., "Combate naval de Iquique," *La Bandera*, IV (1924), 133–135; Manuel Lazo, "A los héroes de Iquique," *La Bandera*, VI (1926), 131.

83 A. de Tera M., "El alcohol i sus inconveniencias," *La Bandera*, I (1921), 87–88; Luis Albornoz M., "El alcoholismo i sus funestas consecuencias," *La Bandera*, I (1921), 231–232; E. Albano, "Perdido por el alcohol," *La Bandera*, II (1922), 50; D. Ortiz, "Las consecuencias del alcohol como microbio de la sociedad," *La Bandera*, V (1925), 111–112; "Conferencia sobre enfermedades venéreas," *La Bandera*, V (1925), 217–218; "Higiene y medicina militar," *La Bandera*, (1925), 231–234; "El terror rojo en Rusia," *La Bandera*, I (1921), 33; "La Cheka Rusa," *La Bandera*, V, (1925), 279; P. Snowden, "El mundo contra el comunismo," *La Bandera*, V (1926), 111–112; "Como llega el suboficial a imponer su autoridad," *La Bandera*, I (1921), 5–7; Muñoz V., "Nuestro peor enemigo," *La Bandera*, VI (1926), 173–174; N. Rivas D., "Ahorrémos," *La Bandera*, I (1921), 233; Luis Molina, "La patria es la expresión de todos los amores," *La Bandera*, I (1921), 31; Alvaro Rivera Matte, "La idea de Patria," *La Bandera*, II (1922), 182; Roberto Camucett, "Todo para la patria," *La Bandera*, V (1925), 171; F. Leiva Torres, "La Patria y la Bandera," *La Bandera*, V (1925), 266–267; Idaluna Arellano A., "Sacrificio por la Patria," *La Bandera*, V (1926), 9–11.

84 G. A. A., "El Sargento Aldea," *El Círculo Militar*, I (1888), 18.

85 P. J. Muñoz Feliú, "El 21 de mayo," *La Bandera*, VI (1926), 134; "La epopeya inmortal," *La Bandera*, VII (1927), 150–151; Luis Caballero C., "Ante el holocausto de Prat," *La Bandera*, IX (1929), 14; "Ecos del 21 de mayo," *RS*, XV (1936), 18–19.

86 "La infancia de Arturo Prat," *La Bandera*, VII (1927), 153; "Visitando la casa en que nació Prat," *La Bandera*, X (1930), 10–13; Miguel de Lanuza, "Anécdotas históricas chilenas," *La Bandera*, XI (1932), 6; "La infancia de Arturo Prat," *RS*, XV (1936), 26–30; "Recuerdos de Prat," *La Patria*, XXIII (1944), 27.

87 A. Muret, "La epopeya de Iquique," *La Bandera*, III (1923), 132; "La epopeya inmortal," *La Bandera*, VII (1927), 150–151; I. Téllez, "El combate de Iquique," *La Bandera*, VIII (1928), 135; "El combate naval de Iquique," *La Bandera*, X (1930), 3–4.

88 Caballero, *op. cit.*, pp. 14–16.

Conclusion

1 *Clarín* (Santiago), May 22, 1970.

2 José Luis Salcedo-Bastardo, "Economic Revolution: Agrarian Reform," in

The Liberator, Simon Bolivar: Man and Image, ed. David Bushnell (New York: Alfred A. Knopf, 1970), pp. 181–186; Juan Bosch, *Bolívar y la guerra social* (Buenos Aires: Editorial Jorge Alvarez, 1966); James Robert Levy, "The Development and the Use of the Heroic Image of José de San Martín, 1840–1900" (Ph.D. diss., University of Pennsylvania, 1964); Germán Carrera Damas, *El culto a Bolívar* (Caracas: Instituto de Antropología e Historia, 1968).

✝ BIBLIOGRAPHY

✝ BIBLIOGRAPHY

I. Primary Sources

Readers are warned that some articles appearing in the *Revista de Marina*, although published in different years, bear the same volume number. This resulted from editorial mistakes in the use of roman numerals. Anyone wishing to use these citations, therefore, would be well advised to rely upon the year of publication rather than the volume number.

A. Newspapers

La Aurora (Curicó). 1878–1879.
La Bandera Roja (Santiago). 1931–1933.
Boletín de la Guerra del Pacífico (Santiago). 1879.
El Centinela (San Carlos). 1879.
El Chicote (Valparaíso). 1876.
The Chilian Times (Valparaíso). 1876–1879.
Clarín (Santiago). 1970.
La Consigna (Santiago). 1934–1941.
El Constituyente (Copiapó). 1876–1879.
El Correo de Quillota (Quillota). 1879.
El Correo de La Serena (La Serena). 1879.
La Crítica (Santiago). 1939–1942 .
El Deber (Valparaíso). 1876–1878.
El Diario de Avisos (Santiago). 1879.
El Diario de la Guerra (Santiago). 1879.
El Diario Ilustrado (Santiago). 1902–1950.
La Discusión (Chillán). 1876–1879.
El Estandarte Católico (Santiago). 1876–1890.
La Federación Obrera (Santiago). 1922–1924.
El Ferrocarril (Santiago). 1876–1902.
El Fígaro (Valparaíso). 1879.
Frente Popular (Santiago). 1936–1939.
El Frente Único (Santiago). 1934–1936.
El Independiente (Santiago). 1878–1879.
La Justicia (Santiago). 1925–1926.
La Libertad (Valdivia). 1876–1879.
La Libertad Electoral (Santiago). 1887–1900.

El Maipo (San Bernardo). 1879.
Mefistófeles (Santiago). 1878.
El Mensajero del Pueblo (Santiago). 1876–1879.
El Mercurio (Santiago). 1900–1950.
El Mercurio (Valparaíso). 1878–1950.
Las Noticias (Talca). 1879.
La Novedades (Santiago). 1879.
El Nuevo Ferrocarril (Santiago). 1879–1880.
El Obrero (Chillán). 1879.
La Opinión (Santiago). 1932–1950.
La Opinión (Talca). 1879.
El Padre Cobos (Santiago). 1877.
La Patria (Valparaíso). 1879.
El Porvenir (Santiago). 1892–1900.
El Pueblo (Santiago). 1876.
La República (Santiago). 1876–1877.
La Revista del Sur (Concepción). 1876–1879.
El Siglo (Santiago). 1941–1948, 1953.
El Sur (Concepción). 1886–1950.
Los Tiempos (Santiago). 1879.
Trabajo (Santiago). 1933–1939.
La Unión (Valparaíso). 1885–1950.

B. Journals

La Bandera. 1921–1933.
Boletín del Consejo de Instrucción Pública. 1900–1902.
Boletín de la Sociedad Nacional de Agricultura. 1876–1879.
Boletín Militar. 1893–1904.
El Círculo Militar. 1888–1891.
Educación. 1922–1923.
La Educación Nacional. 1904–1909.
El Educador. 1890–1905.
La Enseñanza. 1902–1912.
El Ensayo Militar. 1889–1890.
La Ilustración Militar. 1899–1901.
Liga Marítima de Chile. 1915–1916.
Mar. 1944–1950.
Memorial del Ejército de Chile. 1915–1950.
Memorial del Estado Mayor del Ejército de Chile. 1906–1915.
Milicia Republicana. 1933–1935.
Nautilus. 1929–1945, 1949.
La Patria. 1938–1939; 1944–1950.
Revista de la Asociación de Educación Nacional. 1905–1909.
Revista de Educación Nacional. 1911–1926.
Revista de Educación Primaria. 1915.

Revista de Educación Primaria. 1921–1928.
Revista de Educación Secundaria. 1928.
Revista de Instrucción Primaria. 1886–1921.
Revista de Marina. 1885–1950.
Revista Militar de Chile. 1885–1896.
Revista Pedagójica. 1909–1911.
Revista del Suboficial. 1933–1937.

C. Government Documents

Chile. Congreso. Cámara de Diputados. *Proyectos sobre creación de policía rural sometidos a su consideración.* Santiago: Imprenta Nacional, 1878.
Chile. Congreso. Cámara de Diputados. *Sesiones estraordinarias de la Cámara de Diputados en 1877.* Santiago: Imprenta Nacional, 1878.
Chile. Congreso. Cámara de Diputados. *Sesiones estraordinarias de la Cámara de Diputados en 1878.* Santiago: Imprenta Nacional, 1879.
Chile. Congreso. Cámara de Diputados. *Sesiones estraordinarias de la Cámara de Diputados en 1879.* Santiago: Imprenta Nacional, 1880.
Chile. Congreso. Cámara de Diputados. *Sesiones ordinarias de la Cámara de Diputados en 1878.* Santiago: Imprenta Nacional, 1879.
Chile. Congreso. Cámara de Diputados. *Sesiones ordinarias de la Cámara de Diputados en 1879.* Santiago: Imprenta Nacional, 1880.
Chile. Congreso. Cámara de Diputados. *Sesiones ordinarias de la Cámara de Diputados en 1899.* Santiago: Imprenta Nacional, 1900.
Chile. Congreso. Cámara de Diputados. *Sesiones secretas de la Cámara de Diputados en 1879.* Santiago: Imprenta Nacional, 1880.
Chile. Congreso. Senado. *Sesiones estraordinarias de la Cámara de Senadores en 1878.* Santiago: Imprenta Nacional, 1879.
Chile. Congreso. Senado. *Sesiones estraordinarias de la Cámara de Senadores en 1879.* Santiago: Imprenta Nacional, 1880.
Chile. Congreso. Senado. *Sesiones estraordinarias de la Cámara de Senadores en 1913.* Santiago: Imprenta Nacional, 1914.
Chile. Congreso. Senado. *Sesiones ordinarias de la Cámara de Senadores en 1879.* Santiago: Imprenta Nacional, 1880.
Chile. Congreso. Senado. *Sesiones ordinarias de la Cámara de Senadores en 1914.* Santiago: Imprenta Nacional, 1915.
Chile. Congreso. Senado. *Sesiones secretas de la Cámara de Senadores en 1878.* Santiago: Imprenta Nacional, 1879.
Chile. Congreso. Senado. *Sesiones secretas de la Cámara de Senadores en 1879.* Santiago: Imprenta Nacional, 1880.
Chile. *Discurso de S. E. el Presidente de la República en la apertura del Congreso Constituyente de 1891.* Santiago: Imprenta Nacional, 1891.
Chile. *Discurso de su excelencia el Presidente de la República en la apertura del Congreso Nacional en 1877.* Santiago: Imprenta Nacional, 1877.

Chile. *Estadística comercial de la República de Chile correspondiente al año 1877.* Valparaíso: Imprenta del Universo de Gmo. Helfmann, 1878.

Chile. Ministerio de Guerra i Marina. *Memoria de Guerra i Marina presentada al Congreso Nacional por el Ministro del ramo en 1876.* Santiago de Chile: Imprenta de la Librería Mercurio, 1876.

Chile. Ministerio de Guerra i Marina. *Memoria de Guerra i Marina presentada al Congreso Nacional en sus sesiones ordinarias de 1877.* Santiago: Imprenta Nacional, 1877.

Chile. Ministerio de Guerra i Marina. *Memoria de Guerra i Marina presentada al Congreso Nacional en 1878.* Santiago: Imprenta Nacional, 1878.

Chile. Ministerio de Guerra i Marina. *Memoria de Guerra i Marina presentada al Congreso Nacional de 1879.* Santiago: Imprenta de la República de Jacinto Núñez, 1879.

Chile. Ministerio de Hacienda. *Memoria del Ministerio de Hacienda Pública presentado al Congreso Nacional en sus sesiones ordinarias de 1877.* Santiago: Imprenta Nacional, 1877.

Chile. Ministerio de Marina. *Memoria del Ministerio de Marina presentada al Congreso Nacional.* Santiago: Imprenta Nacional, 1892.

Chile. Ministerio de Marina. *Memoria del Ministerio de Marina presentada al Congreso Nacional.* Santiago: Imprenta Nacional, 1893.

Chile. Ministerio de Marina. *Memoria del Ministerio de Marina presentada al Congreso Nacional.* Santiago: Imprenta Nacional, 1894.

Chile. Ministerio de Marina. *Memoria del Ministerio de Marina presentada al Congreso Nacional.* Santiago: Imprenta Nacional, 1895.

Chile. Ministerio de Marina. *Memoria del Ministerio de Marina presentada al Congreso Nacional.* Santiago: Imprenta Nacional, 1896.

Chile. Ministerio de Marina. *Memoria del Ministerio de Marina presentada al Congreso Nacional.* Santiago: Imprenta Nacional, 1897.

Chile. Oficina Central de Estadística. *Sinópsis estadística de la República de Chile.* Santiago: Imprenta Nacional, 1917.

Great Britain. Public Record Office. *Foreign Office 16 (Chile).* Vol. 204.

Peru. Ministerio de Guerra y Marina. *Memoria del Ramo de Guerra presentada al Congreso ordinario de 1878 por el Ministerio de Guerra y Marina.* Lima: Imprenta del Estado, 1878.

United States of America. State Department. *Dispatches from U.S. Ministers to Chile, 1876–1879.*

D. Unpublished Correspondence

Correspondencia de don Rafael Sotomayor a don Aníbal Pinto. *Correspondencia de Pinto.* Vol. I.

Correspondencia de don Alberto Blest Gana a don Aniíbal Pinto. *Fondos Varios.* Vol. 413.

Correspondencia de don José Alfonso a don Aníbal Pinto. *Fondos Varios.* Vol 414.

Correspondencia de don F. Helquera a don Aníbal Pinto. *Fondos Varios.*
Vol. 414.
Correspondencia de don Justo Arteaga a don Aníbal Pinto. *Fondos
Varios.* Vol. 415.
Correspondencia de don Domingo Santa María a don Aníbal Pinto.
Fondos Varios. Vol. 416.
Correspondencia de don Roberto Souper a don Cornelio Saavedra.
Fondos Varios. Vol. 559.

E. Manuscripts

Diario de Bitácora del Buque-Corbeta *Esmeralda.* Archivo Nacional,
Biblioteca Nacional, Santiago, Chile.
Prat, Arturo. "Libreta de gastos de entradas del año 1867 con escepción
de su procedencia de su empleo." In the possession of Dr. Arturo
Prat E.
Velarde, Jorge. "El arca del marino." Archivo Nacional Biblioteca Na-
cional, Santiago, Chile.

F. Books

Ahumada Moreno, Pascual. *Guerra del Pacifico.* 8 vols. Valparaíso:
Imprenta del Progreso. Vols. I, II.
Alfonso, José A. *El parlamentario i la reforma política en Chile.* Santi-
ago: Cabeza i Cía., 1909.
Almeyda Arroyo, Elías. *Lecciones de historia, geografía y educacción
cívica.* Santiago: Imprenta Universo, 1932.
¡Al pueblo de Santiago! Santiago: Imprenta del Independiente, 1879.
Álvarez Bórquez, Pedro J. *Recopilaciones históricas.* 2d ed. Santiago:
Imprenta América, 1945.
Amunátegui, Miguel Luis. *Compendio de la historia política i eclesiás-
tica de Chile.* 11th ed. Santiago: Librería Europea de Nicasio, Ez-
querra, 1881.
———. *Compendio de la historia política i eclesiástica de Chile.* 12th
ed. Santiago: Librería Europea de Nicasio Ezquerra, 1882.
Amunátegui Solar, Domingo. *Historia de Chile.* 2 vols. Santiago: Edi-
torial Nascimento, 1933. Vol. II.
A nuestros amigos i correlijionarios políticos Imprenta La Discusión,
1879.
Arteaga Alemparte, Justo. *Historia del año 75.* Santiago: Imprenta de
El Ferrocarril, 1876.
Arteaga Alemparte, Justo, i José A. 2⁰ Espinosa. *Excelentísimo señor
Aníbal Pinto.* Santiago: Imprenta del Mercurio, 1876.
Arturo Prat i el combate de Iquique. Santiago: Imprenta Gutenberg,
1880.
Baltra Olivares, Luis, y E. Muñoz Yevenes. *Libro de lectura y redac-
ción.* Santiago: Imprenta Universitaria, 1924.

Barrientos Díaz, Pedro. *Compendio de historia de Chile.* Santiago: Imprenta y Encuadernación Lourdes, 1911.

Belmar, Francisco S. *Manual del soldado en defensa de Chile contra Bolivia.* Santiago: Imprenta de "Los Tiempos," 1879.

Benavides Santos, Arturo. *Seis años de vacaciones: Recuerdos de la Guerra del Pacífico.* Santiago: Imprenta Universo, 1929.

Bobadilla Sáenz, Armeliano. *Habitaciones para obreros.* Santiago: Imprenta, Litografía y Encuadernación Bareclona, 1907.

Borgoño, José Manuel. *Silabario.* Santiago: Imprenta y Encuadernación Fiscal de la Penetenciaría, 1918.

Boyd, R. Nelson. *Chili: Sketches of Chili and the Chilians during The War 1879–1880.* London: Wm. H. Allen & Co., 1881.

Bunster, César. *El niño chileno.* Santiago: Imprenta Universitaria, 1944. Vol. I.

Bustos Pérez, Vincente. *Historia de Chile.* 24th ed. Santiago: Imprenta y Litografía Universo, 1942.

————. *Historia de Chile.* 26th ed. Santiago: Imprenta y Litografía Universo, 1944.

————. *Historia de Chile.* 28th ed. Santiago: Imprenta y Litografía Universo, 1945.

————. *Historia de Chile.* 33rd ed. Santiago: Imprenta y Litografía Universo, 1950.

Campos, Silva. *Episodios nacionales.* Santiago: Editorial O'Higgins, 1945.

Carrasco Albano, Adolfo. *La cuestión financiera para 1877.* Santiago: Imprenta de la Librería del Mercurio, 1876.

Carrasco Bascuñán, Camilo. *El proletariado rural en Chile.* Santiago: Sociedad Imprenta y Litografía Universo, 1908.

Carlyle, Thomas. *On Heroes, Hero Worship, and the Heroic in History.* New York: Dolphin, n.d.

Castro Donoso, Luis. *De actualidad.* Santiago: Imprenta Turín. 1901.

Cifuentes, Abdón. *Memorias.* 2 vols. Santiago: Editorial Universitaria, 1936. Vol. II.

Colección H. E. C. *Historia de Chile.* Santiago: Imprenta Franco Chilena, 1913.

————. *Historia de Chile.* 18th ed. Santiago: Editorial La Salle, 1944.

Colegio de los SS. CC. *Historia de Chile.* Santiago: Imprenta Universo, 1926.

Contreras G., Arturo. *El derecho de los pobres.* Santiago: Imprenta Aurora, 1904.

Correspondencia de don Antonio Varas sobre la Guerra del Pacífico. Santiago: Imprenta Universitaria, 1918.

Cristi, Mauricio. *Lectura patriótica: Crónica de la última guerra.* Santiago: Imprenta de El Correo, 1888.

Darío, Rubén. "Canto épico a las glorias de Chile." In *Obras escogidas de Rubén Darío publicadas en Chile*. Ed. Julio Saavedra Molina and Erwin K. Mapes. Santiago: Imprenta y Litografía Universo, 1939.

De un nuevo partido político en Chile. Talca: Imprenta de "La Opiniŏn," 1875.

Díaz Lira, Javier. *Observaciones sobre la cuestión social en Chile*. Santiago: Imprenta Chile, 1904.

Díaz Meza, Aurelio. *Historia de Chile*. Santiago: Sociedad Imprenta-Litografía Barcelona, 1914.

Encina, Francisco Antonio. *La educación y el liceo*. Santiago: Editorial Universitaria, 1962.

———. *Nuestra inferioridad económica*. Santiago: Imprenta Universitaria, 1912.

Errázuriz, Crescente. *Algo de lo que he visto. Memorias de don Crescente Errázuriz*. Santiago: Editorial Nascimento, 1934.

Esposición a nuestros conciudadanos. Santiago, 1878.

Frías V., Francisco. *Historia de Chile*. Santiago: Editorial Nascimento, 1949.

Galdames, Luis. *Educación económica e intelectual*. Santiago: Imprenta Universitaria, 1912.

———. *Estudio de la historia de Chile*. 2d ed. Santiago: Imprenta Universitaria, 1913.

———. *Estudio de la historia de Chile*. 6th ed. Santiago: Imprenta Universitaria, 1925.

———. *Temas pedagójicos*. Santiago: Imprenta Universitaria, 1913.

Garmendia, Félix. *Las elecciones infames*. Santiago: Imprenta de "El Independiente," 1876.

Gonzales, F. S. *Pequeña reseña histórica de Chile*. 2d ed. Antofagasta: Imprenta Castellana, 1921.

González, Marcial. *Estudios económicos*. Santiago: Imprenta Gutenberg, 1889.

González B., Ernesto. *El parto de los montes o la sublevación de la marinería*. Santiago: Talleres Gráficos "Cóndor," 1932.

González von Marées, Jorge. *El mal de Chile*. Santiago: Talleres Gráficos "Portales," 1940.

———. *El problema del hambre*. Santiago: Ediciones Ercilla, 1937.

Guía del elector liberal para las elecciones jenerales de 1876. Santiago: Imprenta de la Librería del Mercurio, 1875.

Guzmán, Leonardo. *Un episodio olvidado de la historia nacional*. Santiago: Editorial Andrés Bello, 1966.

Guzmán Maturana, Manuel. *Libro de lectura*. 8th ed. Santiago: Editorial Minerva, 1948. Vol. II.

Harriet, Ramón 2°. *La verdad de hoi*. Valparaíso: Imprenta de La Patria, 1875.

Hegel, G. W. F. *Lectures on the Philosophy of History*. Trans. J. Sibree. London: George Bell, 1881.

Hertel, Máximo. *Los dirigentes y la ruina de Chile*. Santiago: Imprenta Universitaria, 1915.

Hervey, Maurice. *Dark Days in Chile.* London: Edward Arnold, 1891–1892.

Historia de Chile. 5th ed. Santiago: Librería y Editorial Escolar, n.d. Vol. II.

Hook, Sidney. *The Hero in History.* Boston: Beacon Press, 1955.

Ibáñez, Adolfo. *La diplomacia chileno-argentina, una contestación.* Santiago: Imprenta de Los Teimpos, 1879.

Ibañez, Maximiliano. *El régimen parlamentario en Chile.* Santiago: Imprenta Cervantes, 1908.

König, Abraham. *La constitución de 1833 en 1913.* Santiago: Imprenta Santiago, 1913.

Larraín Zañartu, Joaquín. *El 21 de Mayo. Homenaje de "La Patria" a los héroes de "La Esmeralda" y "La Covadonga" en el primer aniversario del glorioso combate de Iquique.* Valparaíso: Imprenta de "La Patria," 1880.

Lecciones de historia de Chile para el uso de las escuelas públicas. Santiago: Imprenta Cervantes, 1887.

Lefevre M., Ernesto E. *Arqueo.* Santiago: Imprenta y Encuadernación "El Globo," 1907.

La Liga de Acción Cívica, Su fundación en Santiago de Chile. Santiago: Imprenta de A. Hinojosa P., 1912.

MacIver, Enrique. *Discurso sobre la crisis moral de la República.* Santiago: Imprenta Moderna, 1900.

Manifiesto de los secretarios del directorio jeneral del partido conservador dirijen a sus amigos i correligionarios políticos. Santiago: Imprenta de El Independiente, 1878.

Mario, Roberto [Carlos Pinto Durán]. *Cómo se hunde el país! Desgobierno, clericalismo, oligarquía, corrupción, decadencia.* Santiago: Imprenta San Francisco, 1917.

Maza, José. *Sistemas de sufragio i cuestión electoral.* 2d ed. Santiago: Imprenta La Ilustración, 1913.

Méndez M., Javier. *Lecciones históricas de Chile.* Santiago: Imprenta y Encuadernación Chile, 1906.

———. *Lecciones históricas de Chile.* 4th ed. Santiago: Imprenta y Encuadernación Chile. 1912.

Millar, Walterio. *Historia de Chile ilustrada.* Concepción: Imprenta Hispano-Chileno, 1930.

———. *Historia de Chile Ilustrada.* Santiago: Ediciones Orbe, 1938.

Muñoz Donoso, Esteban. *Compendio de historia de América i Chile.* 2d ed. Santiago: Imprenta de R. Varela, 1881.

———. *Compendio de historia de América i Chile.* 4th ed. Santiago: Imprenta de R. Varela, 1890.

———. *Compendio de historia de América i Chile.* 5th ed. Santiago: Imprenta de R. Varela, 1895.

———. *Compendio de historia de América i Chile.* 6th ed. Santiago: Imprenta de R. Varela, 1902.

————. *Compendio de la historia de Chile.* Santiago: Imprenta Emilio Pérez L., 1898.
————. *Compendio de la historia de Chile.* 2d ed. Santiago: Imprenta Emilio Pérez L., 1905.
Muñoz Yurazeck, Marfisa. *Arturo Prat.* Santiago: Imprenta Universitaria, 1914.
Murillo, Adolfo. *La mortalidad urbana en Chile.* Santiago: Imprenta y Encuadernación Roma, 1896.
Oyarzún, Enrique. *Discursos parlamentarios.* Concepción: Tipografía y Litografía José V. Sonlodre, 1913.
Palacios, Nicolás. *Decadencia del espíritu de nacionalidad.* Santiago: Salón Central de la Universidad, 1908.
————. *Nacionalización de la industria salitrera.* Santiago: Salón Central de la Universidad. 1908.
Partes oficiales del combate naval de Iquique. Imprenta de la Armada, 1912.
Peralta Peralta, Juan. *Arturo Prat Chacón: Héroe del mar.* Valparaíso: Imprenta de la Escuela Naval, 1953.
Pérez P., Luis. *Lecciones de Historia de Chile.* 2d ed. Santiago: Editorial Minerva, 1921.
————. *Lecciones de Historia de Chile.* 5th ed. Santiago: Imprenta Universo, 1924.
————. *Lecciones de Historia de Chile.* 6th ed. Santiago: Imprenta Universo, 1925.
————. *Lecciones de Historia de Chile.* 7th ed. Santiago: Imprenta Universo, 1926.
————. *Lecciones de Historia de Chile.* 9th ed. Santiago: Editorial Nascimento, 1927.
————. *Lecciones de Historia de Chile.* 10th ed. Santiago: Editorial Nascimento, 1931.
————. *Lecciones de Historia de Chile.* 11th ed. Santiago: Imprenta Universo, 1932.
————. *Lecciones de Historia de Chile.* 13th ed. Santiago: Imprenta Universo, 1934.
————. *Lecciones de Historia de Chile.* 14th ed. Santiago: Imprenta Universo, 1936.
————. *Lecciones de Historia de Chile.* 15th ed. Santiago: Editorial Nascimento, 1937.
————. *Lecciones de Historia de Chile.* 18th ed. Santiago: Imprenta Universo, 1942.
Pérez Yáñez, Ramón. *Forjadores de Chile.* Santiago: Editorial Zig-Zag, 1953.
Pinochet Le-Brun, Tancredo. *La conquista de Chile en el siglo XX.* Santiago: Imprenta "La Ilustración," 1909.
Pinto, Armando. *Enseñanza de la moral: Dedica a los niños 1, 2, y 3 años de las escuelas primarias.* Santiago: Imprenta y Encuadernación "Claret," 1923.

————. *Historia de Chile.* 4th ed. Santiago: Imprenta Universo, 1926.

————. *Historia de Chile.* 6th ed. Santiago: Imprenta Universo, 1927.

Plekanov, George. *The Role of the Individual in History.* New York: International Publishers, 1967.

Prat Chacón, Arturo. *Observaciones a la lei electoral vijente.* Valparaíso: Imprenta de El Mercurio, 1876.

Préndez, Pedro Nolasco. *La Esmeralda.* Santiago: Imprenta de la República de Jacinto Núñez, 1879.

Ramírez, J. T. *Historia de Chile.* 2d ed. Santiago: Editorial Nascimento, 1937.

Ravinés, Eudocio. *The Yenan Way.* New York: Scribner, 1951.

Reclamo de nulidad de las elecciones del departamento de Casablanca. Santiago: Imprenta de la Librería del Mercurio, 1876.

Reclamo de nulidad de las elecciones del departamento de Putaendo. Santiago: Imprenta de la Librería del Mercurio, 1876.

Reclamo de nulidad de las elecciones del departamento de Quillota. Santiago: Imprenta de la Librería del Mercurio, 1876.

Recopilación de leyes por orden numérico arreglada por la secretaría del Consejo del Estado. Santiago: Litografía y Encuadernación Fiscal de la Penitenciaría, 1917. Vol. VIII.

Representación a la Excma. Comsisión Conservadora. Santiago: Imprenta de la República de J. Núñez, 1876.

Resumen de la hacienda pública desde 1833 hasta 1914. London: Spottiswoode & Co. Ltd., 1914.

La Revolución de 1891: Memorias de don Fanor Velasco. 2d ed. Santiago: Dirección General de Talleres, 1925.

Riquelme, Daniel. *Compendio de historia de Chile.* Valparaíso: Librería e Imprenta Sud Americana de Barra i Cía., 1899.

Roa B., Alejo. *Sexto libro de lectura.* 2d ed. Santiago: Editorial Salesiana, n.d.

Rodríguez Mendoza, Emilio. *Ante la decadencia.* Santiago: Imprenta Moderna, 1899.

Rosales, Justo Abel. *La apoteósis de Arturo Prat i de sus compañeros de heroísmo muertos por la patria el 21 de mayo de 1879.* Santiago: Imprenta de los Debates, 1888.

Rozas, Manuel. *Diccionario cívico chileno.* Santiago: Talleres Gráficos "Cóndor," 1928.

Sáez, Carlos. *Recuerdos de un soldado.* 3 vols. Santiago: Biblioteca Ercilla, 1934. Vol. III.

Salas, Darío. *El problema nacional.* Santiago: Imprenta i Litografía Universo, 1917.

Sanfuentes, Aníbal. *Discurso en la convención celebrada en Santiago el 15 de octubre de 1899.* Santiago: Imprenta de la Alianza Liberal, 1899.

Sierra M., L., y Eduardo Moore. *La mortalidad de los niños en Chile.* Valparaíso: Imprenta Central, 1895.

Silva, Alejandro. *Historia de Chile*. Santiago: Librería de la Federación de Obras Católicas, 1915.

Simpson, Juan. *Algunos rasgos inéditos de la personalidad de Arturo Prat*. Valparaíso: Imprenta Victoria, 1925.

Spencer, Herbert. *The Study of Sociology*. London: Kegan Paul, 1884.

Tornero L., Orestes. *Compendio de la historia de Chile*. 3d ed. Valparaíso i Santiago: Librerías del Mercurio, 1880.

————. *Compendio de la historia de Chile*. 4th ed. Valparaíso: Librería del Mercurio, 1882.

————. *Compendio de la historia de Chile*. 5th ed. Valparaíso: Librería del Mercurio, 1896.

Toro, Gaspar. *Compendio de historia de América i especialmente de Chile*. Santiago: Imprenta Nacional, 1881.

————. *Compendio de historia de América i especialmente de Chile*. 5th ed. Santiago: Imprenta Nacional, 1893.

————. *Compendio de historia de América i especialmente de Chile*. 6th ed. Santiago: Imprenta Nacional, 1904.

————. *Compendio de historia de América i especialmente de Chile*. 7th ed. Santiago: Imprenta Nacional, 1910.

————. *Compendio de historia de Chile*. 2d ed. Santiago: n.p., n.d.

————. *Compendio de historia de Chile*. 3d ed. Santiago: n.p., 1885.

————. *Compendio de historia de Chile*. 5th ed. Santiago: n.p., 1887.

————. *Compendio de historia de Chile*. 6th ed. Santiago: n.p., 1909.

Trotsky, Leon. *The History of the Russian Revolution*. Trans. Max Eastman. Ann Arbor: University of Michigan Press, 1932.

Urzúa, Miguel Rafael. *Prat—drama original en tres actos y en verso*. Santiago: Imprenta "El Globo," 1914.

Valdés Cange, Julio. *Cartas al excelentísimo señor don Pedro Montt sobre la crisis moral de Chile en sus relaciones con el problema económico de la conversión metálica*. Valparaíso: Imprenta Universo, 1909.

————. *Sinceridad: Chile íntimo de 1910*. 2d ed. Santiago: Imprenta Universitaria, 1910.

Valdés Vergara, Francisco. *Historia de Chile para la enseñanza primaria*. 2d ed. Valparaíso: Imprenta del Universo de Gmo. Helfmann, 1898.

————. *Historia de Chile para la enseñanza primaria*. 3d ed. Valparaíso: Imprenta del Universo de Gmo. Helfmann, 1904.

————. *Historia de Chile para la enseñanza primaria*. 17th ed. Valparaíso: Imprenta del Universo de Gmo. Helfmann, 1925.

————. *Historia de Chile para la enseñanza primaria*. 20th ed. Valparaíso: Imprenta del Universo de Gmo. Helfmann, 1927.

————. *Lecturas infantiles preparadas para niños de ocho a doce años de edad*. Santiago: Imprenta Cervantes, 1888.

Valdés Vicuña, Samuel. *La solución del gran problema del día*. Santiago: Imprenta i Encuadernación Roma, 1895.

Valdivieso Araoz, Alberto. *Oportunistas y doctrinarios ante la opinión pública.* Santiago: Imprenta de "El Correo," 1896.

Vásquez, Anjel T. *Nuestra historia nacional al alcance del pueblo.* Santiago: Imprenta La Tracción, 1926.

———. *Nuestra historia nacional al alcance del pueblo.* 2d ed. Santiago: Imprenta La Tracción, 1928.

Vásquez Jara, Efraím. *El trabajador agrícola chileno ante la lei y ante la sociedad.* Santiago: Imprenta y Encuadernación Antigua Iglesia, 1913.

Vergara Ruiz, Eduardo. *El pago del salario en Chile.* Santiago: Litografía y Encuadernación Barcelona, 1914.

Vicuña, Ánjel. *La convención liberal democrática celebrada en Santiago el 28 de noviembre de 1896.* Santiago: Imprenta y Encuadernación Roma, 1896.

Vicuña, Bernardo. *Biografía completa de Arturo Prat.* Valparaíso: Imprenta del Mercurio, 1879.

[Vicuña Mackenna, Benjamín]. *La asamblea de los notables por un liberal sin nota.* Santiago: Imprenta de "El Independiente," 1875.

———. *Las dos Esmeraldas.* Santiago: Imprenta del Centro Editorial, 1879.

———. *El veintiuno de mayo de 1879.* Edited by General Pedro J. Muñoz Feliú. Santiago: Imprenta del Ministerio de Guerra, 1930.

Villalobos, Domingo. *Lecciones de historia de Chile.* Santiago: Imprenta Cervantes, 1893.

———. *Lecciones de historia de Chile.* 2d ed. Santiago: Imprenta y Encuadernación Barcelona, 1895.

———. *Lecciones de historia de Chile.* 3d ed. Santiago: Imprenta i Encuadernación Barcelonia, 1896.

———. *Lecciones de historia de Chile.* 4th ed. Santiago: Imprenta y Encuadernación Barcelona, 1898.

———. *Lecciones de historia de Chile.* 5th ed. Santiago: Imprenta y Encuadernación Barcelona, 1911.

———. *Tratado elemental de historia de Chile.* Santiago: Imprenta y Encuadernación Barcelona, 1896.

———. *Tratado elemental de historia de Chile.* 2d ed. Santiago: Imprenta i Encuadernación Barcelona, 1898.

———. *Tratado elemental de historia de Chile.* 3d ed. Santiago: Imprenta y Encuadernación Barcelona, 1903.

———. *Tratado elemental de historia de Chile.* 5th ed. Santiago: Imprenta y Encuadernación Barcelona, 1908.

Villalón Madrid, Lorenzo. *Combate naval de Iquique, Valparaíso. 21 de mayo de 1925.* Valparaíso: Fisher e Ihnen impresores, 1925.

von Schroeders, Edgardo. *El delegado del gobierno y el motín de la escuadra.* Santiago: Imprenta y Litografía Universo, 1933.

Williams Rebolledo, Juan. *Operaciones de la escuadra chilena mientras estuvo a las órdenes del contra-almirante Williams Rebolledo.* Valparaíso: Imprenta Progreso, 1882.

X. [pseud.]. *La Patria está en peligro.* 1879.
X. X. [pseud.]. *La crisis económica.* La Serena: Imprenta Encuadernación y Litografía Americana, 1913.

G. Articles

Aeta Astorga, Daniel. "Paseos escolares," *Revista de Instrucción Primaria,* XV (1901), 185–202.
Alarcón S., Francisco 2⁰. "Clase de historia de Chile," *Revista de Instrucción Primaria,* XIV (1900), 477–484.
Albano, E. "Perdido por el alcohol," *La Bandera,* II (1921), 50.
Albornoz G., J. "La educación del carácter," *La Educación Nacional,* IV (1908), 153–156.
Albornoz M., Luis. "El alcoholismo i sus funestas consequencias," *La Bandera,* I (1921), 231–232.
[Altamirano, Eulogio]. "Cartas a don Aníbal Pinto," *Revista Chilena,* XIII (1921), 225–255.
Alvarez B., Arcadio. "Nuestra independencia económica," *La Educación Nacional,* VIII (1912), 4–6.
———. "Los nuevos libertadores de Chile," *Revista de Eduación Nacional,* XII (1916), 176–181.
Andrade L., Luis. "Nuestro problema económico," *Revista de Marina,* LIV (1940), 693–707.
"El aniversario del combate de Iquique en la Escuela Normal de Preceptores de Santiago," *El Educador,* VI (1896), 22–26.
"El aniversario glorioso. 21 de mayo," *Revista de Marina,* XLII (1907), 449–450.
"Aniversario patrio: el 21 de mayo," *Revista Pedagójica,* VII (1911), 146–150.
Arellano A., Idaluna. "Sacrificio por la Patria," *La Bandera,* V (1926), 9–11.
Arellano, E. "La Patria," *El Educador,* V (1895), 97–98.
Arias Lillo, Anjel A. "Programa de instrucción cívica, economía política, i social para la Escuela Normal de Preceptores de Curicó," *La Educación Nacional,* IV (1908), 324–333.
Arrendondo, Oscar. "Crónica nacional," *Revista de Marina,* LVIII (1944), 562–564.
Beaugancy A., R. "Oficiales para la armada," *Revista de Marina,* VIII (1889), 276–279.
Becerra, Manfredo. "El concepto del deber en las instituciones armadas," *Revista de Marina,* LXXI (1926), 643–648; LXXI (1926), 795–819.
———. "Espíritu de cuerpo," *Revista de Marina,* LXXI (1926), 627–643; LXXII (1927), 1–19.
Berríos, Luis. "El maestro i el momento nacional," *Revista de Educación Nacional,* XV (1919), 139–144.

Bórquez Solar, Antonio. "La epopeya olvidada," *Revista Pedagójica,* V (1909), 161–163.

———. "Prat i su pléyade," *Revista de Educación Primaria,* XXXI (1921), 204–207.

Brown, A. "Nuestras construcciones navales," *Revista de Marina,* XXX (1902), 347–354.

Bunster, Enrique. "Arturo Prat, abogado," *Mar,* XX (1949), 53–58.

Caballero C., Luis. "Ante el holocausto de Prat," *La Bandera,* IX (1929), 14–16.

Cabrinety y G., Manuel. "La marina mercante en Chile," *Revista de Marina,* XXIV (1899), 1004–1007.

Camucett, Roberto. "Toda para la patria," *La Bandera,* V (1925), 171.

Cannobio, Enrique. "Defensa de la Escuela de Artes i Oficios," *Revista de Educación Nacional,* X (1914), 414–416.

———. "Discursos," *Revista de Educación Nacional,* X (1914), 414–416.

Carrasco Bascuñán, Camilo. "El proletariado rural en Chile." In *Contribución del Centro Industrial y Agrícola al IV Congreso Científico y 1° Pan Americano,* pp. 35–45. Santiago: Imprenta y Litografía Universo, 1908.

Carriola, Luis A. "El 21 de Mayo en crónicas," *Revista de Educación Primaria,* XXXI (1921), 186–188.

"Carta de David Montt a Sr. Dr. Carlos Fernández Peña," *Revista Pedagójica,* VI (1910), 162.

Chaigneux, J. Federico. "Medida económica para el armamento o desarme de nuestra escuadra," *Revista de Marina,* XIV (1893), 134–138.

Chauiedez, E. T. "El 21 de mayo," *Revista de Marina,* XXXI (1901), 32–42.

Chávez, Capitán. "El 21 de mayo," *Memorial del Ejército de Chile,* XXVI (1933), vii–viii.

"La Checka Rusa," *La Bandera,* V (1925), 275.

Chile, Pierre. "El almirante Arturo Wilson y el hogar de la marina mercante," *Nautilus,* VIII (1937), 3–5.

Chouteau, E. "A nuestros lectores," *Revista de Marina,* I (1885), 1–7.

———. "Arturo Prat," *Revista de Marina,* II (1886), 711–713.

Cid, Pío. "La boya de la *Esmeralda,"* *Revista de Instrucción Primaria,* XXV (1911), 255–259.

Claro, J. "Chile en el mar," *Revista de Marina,* LIII (1939), 613–615.

Claro Velasco, Benjamín. "La lección del héroe. Mayo de 1943." In *Mensajes a los niños de Chile.* Santiago: Imprenta de la Universidad de Chile, 1945. Pp. 27–37.

Colombo, I. D. Romildo. "Discurso patriótico pronunciado el 21 de mayo," *La Enseñanza,* I (1902), 108–113.

"El combate de Iquique," *La Bandera,* I (1921), 21.

"El combate naval de Iquique," *La Bandera,* X (1930), 3–4.

"El combate de Iquique," *Revista de Marina,* LXVI (1921), 353–354.

"El combate de Iquique el 21 de mayo y la excursión de la escuadra al Callao," *Revista Chilena*, XIV (1922), 30–38.

"Como llega el sub oficial a imponer su autoridad," *La Bandera*, I (1921), 5–7.

"El Congreso Nacional de Enseñanza Secundaria," *Revista de Educación Nacional*, VIII (1912), 431–506.

Condell, Carlos. "Defensa de nuestro litoral," *Revista de Marina*, I (1885), 134–138.

"Conferencias sobre enfermedades venéreas," *La Bandera*, V (1925), 217–218.

"El Congreso Nacional de enseñanza secundaria," *Revista de Educación Nacional*, XIII (1912), 431–506.

"La conmemoración del aniversario del combate naval de Iquique," *Revista de Marina*, LXIV (1950), 365–366.

"La conmemoración del 66⁰ aniversario de la epopeya del 21 de mayo de 1879," *Revista de Marina*, LIX (1945), 559–560.

"Coronel Enrique Caballero ante la tumba del soldado desconocido durante la ceremonia conmemorativa del combate naval de Iquique," *Memorial del Ejército de Chile*, XXVIII (1935), 337–341.

"Correspondencia de don Rafael Sotomayor con don Aníbal Pinto sobre la Guerra del Pacífico," *Revista Chilena*, XV (1922), 178–193.

"Correspondencia de don Rafael Sotomayor con don Aníbal Pinto durante la Guerra del Pacífico," *Revista Chilena*, XV (1922), 285–294.

"Correspondencia de don Rafael Sotomayor con el General don Justo Arteaga Alemparte y don Aníbal Pinto sobre la Guerra del Pacífico," *Revista Chilena*, XVII (1924), 410–430.

"Crónica militar," *El Ensayo Militar*, I (1889), 138–140.

"Crónica nacional," *Revista de Marina*, L (1934), 415–416.

"Crónica nacional," *Revista de Marina*, LIX (1945), 559–562.

"Crónica nacional: 21 de Mayo," *Revista de Marina*, LIV (1914), 423–424.

"Crónica pedagógica," *Revista Pedagógica*, V (1909), 175–177.

"Crónica pedagógica, La conquista de Chile en el Siglo XX," *Revista Pedagógica*, V (1909), 180.

Daza Lira, Rafael Luis. "Necesidades de la instrucción primaria," *Revista de Educación Nacional*, IX (1913), 313–316.

"Deberes de la hora presente," *Revista de Marina*, XLVI (1909), 457–460.

"Decadencia de la Raza," *Revista de Educación Nacional*, XII (1916), 145–148.

De la Sotta, Nicanor. "El ejército de Chile," *El Ensayo Militar*, II (1890), 306.

de Teras M., A. "El alcohol i sus inconveniencias," *La Bandera*, I (1921), 87–88.

"El día de la gloria," *Revista de Marina*, XLIX (1933), 174–176.

"El 18 de Setiembre i el 21 de Mayo," *La Enseñanza*, VII (1909), 172–173.

"1879–1931," *Nautilus*, III (1931).

Dirección. "Iquique, 21 de mayo de 1879," *Memorial del Ejército de Chile*, X (1914), I–II.

La Dirección. "21 de mayo de 1879," *Memorial del Ejército de Chile*, IX (1914), I–II

E. A. S. "Los armamentos navales en Sud América," *Revista de Marina*, XLI (1906), 337–342.

E. C. S. "La marina mercante como arma auxiliar de la Armada," *Nautilus*, II (1924).

————. "Rendención," *Nautilus*, II (1929).

————. "21 de mayo de 1879," *Nautilus*, II (1929), 1–2.

Echavarría, Agustín. "El 21 de mayo de 1879," *Memorial del Ejército de Chile*, XI (1916), I–IV.

"Ecos del 21 de mayo," *Revista de Suboficial*, XV (1936), 17–20.

"Educación cívica," *Revista de Educación Nacional*, XI (1915), 187–189.

"Educación económica del país," *Revista de Educación Nacional*, VII (1911), 400–404.

Edwards, Monseñor. "Por la salvación de la raza," *Revista de Educación Nacional*, XIII (1917), 436–453.

Encina, Francisco Antonio. "Reforma de nuestra educación nacional," *Revista Pedagógica*, VII (1911), 4–6.

Enlufe, José S. "Programas," *La Educación Nacional*, V (1909), 117–122.

"La epopeya inmortal," *La Bandera*, VII (1927), 150–151.

"La epopeya naval de Iquique," *Nautilus*, VIII (1938).

"Fallecimiento de don José Bernardo Suárez," *La Enseñanza*, XI (1912), 43–52.

"La fecha gloriosa," *Revista de Marina*, XXXVI (1904), 489–491.

Fernández Peña, Carlos. "Defensa de la Escuela de Artes i Oficios," *Revista de Educación Nacional*, X (1914), 353–365.

————. "Necreolojía a don José Bernardo Suárez," *Revista de Educación Nacional*, VIII (1912), 165–167.

Fernández V., Arturo. "Parte del jefe de la escuadrilla de evoluciones," *Revista de Marina*, XIII (1892), 290–305.

Frías, W. "Economías de nuestra escuadra con relación a su disciplina e instrucción," *Revista de Marina*, I (1885), 452–459.

Fuenzalida A., F. "Combate naval de Iquique," *La Bandera*, IV (1924) 133–135.

G. A. A. "El Sargento Aldea," *El Círculo Militar*, I (1888), 17–18.

Galdames, Luis. "Los movimientos obreros en Chile." In *Ciencias Económicas y Sociales*. Volúmen VIII de *los Trabajos del Cuarto Congreso Científico (1º Pan-Americano)*, ed. Julio Philippi. 14 vols. Santiago: Imprenta, Litografía y Encuadernación "Barcelona," 1911. Pp. 361–381.

————. "El nacionalismo en la educación," *Revista de Instrucción Primaria*, XXVI (1912), 121–142.

"La gesta heroica," *Revista de Marina*, LXII (1948), 529.
"La gloria inmarcesible de Iquique," *Revista de Marina*, LIX (1945), 407.
"Las glorias de Chile," *Nautilus*, VI (1934).
Goñi, Luis A. "Comparativo de los tipos de blindados que pertenecen a la República Arjentina y a Chile," *Revista de Marina*, I (1885), 500–515.
González Lynch, Edmundo. "Prat, modelo de civismo," *Nautilus*, IV (1932).
González Rocuant, Félix. "Qué es la Patria?" *Revista de Educación Nacional*, XII (1916), 179–181.
"La gran fecha de la Armada," *Revista de Marina*, LVIII (1944), 351–353.
"Un gran movimiento chileno para salvar la raza i proteger el hogar," *Revista de Educación Nacional*, XVI (1920), 391–417.
"La guerra al alcohol," *Revista de Instrucción Primaria*, XIV (1900), 449–456.
Hernández, Victor. "El 21 de Mayo en la Escuela Normal de Preceptores de Santiago," *Revista de Instrucción Primaria*, IV (1890), 618–623.
"Los héreos del Pacífico," *Nautilus*, II (1930).
"Higiene y medicina militar," *La Bandera*, V (1925), 231–234.
Ignotus (Marcial González). "El meeting de obreros en Santiago," *Revista Chilena*, VII (1877), 281–290.
"La infancia de Arturo Prat," *La Bandera*, VII (1927), 153.
"La infancia de Arturo Prat," *Revista de Suboficial*, XV (1936), 26–30.
"Iquique y Punta Gruesa," *Revista de Marina*, L (1936), 293–294.
J. F. C. "Protección a la marina mercante nacional," *Revista de Marina*, XXVIII (1900), 337–341.
———. "La protección de nuestras costas," *Revista de Marina*, XXVIII (1900), 449–451.
Johnson, Ana. "Educación cívica," *La Revista Pedagógica*, III (1907), 236–239.
L. E. C. A. "A los héroes de Iquique," *La Bandera*, II (1922), 135–136.
Labarca H., Amanda. "Educación nacional," *Revista de la Asociación de Educación Nacional*, III (1907), 118–122.
Laboremus. "Reclutamiento," *Revista de Marina*, XII (1897), 507–514.
Lagos, Gutenberg C. "Estudios sobre la educación moral," *Revista de Instrucción Primaria*, XVIII (1904), 22–29.
Lanuza, Miguel de. "Anécdotas históricas chilenas," *La Bandera*, XI (1932), 5–7.
Lazo O., Manuel. "A los héroes de Iquique," *La Bandera*, VI (1926), 131.
Leiva Torres, F. "La Patria y la Bandera," *La Bandera*, V (1925), 266–267.
Lenz, Rodolfo. "Memoria sobre las tendencias de la enseñanza del idioma patrio en Chile," *El Educador*, X (1902), 65–70.

Lira, Adela. "Sección práctica," *La Educación Nacional*, IV (1907), 18–23.

López Pinto, Ramón L. "Memorias del alumno normalista pensionista en los Estados Unidos," *Revista de Instrucción Primaria*, III (1888), 352–375.

López V., Matías. "La falta de personal en nuestra Armada," *Revista de Marina*, XLIV (1908), 298–301.

M. V. Z. "El problema de los sueldos en la armada," *Revista de Marina*, LXV (1920), 199–216.

Machuca, Francisco A. "Principios de instrucción cívica," *Revista de Instrucción Primaria*, XX (1906), 92–100.

Madrid, Juan. "La instrucción cívica debe figurar en el programa de estudios de las escuelas elementales i superiores," *Revista de Instrucción Primaria*, IV (1891), 705–709.

"La marina mercante y la marina de guerra de Chile," *Nautilus*, VI (1934).

Marfán, Alejo. "El 21 de mayo," *Revista de Marina*, LXX (1925), 484–487.

Martínez, P. N. "Composición de nuestro material naval," *Revista de Marina*, XXXI (1901), 143–145.

Marx, Karl. Preface to "A Contribution to the Critique of Political Economy." In Karl Marx and Frederick Engels, *Selected Works in Two Volumes* (Moscow: Foreign Languages Publishing House, 1955). I, 361–366.

Maza, Julio. "El sistema de elección presidencial," *Revista de Educación Nacional*, XI (1915), 173–179.

"Memoria del Presidente de la Asociación de Educación Nacional, correspondiente a 1911," *Revista de Educación Nacional*, VII (1912), 67–104.

"Memoria del Presidente de la Asociación de Educación Nacional," *Revista de Educación Nacional*, IX (1913), 50–139.

Méndez, Rodolfo. "Enseñanza anti alcohólica," *La Enseñanza*, I (1902), 58–60.

"Miscelánea: Escuela Normal de Preceptores de Santiago," *El Educador*, VII (1897), 26–27.

Molina, Juan A. "Las enfermedades venéreas," *La Bandera*, V (1926), 57–58.

Molina, Luis. "La Patria es la expresión de todos los amores," *La Bandera*, I (1921), 31.

"Monumento conmemorativo de la batalla de San Francisco," *El Ensayo Militar*, I (1889), 302–305.

Morales, F. J. "Iquique en la Escuela Normal de Preceptores de Santiago," *Revista de Instrucción Primaria*, VI (1892), 631–635.

Morales Vera, D. P. "La instrucción cívica en la escuela primaria," *Revista de Instrucción Primaria*, IX (1895), 558–561.

Muñoz, Jermán. "Necesidades de fundar una sociedad que se ocupe de proteger a la Raza Chilena," *Revista Pedagógica*, VI (1910), 201–206.

Muñoz, José María. "El deber," *Revista de Instrucción Primaria*, XXIII (1909), 321–329.

———. "La enseñanza de la historia i la formación del carácter," *Revista de Instrucción Primaria*, VIII (1893), 65–70.

———. "Observaciones sobre la enseñanza de la instrucción cívica, la economía doméstica," *Revista de Instrucción Primaria*, VIII (1894), 577–588.

———. "La Patria," *Revista de Instrucción Primaria*, XXIII (1909), 417–429.

———. "El patriotismo en la escuela," *Revista de Instrucción Primaria*, VIII (1893), 210–217.

Muñoz Feliú, P. J. "El 21 de mayo," *La Bandera*, VI (1926), 132–134.

Muñoz V. "Nuestro peor enemigo," *La Bandera*, VI (1926), 173–174.

Muñoz Yurazeck, Marfisa. "Conferencia sobre Arturo Prat," *Revista de Educación Nacional*, X (1914), 188–194.

Muret, A. "La epopeya de Iquique," *La Bandera*, III (1923), 129.

"El museo naval," *Revista de Marina*, XLVI (1909), 607–610.

Náuta. "La renovación de la escuadra," *Revista de Marina*, XXXX (1906), 1061–1064.

———. "El 21 de mayo," *Revista de Marina*, XXXII (1902), 457–461.

———. "El 21 de mayo," *Revista de Marina*, XXXVII (1905), 455–458.

"Nuestro saludo al 21 de Mayo de 1879," *Liga Marítima de Chile*, II (1916).

"Las nuevas construcciones navales," *Revista de Marina*, L (1911), 85–98.

Orompello. "Los sueldos en la armada," *Revista de Marina*, XXXVIII (1905), 131–136.

Oroz, Ruperto. "El amor a la patria," *El Educador*, XII (1902), 35–41.

———. "El amor patrio," *La Enseñanza*, I (1902), 7–12, 40–43.

———. "La enseñanza educativa," *Revista de Instrucción Primaria*, XIII (1899), 11–16.

Ortiz, D. "Las consecuencias del alcohol como microbio de la sociedad," *La Bandera*, V (1925), 111–112.

"El otro Arturo Prat," *Nautilus*, XXII (1950).

"Otro 21 de mayo," *Nautilus*, XIV (1942).

P. N. M. "La marina de guerra es indispensable a la defensa militar del país," *Revista de Marina*, XLVI (1909), 90–99.

"La patria i la familia," *La Enseñanza*, XI (1912), 100–109.

"El patriotismo i las virtudes cívicas en la educación," *Revista Pedagógica*, VII (1911), 185–188.

Peña, Rómulo J. "La reforma de nuestro sistema educacional," *Revista de Educación Primaria*, XXXII (1922), 215–221.

Pérez, F. "Aniversario de la Batalla de Buin," *Revista Militar*, II (1887), 307–311.

Pérez G., Lindor. "Un programa," *Revista de Marina*, XXV (1898), 1725–1727.

"Petición inicial al Gobierno sobre reforma de la enseñanza pública de la Asociación de Educación Nacional," *Revista de Eduación Nacional*, XVII (1921), 6–11.

"Petición para establecer la educación cívica i la continuidad de nuestra Educación Nacional de acuerdo con la Memoria de Instrucción pública en 1907," *Revista de Educación Nacional*, VIII (1912), 403–406.

Pinochet Le-Brun, José. "La evolución de nuestro régimen político y la educación nacional," *Revista de Educación Nacional*, XXI (1925), 6–35.

Pinto, Aníbal. "Apuntes," *Revista Chilena*, XIII (1921), 337–373.

"Por la salvación de la raza," *Revista de Educación Nacional*, XIII (1917), 436–453.

"Porqué alarmarse?" *Revista de Marina*, L (1911), 1–5.

Porto Carrero, Eusebio. "21 de Mayo," *Revista de Marina*, IV (1887), 597–599.

"Programa de acción cívica de la Asociación de Educación Nacional del Departamento de Extensión Universitaria i Secundaria en 1915," *Revista de Educación Nacional*, XI (1915), 43–50.

"Programa de historia," *Revista de Instrucción Primaria*, XXVII (1913), 22–34.

R. O. "Crónica escolar," *Revista de Instrucción Primaria*, XXVII (1913), 361–368.

———. "El 21 de Mayo i la educación cívica de los niños en las escuelas públicas," *Revista de Instrucción Primaria*, XXVIII (1914), 238–240.

Ramírez, J. A. "Tradiciones navales," *Revista de Marina*, XLIX (1933), 177–178.

Ramírez, Julio. "Crónica nacional," *Revista de Marina*, XLIX (1933), 474–475.

"La reconstrucción de la escuadra," *Revista de Marina*, XXXIX (1905), 1–4.

"Recuerdos de Prat," *La Patria*, XXIII (1944), 27.

La Redacción. "Economías en los presupuestos de guerra y marina," *Revista de Marina*, XXVIII (1899), 385–388.

———. "La reforma de la educación nacional," *Revista de Educación Primaria*, XXXII (1922), 209–213.

"Redención," *Nautilus*, II (1929).

"Reformas prácticas de actualidad en la marina," *Revista de Marina*, XXXVIII (1904), 218–236.

"La renovación de nuestra escuadra i la campaña contra los Dreadnoughts," *Revista de Marina*, XLIX (1910), 441–451.

"Responsabilidad histórica," *Mar*, XX (1944), 51–52.

Rivas D., N. "Ahorremos," *La Bandera*, I (1921), 233.

Rivera Matte, Alvaro. "La idea de Patria," *La Bandera*, I (1921), 182.

Robinet, Carlos. "Los deberes cívicos," *El Educador*, VIII (1898), 100–104.

Rodríguez Mendoza, M. "La enseñanza de la historia en las escuelas del estado," *Revista de Instrucción Primaria*, I (1887), 605–609.

Saavedra, Julio. "La educación cívica en Chile," *Revista Pedagógica*, III (1907), 67–75.

———. "Nuestro idioma patrio," *Revista de la Asociación de Educación Nacional*, III (1907), 118–122.

Salas Marchan, Maximilano, y José Pinochet Le-Brun. "La reforma de la enseñanza pública en la asamblea de la Asociación de Educación Nacional," *Revista de Educación Nacional*, XVII (1921), 52–72.

Santa Cruz, José María. "Reseña de defensa," *Revista de Marina*, I (1885), 428–433.

Santa María, Domingo. "Cartas de don Domingo Santa María a don José Victorino Lastarria," *Revista Chilena*, VI (1918), 249–261.

Santibáñez, Rafael. "Crónica nacional," *Revista de Marina*, LI (1934), 415–416.

Schlott, Otto. "El libro de lectura," *Revista de Instrucción Primaria*, III (1888), 171–184.

"Se impone la acción," *Revista de Educación Nacional*, XII (1916), 3–4.

"Significado del 21 de Mayo," *Mar*, XX (1949), 51–52.

Silva, Víctor Domingo. "El himno de la raza," *Revista de Educación Nacional*, XVI (1920), 198–200.

Snowden, P. "El mundo contra el comunismo," *La Bandera*, V (1925), 111–112.

"Solicitud de la Asociación de Educación Nacional a S.E. el Presidente de la República, Octubre 31, 1907," *Revista de la Asociación de Educación Nacional*, III (1907), 251.

Stream, Juan. "Tomando el nivel," *Revista de Marina*, LXXVII (1932), 121–124.

Streeter V., Edgardo. "Crónica nacional," *Revista de Marina*, L (1936), 390–391.

Subercaseaux, Guillermo. "Educación moral i religiosa en la enseñanza del estado," *Revista de Educación Nacional*, XIII (1917), 219–230.

———. "Política nacionalista," *Revista de Educación Nacional*, IX (1913), 267–277.

Submarino. "Deberes de la hora presente," *Revista de Marina*, XLVI (1909), 457–460.

———. "En qué estado ha quedado la proyectada reconstrucción de nuestra armada?" *Revista de Marina*, XXXX (1906), 986–992.

Téllez, I. "El combate de Iquique," *La Bandera*, VIII (1928), 132–137.

"El terror rojo en Rusia," *La Bandera*, I (1921), 33.

"Tradición," *Revista de Marina*, LV (1941), 281.

U. A. F. "Correspondencia especial para *La Revista Militar*: La apoteósis de los héroes," *Revista Militar*, V (1888), 452–472.

"Un año más," *Revista de Marina*, LVI (1942), 263.

"Un año nuevo," *Revista Pedagógica*, VII (1911), 1–3.

Valdés C., S. "La renovación de nuestra escuadra: Los Dreadnoughts i el ABC Sud Americano," *Revista de Marina*, XLIX (1910), 445–451.

Valdivieso, Rafael Valentín. "Proyectos de lei de cementerios," *Boletín Eclesiástico*, VI (1880), 548–549.

Varela, José 2⁰. "De la educación en jeneral," *Revista de Instrucción Primaria*, XV (1901), 58–66.

"24 de mayo de 1885," *Revista Militar*, I (1885), 177–178.

"21 de mayo," *Liga Marítima de Chile*, I (1915), 1–4.

"21 de mayo de 1879," *Memorial del Ejército de Chile*, VIII (1913), 551–552.

"21 de mayo de 1879," *Memorial del Ejército de Chile*, XXIII (1928), 7–9.

"21 de mayo," *Nautilus*, VIII (1937).

"21 de mayo de 1879," *Nautilus*, XII (1941).

"21 de mayo," *Revista de Marina*, L (1911), 337–338.

"21 de mayo," *Revista de Marina*, LIV (1913), 420–422.

"21 de mayo," *Revista de Marina*, LXV (1920), 351–352.

"21 de mayo," *Revista de Marina*, LII (1938), 295–297.

"21 de mayo," *Revista de Marina*, LIII (1939), 253–254.

"21 de mayo," *Revista de Marina*," LIV (1940), 289.

"21 de mayo," *Revista de Marina*, LVII (1943), 1–2.

"21 de mayo de 1879," *Revista de Marina*, LI (1935), 297–301.

"El 21 de mayo de 1879," *Revista de Marina*, LI (1937), 261–263.

"El 21 de mayo en la Escuela Normal de Preceptores de Santiago," *Revista de Instrucción Primaria*, IV (1890), 618–623.

Vergara M., Capitán Marcial. "El 21 de Mayo," *Memorial del Ejército de Chile*, XXVII (1934), 401–403.

Vergara Z., Mario. "Comentarios sobre la historia de la Guerra del Pacífico," *Revista de Marina*, LXIV (1919), 337–340.

Vial Solar, Alfredo. "Necesidad de fortificar nuestros puertos," *Boletín Militar*, I (1894), 355–365.

Vigía. "El futuro desarme," *Revista de Marina*, XXII (1897), 341–343.

Villalobos, D. "La enseñanza de historia en la escuela pública," *El Educador*, II (1890), 20–24.

"Visita de honor," *Nautilus*, V (1933).

"Visitando la casa en que nació Prat," *La Bandera*, X (1930), 10–13.

Von Schroeders, Edgardo. "Crónica," *Revista de Marina*, LXXVI (1931), 646–647.

Wilson, Arturo. "Recuerdos del combate naval de Iquique," *Revista de Marina*, LXXVI (1931), 308–325.

———. "Recuerdos del combate naval de Iquique el 21 de mayo de 1879," *Revista de Marina*, LXXI (1926), 473–493.

Zavala, Santiago. "Crónica nacional," *Revista de Marina*, LVI (1942), 428–429.

Zegers, Vicente. "Organización del personal naval en las distintas potencias del globo," *Revista de Marina*, XIII (1892), 542–549.

Zenteno Araya, Samuel. "Lo que significa la bandera chilena," *Revista de Educación Nacional*, VIII (1912), 252–255.

II. Secondary Sources

A. Books

Alexander, Franz. *Our Age of Unreason*. Philadelphia: Lippincott, 1942.

Amunátegui Solar, Domingo. *La democracia en Chile*. Santiago: Universidad de Chile, 1946.

————. *El progreso intelectual y político de Chile*. Santiago: Editorial Nascimento, 1936.

Arosamena Garland, Geraldo. *El contralmirante Miguel Grau*. Lima: San Martí y Compañía, 1946.

Barros Arana, Diego. *Obras Completas*. Vol. XVI. *Historia de la Guerra del Pacífico*. Santiago: Imprenta, Litografía, i Encuadernación "Barcelona," 1914.

Barros Borgoño, Luis. *Caja de crédito hipotecario*. Santiago: Librería y Imprenta Artes y Letras, 1930.

Bertrand, Alejandro. *La crisis salitrera*. Paris: Louis Michaud, 1910.

Blanlot Holley, Anselmo. *Perfiles de la situación*. Santiago: Imprenta Franco Chilena, 1893.

Bosch, Juan. *Bolívar y la guerra social*. Buenos Aires: Editorial Jorge Alvarez, 1966.

Bravo Kendrick, Aníbal. *La revolución de 1891*. Santiago, 1946.

Bulnes, Gonzalo. *Guerra del Pacífico*. 3 vols. Valparaíso: Sociedad, Imprenta, y Litografía Universo, 1911. Vol. I.

Burr, Robert N. *By Reason or Force*. Berkeley: University of California Press, 1965.

Campos Harriet, Fernando. *Desarrollo educacional 1810–1910*. Santiago: Editorial Andrés Bello, 1960.

Carrera Damas, Germán. *El culto a Bolívar*. Caracas: Instituto de Antropología e Historia, 1968.

Ceriana Bórquez, Eliana. *Arturo Prat, abogado*. Santiago: Editorial Universitaria, 1964.

Civiti Bernesconi, Edmundo H. *Guerra del Pacífico (1879–1883)*. 2 vols. Buenos Aires: Círculo Militar, 1946. Vol. I.

Cortés, Lía, and Jorge Fuentes. *Diccionario político de Chile*. Santiago: Editorial Orbe, 1967.

Cotapos Aldunate, F. Javier. *El aporte del capital extranjero en la industria minera de Chile*. Santiago: Talleres Gráficos "Simiente," 1947.

Cuevas, Arturo. *Estudio estratéjico sobre la campaña marítima de la Guerra del Pacífico*. Valparaíso: Talleres Tipográficos de la Armada, 1901.

Dellepiane, Carlos. *Historia militar del Perú*. 2 vols. Buenos Aires: Círculo Militar, 1941. Vol. II.

Donoso, Ricardo. *Alessandri Agitador y Demoledor*. 2 vols. México: Fondo de Cultura Económica, 1954. Vol. II.

Elson, Ruth Miller. *Guardians of Tradition*. Lincoln: University of Nebraska Press, 1964.

Encina, Francisco Antonio. *Historia de Chile desde la prehistoria hasta 1891*. 20 vols. Santiago: Editorial Nascimento, 1949–1952. Vol. XVI.

Fenichel, Otto. *The Psychoanalytic Theory of Neurosis*. New York: Norton, 1945.

Fetter, Frank W. *Monetary Inflation in Chile*. Princeton, N.J.: Princeton University Press, 1931.

García Castelblanco, Alejandro. *Estudio crítico de las operaciones navales en Chile*. Santiago: Imprenta de la Armada, 1929.

Gil, Federico. *The Genesis and Modernization of Political Parties in Chile*. Gainesville: The University of Florida Press, 1962.

Guerrero Vergara, Ramón, and José Toribio Medina. *El Capitán de Fragata Arturo Prat. Estudios de su vida*. Valparaíso: Imprenta de la Armada, 1952.

Guilisasti Tagle, Sergio. *Partidos políticos chilenos*. 2d ed. Santiago: Editorial Nascimento, 1964.

Guzmán Rosales, Miguel, y Octavio Vió Henriquez. *Don Francisco de Paula Taforó y la vacancia arzobispal de Santiago, 1878–1887*. Santiago: Editorial Universidad Católica, 1964.

Hirschman, Alberto O. *Journey's Toward Progress*. New York: Doubleday & Company, Inc., 1965.

Jobet, Julio César. *Ensayo crítico del desarrollo económico-social de Chile*. Santiago: Editorial Universitaria, 1955.

Jofré Ramírez, Hilda. *Las primeras sociedades anónimas*. Santiago: Editorial Universitaria, 1964.

Jung, C. G. *Essays on Contemporary Events*. London: Kegan Paul, 1947.

Körner, Emilio, and Boonen Rivera, J. *Estudios sobre historia militar*. 2 vols. Santiago: Imprenta Cervantes, 1887. Vol. II.

Labarca Hubertson, Amanda. *Historia de la enseñanza en Chile*. Santiago: Imprenta Universitaria, 1939.

López U., Carlos. *La historia de la marina de Chile*. Santiago: Editorial Andrés Bello, 1969.

McBride, George. *Chile: Land and Society*. New York: American Geographical Society, 1936.

McClelland, David. *The Achieving Society*. Princeton. N.J. D. Van Norstrand Company, Inc., 1961.

Machuca, Francisco A. *Las cuatro campañas de la Guerra del Pacífico*. 4 vols. Valparaíso: Imprenta Victoria, 1926. Vol. I.

Martner, Daniel. *Estudio de Política Comercial Chilena e Historia Económica Nacional.* 2 vols. Santiago: Editorial Universitaria, 1923. Vol. II.

Menéndez Pidal, Ramón. *The Spaniards in Their History.* Trans. Walter Starkie. New York: Norton, 1966.

Money-Kyrle, Roger. *The Meaning of Sacrifice.* London: Hogarth Press, 1930.

Nunn, Frederick M. *Chilean Politics 1920–1931.* Albuquerque: University of New Mexico Press, 1970.

Paz Soldán, Mariano Felipe. *Narración histórica de la Guerra de Chile contra el Perú y Bolivia.* Buenos Aires: Imprenta y Librería de Mayo, 1884.

Pereira Salas, Eugenio. *Historia de la música chilena.* Santiago: Universidad de Chile, 1957.

Pike, Frederick. *Chile and the United States, 1880–1962.* Notre Dame, Ind.: University of Notre Dame Press, 1965.

Pinto Santa Cruz, Aníbal. *Chile un caso de desarrollo frustrado.* Santiago: Editorial Universitaria, 1962.

Ramírez Necochea, Hernán. *Origen y formación del partido comunista de Chile.* Santiago: Editorial Austral, 1965.

Rank, Otto. *The Myth of the Birth of the Hero and Other Essays.* Edited by Phillip Freund. New York: Vintage, 1959.

Rojas, Francisco. *Administración naval en Chile.* Santiago: Imprenta Chile, 1934.

Ross, Agustín. *Chile 1851–1910.* Santiago de Chile: Imprenta Barcelona, 1911.

Segall, Marcelo. *Desarrollo del capitalismo en Chile.* Santiago, 1953.

Scheidlinger, Saul. *Psychoanalysis and Social Behavior.* New York: Norton, 1952.

Semper and Michels. *La industria del salitre en Chile.* Translated by Javier Gandarillas and Orlando Ghigliotto Salas. Santiago: Imprenta, Litografía y Encuadernación Barcelona, 1908.

Silva Castro, Raúl. *Prensa y periodismo en Chile 1812–1956.* Santiago: Ediciones de la Universidad de Chile, 1958.

Sepúlveda, Sergio. *El trigo chileno en el mercado mundial.* Santiago: Universidad de Chile, 1959.

Smelser, Neil J. *Theory of Collective Behavior.* New York: The Free Press, 1962.

Stevenson, John Reese. *The Chilean Popular Front.* Philadelphia: The University of Pennsylvania Press, 1942.

Subercaseaux, Guillermo. *El sistema monetario i la organización bancaria de Chile.* Santiago: Imprenta Universo, 1920.

Téllez, Indalicio. *Historia de Chile—Historia militar.* 2 vols. Santiago: Balcells i Cía., 1925. Vol. I.

Uribe Orrego, Luis. *Los combates navales en la Guerra del Pacífico.* Valparaíso: Imprenta "La Patria," 1886.

Urzúa Valenzuela, Germán. *Los partidos políticos chilenos.* Santiago: Editorial Jurídica de Chile, 1968.

Vegas G., Manuel. *Historia de la marina de guerra del Perú.* Lima: Imprenta "Lux" de E. L. Castro, 1929.

Wilde Cavero, M. Fernando. *Historia militar de Bolivia.* La Paz, 1963.

B. Articles

Ackerman, Nathan W. "Interaction Processes in a Group and the Role of the Leader." In *Psychoanalysis and the Social Sciences,* edited by Geza Roheim. Vol. IV. New York: International Universities Press, 1955. Pp. 111–121.

Alexander, Franz. "On the Psychodynamics of Regressive Phenomena in Panic State." In *Psychoanalysis and the Social Sciences,* edited by Geza Roheim. Vol. IV. New York: International Universities Press, 1955. Pp. 104–111.

————. "Psychology and Social Disorganization," *The American Journal of Sociology.* XLII (1937), 781–814.

Ballesteros, Marto. "Desarrollo agrícola chileno, 1910–1955," *Cuadernos de Economía,* II (1965), 7–41.

Blakemore, Harold. "The Chilean Revolution of 1891 and its Historiography." *The Hispanic American Historical Review,* XLV (1965), 393–422.

Burns, E. Bradford. "The Black in Brazilian History," *West Georgia College Studies in the Social Sciences,* VIII (1969), 52–61.

Carvajal, M. Meliton. "Reseña de la campaña del Huáscar contra Chile en 1879," *Revista Chilena,* XV (1922), 79–89.

Devereux, George. "Charismatic Leadership and Crisis." In *Psychoanalysis and the Social Sciences.* Ed. Geza Roheim. Vol. IV. New York: International Universities Press, 1955. Pp. 145–157.

Echeñique Gandarillas, José M. "La declaración de guerra del 5 de abril de 1879," *Revista Chilena,* XI (1927), 51–88.

Elson, Ruth Miller. "American Schoolbooks and 'Culture' in the Nineteenth Century." In *The National Temper.* Ed. Lawrence W. Levine and Robert Middlehauff. New York: Harcourt, Brace & World, Inc. 113–135.

Espinosa Moraga, Oscar. "Arturo Prat, agente confidencial," *Boletín de la Academia Chilena de la Historia,* XVII (1950), 65–80.

Grez, Carlos. "La supuesta preparación de Chile para la Guerra del Pacífico," *Boletín de la Academia Chilena de la Historia,* III (1935), 111–139.

Hernández C., Roberto. "Estudio y prólogo de Roberto Hernández C." In *El Capitán de Fragata Arturo Prat: El Vice-Almirante Patricio Lynch.* Commandancia en Jefe de la Armada, 1952. Pp. 1–78.

Lipset, Seymour Martin. "Values, Education, and Entrepreneurship." In *Elites in Latin America.* Ed. Seymour Martin Lipset and Aldo Solari. New York: Oxford University Press, 1967. Pp. 3–61.

Money-Kyrle, Roger. "Varieties of Group Formation." In *Psychoanalysis and the Social Sciences*. Ed. Geza Roheim. Vol. IV. New York: International Universities Press, 1955. Pp. 313–329.

Muensterberger, Warner. "Observations on the Collapse of Leadership." In *Psychoanalysis and the Social Sciences*. Ed. Geza Roheim. Vol. IV. New York: International Universities Press, 1955. Pp. 158–169.

Redl, Fritz. "The Phenomenon of Contagion and 'Shock Effect' in Group Therapy." In *Searchlights on Delinquency*. Ed. K. R. Eissler. New York: International Universities Press, 1948. Pp. 315–328.

Salcedo-Bastardo, José Luis. "Economic Revolution: Agrarian Reform." In *The Liberator, Simon Bolívar: Man and Image*. Ed. David Bushnell. New York: Alfred Knopf, 1970. Pp. 181–186.

Saussure, Raymond. "Psychoanalysis and History." In *Psychoanalysis and the Social Sciences*. Ed. Geza Roheim. Vol. II. New York: International Universities Press, 1950. Pp. 7–67.

Schmideberg, Melitta. "The Role of the Psychotic Mechanisms in Cultural Development," *The International Journal of Psychoanalysis*, XI (1930), 387–418.

Segall, Marcelo. "Biografía social de la ficha salario," *Revista Mapocho*, II (1964), 97–131.

Simmel, Ernst. "Anti-Semitism and Mass Psychopathology." In *Anti-Semitism*. New York: International Universities Press, 1946. Pp. 33–79.

Sternbach, Oscar. "The Dynamics of Psychotherapy in the Group," *The Journal of Child Psychiatry*, I (1947), 91–112.

Weigert, Edith. "Conditions of Organized and Regressive Responses to Danger." In *Psychoanalysis and the Social Sciences*. Ed. Geza Roheim. Vol. IV. New York: International Universities Press, 1955. Pp. 121–127.

III. Other Sources

Levy, James Robert. "The Development and the Use of the Heroic Image of José de San Martín, 1840–1900." Ph.D. dissertation. University of Pennsylvania, 1964.

Personal communication with Dr. Arturo Prat Echaurren. August 1966. Santiago, Chile.

INDEX

Acuña, Pedro, 119
Aguirre Cerda, Pedro, 97, 109, 111; death of in 1941, 101; election of in 1938, 98; nomination of, 97; policies of, 101–102
Aldea, Juan de Dios, 18, 61, 117, 152–153
Alessandri, Arturo, 105, 109, 111, 143; election of in 1920, 90; election campaign of in 1931, 95; election of in 1932, 95–96; first government of, 90–91; and Milicia Republicana, 96; overthrow of, 91; second regime of, 96–97. See also Arturo Prat, and regime of Arturo Alessandri
Alessandri, Fernando, 102
Alfonso, José, 32, 49, 180n
Allende, Salvador, 156
Altamirano, Eulogio, 19
Amunátegui, Luis Miguel, 119–120
Angamos, battle of, 43, 111
Anticlericalism, 30–31
Anti-Semitism. See Movimiento Nacional Socialista
Argentina, 76; claims by to Patagonia, 32–33; naval rivalry of with Chile, 135, 137–138; relations of with Chile, 80; trade competition with Chile, 28–29, 78
Arteaga Alemparte, Justo, 52–53
Arteaga Cuevas, General Justo, 19, 42

Balmaceda, José Manuel, 2, 80, 83, 86, 105, 111, 114, 130, 136; attitude of toward War of the Pacific, 22; overthrow of, 74
Bandera, La, 152–153
Barrientos, Pedro, 131
Barros Arana, Diego, 32
Becerra, Manfredo, 143–144
Belmar, Francisco, 54
Blanche, General Bartolomé, 95

Blanco Encalada, Miguel, 144
Blest Gana, Alberto, 28, 31
Boletín Militar, El, 150
Bolívar, Simón, 2, 156. See also Heroes and heroism
Bolivia, 33–35, 43, 138; economic exploitation of by Chile, 24; relations of with Chile, 80. See also War of the Pacific
Bórquez Solar, Antonio, 128
Brazil, 135, 137–139
Bulnes, Gonzalo, 140
Bulnes, Manuel, 130
Bunster, César, 131

Carlyle, Thomas, 3–5. See also Heroes and heroism
Carrasco, Manuel Hidalgo, 70
Carrera, José Miguel, 56, 127, 130
Carriola, Luis, 130
Caupolicán: compared with Prat, 56; as symbol of Chilean culture, 55, 130
Centinela, El, 61, 66
Chamúdez, Marcos, 106
Chauviedez, E. T., 141
Chilian Times, The, 26, 53
Chipana, battle of, 40, 44, 58; compared with battle of Iquique, 52–53
Círculo Militar, El, 152
Clarín, 156
Cochrane, Lord Thomas, 113, 144
Colombo, Romildo, 128
Communist party, 92, 97, 101, 104; fear of, 99, 103; history of, 110; persecution of, 102. See also Arturo Prat, and Communist party; Popular Front
Condell, Carlos, 17, 21, 48–49, 67, 87, 116, 125, 140; career of, 50; compared with Arturo Prat, 53; conduct of at battle of Iquique, 19, 50–51, 187n

Conservative party, 26, 65, 97, 102; attitude of toward Pinto, 30, 154; and Arturo Prat, 62–63; support of for Williams Rebolledo, 42, 49, 67

COSACH, 96, 111

Cristi, Mauricio, 20

Cruz Coke, Eduardo, 102

Darío, Rubén, 70

Dávila, Carlos, 95

de la Barra, Eduardo, 57

del Campo, Máximo, 84

de Valdivia, Pedro, 56. *See also* Arturo Prat

Diario Ilustrado, El, 84, 92, 99–101

Díaz, Joaquín, 54

Echavarría, Agustín, 151

Education: emphasis on civics in, 124–125, 199n; nationalism in, 121–123. *See also* Arturo Prat, and education

Elson Ruth Miller, 132

Encina, Francisco Antonio, 123

Ensayo Militar, El, 150

Errázuriz, Federico, 22, 30, 138; intervention of in election of 1876, 23–24

Esposición a nuestros conciudadanos, 31

Estandarte Católico, El, 31, 67, 70–72

Ferrocarril, El, 30, 43, 57, 71, 83

Fierro-Sarratea Treaty, 32, 36

Figueroa Larraín, Emiliano, 93

Franklin, Benjamin, 125; compared with Arturo Prat, 133; in American schools, 132. *See also* Arturo Prat, and education

Freire, Ramón, 56, 114

Frente Popular, 110–112

Galdames, Luis, 121–123

Gonzales, S., 131

González, Ernesto, 146

González, Félix, 128

González Videla, Gabriel, 102

González von Mareés, Jorge, 104; alliance of with Ibáñez, 98; philosophy of, 105–106; and Popular Front 98

Gorigoitía, Luis, 120

Grau, Miguel, 18, 40–41, 43, 125; compared with Prat, 204n; naval campaign of, 41, 60–61

Great Britain, 110, 135, 138–139, 149; involvement of in War of the Pacific, 39; private economic interests of in Chile, 28, 78, 112

Grez, Vicente, 72

Grove, Marmaduque, 95

Hegel, Georg, 3, 6. *See also* Heroes and heroism

Hernández, Roberto, 142–143

Hernández, Víctor, 127–128

Heroes and heroism: concept of, 1–3, 5–6, 156–157; Marxist interpretation of, 4; psychological interpretation of, 6–8; sociological interpretation of, 8–9

Hook, Sidney, 5, 90. *See also* Heroes and heroism

Hozven, Alberto, 145

Ibáñez, Adolfo, 32–33

Ibáñez, Bernardo, 102

Ibáñez del Campo, Carlos, 105, 110, 145; as candidate for presidency in 1938, 98; election of in 1927 91; government of 91, 93–94; overthrow of, 95. *See also* Arturo Prat, and regime of Carlos Ibáñez

Independiente, El, 60–61, 67

Iquique: battle of, 17–19; description of, 11

Irarrázaval Zañartu, Alfredo, 70

Izquierdo, Domingo, 56, 69

Johnson, Ana, 81, 121

Kelley, Colin, 156–157. *See also* Heroes and heroism

König, Abraham, 83

Las Casas, Aníbal, 60

Latorre (battleship), 145–147

Latorre, Juan: compared with Prat, 52, 144; in Revolution of 1891, 136

Lautaro, 55–56

League of Civic Action, 85

Lecciones de historia de Chile para el uso en las escuelas públicas, 120
Leonidas, 73, 150; compared with Prat, 58, 115; as hero, 6
Liberal Democrats, 23, 63, 154
Lillo, Samuel, 72
Lincoln, Abraham, 5, 125
Lipset, Seymour, 132
Lira, Fernando, 107
Lisboa, Francisco, 32

Mac-Iver, Enrique, 82, 90
Mahan, Alfred Thayer, 135
Mario, Roberto, 89
Maritime League of Chile, 132
Martínez, P. N., 137
Matte, Eugenio, 95
Memorial del Estado Mayor del Ejército de Chile, 150
Menéndez Pidal, Ramón, 55
Mercurio, El (Santiago), 89, 92, 99–100
Mercurio, El (Valparaíso), 61–62, 70–72, 84, 86, 92, 99, 139, 141
Milicia Republicana, 96, 101
Millar, Walterio, 131
Molinare, Nicanor, 89
Montero, Juan Esteban, 95
Montt, Enrique, 119
Montt, Jorge, 86
Movimiento Nacional Socialista (Nazi party), 104, 106, 155–156; attempted coup by, 98, 109; hostility of toward Alessandri government, 107–108; and Popular Front, 109. *See also* Arturo Prat, and *Movimiento Nacional Socialista*
Muñoz, José María, 129
Muñoz, Marfisa, 128
Muñoz Donoso, Esteban, 53–54, 57, 120

"Nauta," 143
Navarrete, Benjamín, 67
Navy: decline of, 136–138; growth of, 135, 138–139; mutiny of in 1931, 145–147; role of in 1891 Revolution, 136
Nelson, Lord Horatio, 17, 150; compared with Prat, 58, 73; compared with Williams, 68
Novedades, Las, 30, 45

Novoa, Manuel, 65
Nuevo Ferrocarril, El, 66

Opinión, La, 115–118
Orella, Manuel, 125, 172n
Oroz, Ruperto, 129
Orrego Barros, Antonio, 72
Owen, Ricardo, 15

Pacheco, Ramón, 70
Palacios, Nicolás, 73
Parliamentary regime: economic conditions during, 75–79; loss of faith in, 81–85; political changes during, 74–75; social conditions during, 79–80. *See also* Arturo Prat, and Parliamentary regime
Patria, La (military journal), 152–153
Patria, La (newspaper), 53, 66
Peru, 13–14, 41, 44–45, 80. *See also* War of the Pacific
Pinochet Le-Brun, Tancredo, 81, 121
Pinto, Aníbal, 20, 26, 34–36, 42–43, 59, 63–66, 130, 154; career of, 22–23; economic policies of, 26–29; election of in 1876, 23; foreign policy of, 32–33; hostility toward, 23–24, 27, 30, 44–47, 59–61; compared with Prat, 61–62; relations with clergy, 30–32; war policy of, 40
Pinto, Armando, 131
Pinto Riesco, Jaime, 95
Plekhanov, George, 4, 6. *See also* Heroes and heroism
Popular Front: attitude toward, 98–99; collapse of, 101; growth of, 97; policies of, 101–102
Portales, Diego, 30, 45, 59, 105, 130
Porvenir, El, 87, 136
Prat Carvajal, Arturo (son), 147
Prat Chacón, Arturo, 1, 6, 9, 48, 151; and army enlisted men, 152–153; and army officer corps, 150–151; career and life of, 14–16; changing image of, 73–74, 86, 92, 103–104, 154–156; and Communist party, 110–115, 195–196n; declining popularity of, 69–72; described as religious figure, 55, 57, 72–73; and education, 119–121, 132–133; as

force for morality, 73–74, 86, 89;
as force for unity, 86, 92–93, 100–
103; initial popularity of, 20–21,
52, 56–59; as martial figure, 56–
58; as martyr, 54–55; and merchant
marine, 141–143, 204–204n; and
Milicia Republicana, 101; and *Movimiento Nacional Socialista*, 106–
109; and navy, 134, 139–150; and
Parliamentary regime, 86–89, 185n,
189–191n; and political parties,
62–65, 68, 154–155; and Popular Front, 99–101; and regime of
Arturo Alessandri, 91–93, 192n;
and regime of Carlos Ibáñez, 93–
94, 192–193n; and regime of Aníbal Pinto, 59–62; resurrection of,
72, 86; role of at Battle of Iquique,
14, 17–18, 53; and Socialist party,
115–118, 155–156, 196n; as symbol of Chilean culture, 55–56, 73;
as symbol of sacrifice, 52–53, 92,
99–100; and textbooks, 120–121,
125–126, 130–132
Pretoto Freir, Roberto, 142
Pueblo, El, 27

Radical party, 96–97, 102, 110. *See
also* Popular Front
Ravines, Eudocio, 110
Recabarren, Luis Emilio, 110, 114
Revista de Marina, 72, 134, 137–138,
140, 143, 148–149
Revista del Suboficial, La, 152–153
Revista del Sur, La, 25–26
Revista Militar de Chile, La, 150
Reynolds, Enrique, 136
Rimac: reaction to capture of, 61;
riots precipitated by capture of, 46
Ríos, Juan Antonio, 102
Riquelme, Ernesto, 19, 64
Riverso, Galvarino, 42
Roa, Alejo, 131
Rosales, Justo Abel, 70
Ross Santa María, Gustavo: as candi-
date for presidency 97–98; as Min-
ister of Finance, 96–97

Saavedra, Julio, 81, 121–122
Salas, Darío, 128
Sánchez, Francisco, 136, 171n

Sanfuentes, Aníbal, 84
San Martín, José, 2, 56, 156
Santa María, Domingo, 30, 75
Sanz, Miguel, 136, 172n
Schlott, Otto, 130–131
Serrano, Ignacio, 19, 64, 70, 125,
171n
Siglo, El, 112–114
Silva, Alejandro, 131
Simpson, Juan, 49, 180n
Socialist party, 92, 97, 104, 110, 115,
155–156. *See also* Arturo Prat, and
Socialist party
Socialist Republic of 100 Days, 95
Sotomayor, Rafael, 27, 181n
Spencer, Herbert, 3, 6. *See also* He-
roes and heroism
Suárez, José Bernardo, 126
Subercaseaux, Guillermo, 123, 142
"Submarino," 138
Sur, El, 71

Taforó, Francisco de Paula, 31–32
Thompson, Manuel, 16
Tiempos, Los, 64
Tocornal, Enrique, 52, 64
Tomic, Raimundo, 156
Tornero, Orestes, 120
Toros, Gaspar, 120
Trabajo, 106–110

Unión, La, 87, 94, 98–101, 141, 145
United States, 17, 24, 28, 78, 112,
135, 138
Uribe, Luis, 15, 38, 51, 139–140,
171n
Uruguay, 28
Urzúa, Miguel, 72

Valdés Vicuña, Samuel, 79
Valdivieso, Ramon, 31. *See also* Anticlericalism
Varas, Antonio, 42
Vicuña, Anjel, 81, 83
Vicuña Mackenna, Benjamín, 63, 65;
attitude of toward Arturo Prat, 61,
70; as defender of Williams Rebolledo, 67–68; election campaign
of 1876, 23
Viel, Oscar, 136

Villalobos, Domingo, 126
von Schroeders, Edgardo, 146–147

Walker Martínez, Carlos, 67
War of the Pacific, 33; Bolivian preparations for, 37–38; causes of, 34–
36; Chilean preparations for, 36–
39; Chilean reaction to, 43–46;
conclusion of, 43; Peruvian preparations for, 37, 39; threatened Argentine intervention in, 39–40
War of the Peruvian-Bolivian Confederation (1836–1839), 46, 56,
59, 113
War with Spain (1865–1866), 17,
56, 113
Washington, George, 125; in American schoolbooks, 132; compared
with Arturo Prat, 133. *See also*
Arturo Prat, and education; Arturo
Prat, and textbooks
Williams Rebolledo, Juan, 44, 46,
67–68, 136; attack of on Callao,
12–13, 48–50, 180–181n; attitude
toward Arturo Prat, 16–17, 171–
172n; defense of by friends and allies, 66–68; hostility toward, 60,
65–66; naval strategy of, 12, 40–
42, 171–172n, 180n; personality of,
42; political aspirations of, 42, 49,
67–68; relations of with army, 42
Wilson, Arturo, 136, 171n; on Battle
of Iquique, 55; during 1931 naval
mutiny, 147; as supporter of Ibáñez, 94

Zañartu, Sady, 106
Zegers, Vicente, 135, 172n